EDUCATIONAL AND GLOBAL SURVIVAL

MODERN TECHNIQUES OF TEACHING SERIES

EDUCATION AND GLOBAL SURVIVAL

V. K. NANDA

ANMOL PUBLICATIONS PVT. LTD.
NEW DELHI-110002 (INDIA)

ANMOL PUBLICATIONS PVT. LTD.
4374/4B, Ansari Road, Daryaganj
New Delhi-110 002

Educational and Global Survival

First Edition 1998

ISBN 81-261-0021-4

PRINTED IN INDIA

Published by J. L. Kumar for Anmol Publications Pvt. Ltd., New Delhi-110 002 and Printed at Mehra Offset Press, Delhi.

Contents

Preface

Advancement of any society or nation depends on the—quality of education' being imparted there. For quality of education we have to adopt modern and easily understandable techniques of teaching. Though plenty of literature is there on techniques of teaching-learning—the present work in five volumes is unique—as it contains valuable relevant matter on diverse aspects of teaching. The material have been judiciously collected from authoritative and reliable sources.

Volume-wise organisation of the work is: Educational Technology for Adults; Education and Global Survival; Teaching of General Science in Elementary Schools; Typology of Distance Teaching Systems; and Adult Education and Human Resource Development.

Students, teachers, educationists and educational administrators besides the policy planners and teacher-trainers in different pedagogical institutes will find this work most useful and informative.

We are deeply beholden to all the learned educationists and writers whose writings are cited or substantially made use of in these volumes.

V. K. Nanda

1

Global Survival

Dimensions of the Problem

Even a cursory review of the popular press in the last quarter of the twentieth century gives the reader some understanding of the dimensions of the problems facing mankind. Excessive population growth and the resultant malnutrition and starvation are no longer Malthusian predictions of the future, but are the reality of today. Population estimates for the year 2000 are for 7.5 billion people. Robert Heilbroner in his 1974 book *An Inquiry into the Human Prospect* predicted the possibility of 20 billion people by the year 2050. Moreover, the growth is unequally distributed, with the largest numbers of people being born into the poorer nations of the world.

Whereas some of the developed countries have reached near zero population growth, many poor nations have birth rates in excess of 3 and 4 percent per year. Further, the world's population is becoming increasingly urbanized, not just in the developed nations of the Western world, but also in the poorer nations of the Southern hemisphere and Asia. Some experts have predicted that by 1990 over half of the world's people will be living in cities of 100,000 or more.

Energy

Although the world has been moving towards a crisis in energy for a long time, it was not until the 1970s that the dimensions of the problem became obvious. With the Arab oil boycott and the resultant rapid rise in prices for petroleum, it became increasingly clear that energy was a limited resource and the nations of the world must move to conserve it in all its forms, and in particular the fossil fuels such as coal, oil, and natural gas. The energy crisis helped to make the interdependence of nations more obvious, and the world was thrust into an international recession, partially due to the increased cost of energy. The industrialized nations of the world are seeking to become energy self-sufficient and have funded research in nuclear fusion, solar, and hydroelectric energy, and other forms which cannot be cut off by an oil cartel or in times of war. With the rapid increase in the cost of energy, the poor nations suffered the most, with inflation rates of upwards of 30 to 50 percent.

Quality of Life

A problem related to the world population growth and energy shortages is the worsening quality of life for much of humanity. This can be measured by the polluted air and water, lack of adequate health care, unemployment and underemployment, lack of protein, and malnutrition and starvation. It has become increasingly obvious that these problems do not stop at national boundaries, but are worldwide in scope. Air pollution is carried across continents and over the oceans.

A nuclear holocaust would spread radioactive death throughout most of the northern hemisphere and possibly cover the whole earth. It has slowly been dawning upon the people and power structures of the rich nations that their excessive consumption of the world's resources means less available for the poor, and the continued despoliation of the environment. Quality of life is also affected by wars, crimes in the streets, bombings, hijackings, assassinations, dishonesty in the highest levels of government, and numerous other events that indicate that much of the glue holding together the societies of the world appears to be disintegrating.

Maldistribution of Wealth

Per capita income figures give some indication as to the gross inequities which exist in the last quarter of the twentieth century. The United States and some of the newly rich oil nations lead the world with per capita incomes of $ 4,000 or more. They are followed by other European countries, Australia, Japan, and the Soviet Union with $ 1,000 to $ 3,000 per person, with the nations of what has been called the Third World having per capita income of $ 100 to $ 1,000 per year. There now has been added another group called the Fourth World countries, who have been described by at least one international statesman as economic basket cases, due to the extreme nature of their poverty, with per capita incomes of under $ 100 per year. It has been estimated by some economists that upwards of half the woıld's population fall into the last category. Within individual countries, too, there are gross inequalities and inequities. Many nations with per capita incomes of $ 2,000 to $ 4,000 a year have within them large numbers of people living at near starvation levels. Traditional economic viewpoints suggested that with the development of a nation's total economy, the poor would be brought up with the rest of the population to a decent standard of living. There seems to be considerable evidence, however, in recent years, that both the gap between nations and the gap between rich and poor individuals are growing, so that in the 1970s much of the world found itself in worse condition than thirty years previously.

War and Violence

Other major areas of concern are international war and internal violence. Partly because of overpopulation government after government has resorted to military power, police-state tactics and the destruction of civil liberties in order to control their own populations. This has led to rapid increases in the expenditures of military hardware and in the levels of violence, both internal and external throughout much of the world. In spite of the nonproliferation treaty, numerous nations have joined the nuclear club, with the resultant threat not only to their enemies, but ultimately to the whole world.

The United States has been unable to bring about an age of peace in the world, and as the number of new nation states grows each year, calls for world federalism are increasingly resisted. During the 150-year period from 1816 to 1957 there were a total of ninety-three wars, fifty of them between countries, and war was in progress during 126 of the 150 years. Twenty-nine million battle deaths were recorded or reported during the same period. The United States in 1970 was spending an estimated $ 72 billion on its military budget, the Soviet Union $ 40 billion, with France, Britain, and West Germany each spending more than $ 5 billion.

In the same year the United States had over 7500 warheads deliverable by missiles, the Soviet Union, some 5600. In the nuclear arsenals of the United States, the U.S.S.R., Great Britain, France, and China there were over 50,000 megatons of explosive force or the equivalent of fifteen tons of TNT for each man, woman, and child in the world. With a disastrous history of peace and with such incredible levels of violence now available to mankind, war and the threat of war must be a major concern of every nation and of every educational system.

Education: Problems and Solutions

The educational systems of the world are generally looked upon as one of the major solutions to the problems of overpopulation, consumptive values, economic problems, and war. However, education also can be part of the problem. Through a study of education in four Third World nations, education as both "problem" and "solution" will be analysed.

The American model of compulsory schooling has been or is being adopted by most nations. At one time, Great Britain, France, and other Western European countries served as the models for the educational systems of the Third World, and the elite of Africa, Asia, and Latin America were trained at Oxford and the Sorbonne. Since World War II, however, the United States has become a model. It is a tragedy that a model with so many flaws and in such a wealthy nation is being adopted by others who cannot even afford to provide decent housing, food, clothing, and health care for their people.

There are more illiterates in the world today than at any point in the history of mankind. According to the *Population Bulletin,* the world's illiterate population rose from 700 to 782 million adults between 1950 and 1970. In spite of a drop in the percentage of the world's illiterates during the same period from 44 percent to 34 percent, the nations of the Third World were, with few exceptions, unable to keep up with their population growth.[1] Famine stalks hundreds of millions of people in the developing nations. The poor are getting poorer, as evidenced by the August, 1976, economic predictions from the World Bank, which indicate that the poorest nations, those with average incomes of under $ 200 per person, will grow at an annual rate of less than 1 percent for the rest of the twentieth century. That the educational systems of the world are also in crisis is attested to by educational conservatives and liberals alike. Philip Coombs, director of UNESCO's Educational Planning Agency, entitled his 1968 book *The World Education Crisis,*[2] and things have not improved much, if at all, since that time. The model of schooling found in the United States, Western Europe, and the Soviet Union is involved in the process of keeping people illiterate, poor, hungry, and ignorant. What evidence bears out such an outrageous statement? Let us share the example of two countries which have followed the United States, Western European or Soviet models of schooling, and two which have rejected them. References will also be made to programs and experiments in other Third World Countries in an attempt to indicate possible connections between formal, Western-style schooling and the problems of illiteracy and poverty.

Nicaragua

One country which has followed the United States model

of education is the Central American country of Nicaragua. Although it can hardly be called prototypical of all developing nations, it does contain within its social, political economic, and educational systems similarities to much of the rest of the Third World. There are a variety of reasons why Nicaragua has chosen to follow the U.S. Model of education.

American involvement in the country goes back to the Clayton-Bulwer Treaty of 1850, which gave Cornelius Vanderbilt, the American financier, the opportunity which he had been looking for to construct an interoceanic canal across the country. Although the canal was never built, many hundreds of "forty-niners" heading for California, were transported by Vanderbilt's steamship company across the country of Nicaragua and up the west coast to California. In 1855, an American soldier of fortune, William Walker, had himself elected president of the country, but two years later, the combined forces of Central America, supported by Great Britain and by Vanderbilt, brought Walker's short reign to an end. The next major American involvement was in 1912, when U.S. Marines were called in to "protect foreign lives and property" during a rebellion by the opposition party. The Marines remained in Nicaragua from 1912 until 1925 and returned again from 1927 to 1933, during which time they were involved in guerrilla warfare against Augusto Sandino, a man who has since become a symbol of revolution throughout Latin America. In 1933, Sandino was killed by members of the Nicaraguan National Guard led by General Anastasio Somoza, the commander of the Guard and Minister of War, who was elected president of the country in 1936, with U.S. support. Although others have been elected to the presidency since that time, the Somoza family has remained in power behind the scenes for forty years. The current President is the son of General Anastasio Somoza[3] In addition to the historic U.S. involvement in the country, there have been large American investments, many Nicaraguan industries and agribusiness firms having either American partners or American control.

Like many Third World nations, Nicaragua has been plagued with natural disasters, the most recent and famous being the December 23, 1972, earthquake which destroyed the capital city, Managua. There have also been volcanic eruptions, hurricanes, droughts, and other natural disasters, during which time the United States has been active in relief efforts. These have been welcomed and desperately needed by the Nicaraguans, but have been one more penetration by the United States into the country.

With a high percentage of its foreign trade being conducted with the United States, large numbers of American television programs being shown on its nationalized system, American movies dominating its theaters, American corporations controlling many of its businesses, and large numbers of Peace Corps volunteers and missionaries working among its people, the Americanisation of Nicaragua can only be described as extensive. All of these are evidence of the reasons why Nicaragua has adopted an American model of schooling for its society. With tens of millions of dollars in U.S. backed loans to help rebuild their earthquake-shattered schools and industries, it is unlikely that there will be any shift in this direction during the coming years.

The constitution of Nicaragua, like the constitutions of most Third World nations, contains legislation very similar to that found in the United States and Western Europe. Some of the articles are as follows: Public Education is a State duty; primary education is obligatory and both primary and secondary education shall be free; the National University will have autonomous status; academic freedom is guaranteed; teaching is nonpolitical.[4] In its stated *goals and objectives*, the Nicaraguan educational system also reflects the influence of the United States and other societies. Some of its goals for education are as follows: strengthening national unity, cultivating the capacity to understand and appreciate spiritual values; forming a democratic conscience; teaching the rational distribution of time between work, rest, and recreation; and facilitating the acquisition of basic knowledge and cultivating a scientific attitude to banish superstition, prejudice and fanaticism.[5]

In and of themselves, the laws governing the Nicaraguan system and the goals for education are hard to fault. It is only when one looks at the realities of the society that the laws and goals can be brought into question. To have as a law that primary education is obligatory is all well and good; however, in 1974 only 54 out of every 1,000 students who entered rural primary schools in 1969 were graduating from sixth grade. In the urban areas it was considerably better, where 440 of every 1000 entrants were completing primary school.[6] Many students, however, never enter the formal educational system at all, so that the numbers actually receiving an education up to the sixth grade are considerably less than the 39 percent average given in 1974.[7] Free education is also desirable for a society; however, in a country where 50 per cent of the families have incomes of between $ 100 and $ 300 annually,[8] any costs, such as school fees, books, or uniforms, almost automatically eliminate the poor from attending. The autonomous status of the national university and the guarantee of academic freedom are to be found in most constitutions in the Third World. When faced with a lack of jobs and meaningful work following graduation and the injustices which they see all around them, students at both the secondary and university levels in Nicaragua, and throughout most of the Third World, tend to be the centers of dissent and opposition to the government. As a result the national universities are often threatened with cuts in their governmental subsidies and the actual amount of academic freedom is suspect.

Goals of national unity and understanding and appreciating spiritual values are important. To speak, however, of forming a democratic conscience in Third World nations controlled by elite groups is to raise a sense of disbelief in the young people of such societies. To talk of a rational distribution of time between work, rest, and recreation in poor countries where a majority of the people are unemployed or underemployed is making a mockery of an educational goal. This is not to deny the importance of having ideals or goals; but the society must have within it some semblance of actively seeking to achieve those ideals, or they can only lead to a great deal of disillusionment.

In addition to the dissonance between the society and its educational laws and goals, a major educational problem facing a country such as Nicaragua can be seen through its literacy rates. Although a comparative analysis of census data from 1950 to 1971 indicates a progressive decrease in illiteracy from 63 percent of the population ten years of age and over in 1950 to 42 percent in 1971, in terms of absolute numbers of illiterates, the figures show an increase from 369,000 in 1950 to 511,000 in 1970, and a projected 630,000 by 1980. Thus, even with a rapid expansion of the schools within the society, the number of adult illiterates will continue to grow.[9] This is true not only of Nicaragua but of most of the nations of the Third World. It is not for lack of effort that the formal schools have failed to solve the problem of illiteracy. Primary enrollments in Nicaragua rose dramatically in the 1960s, 144,000 to 283,000, while in secondary education the numbers increased from 26,000 to 51,000, and in higher education in the five years from 1965 to 1970, from 3,300 to over 9,000.[10] Even with this massive increase in formal schooling,there will continue to be a growing number of illiterates in the Nicaraguan society.

Following the earthquake of 1972, some of the first buildings rebuilt were the public schools. This was partially due to the Nicaraguan government's adoption of the Western value of formal education, but also due to the pressures of CARE, World Bank, USAID, and other international organisations, which loaned and gave millions of dollars to replace the thousands of classrooms destroyed in that disaster.

Little if any thought was given to whether the schools should be rebuilt first, or if money could not perhaps be better spent in nonformal methods of education or no other sectors of the economy.

The aid given to Nicaragua for its schools is no exception to the policies governing U.S. aid to the rest of the world. One criteria is that, wherever possible, funds will be spent in the United States in the form of purchases of goods or services given by American citizens. American firms provide the printing machines to print textbooks. American firms contract to build schools, often using American-made materials. U.S. advisors are hired to consult on all aspects of the system, and Peace Corps volunteers are provided to develop programs for which there are no trained personnel in the country. In this manner, the Nicaraguan educational system and those of many Third World countries, look suspiciously like those found throughout the United States.

In the mid 1960s, a team of educators was brought together to produce textbooks for all of Central America, financed through grants from the U.S. government. Although the textbooks are generally of quite high quality, it is obvious that if they are funded by the U.S., they will tend to represent, to some extent, American perspectives of reality. American foundation funds have gone into the development of testing techniques and standardized examinations, through a program being developed in Guatemala. Nicaraguan educators, along with those from other Central American countries, are now developing tests based on the College Entrance Board Examinations and using American testing techniques.

In the late 1960s, an American team of educators went to Colombia in South America to develop a series of comprehensive secondary schools for that nation. American administrators helped to design the school, develop the curricula, train the teachers and produce an institution very similar to the suburban U.S. high school, In 1973, a Colombian

UNESCO advisor began work with the Nicaraguans on instituting and building a comprehensive secondary school. Thus, by way of Colombia, another American invention, the comprehensive secondary school, is coming to a Central American country. In the United States, the comprehensive secondary school was seen as a mechanism for providing a variety of educational experiences under one roof while at the same time breaking down class barriers and the stigma attached to vocational programmes. To a certain extent this has been accomplished, although numerous research studies have pointed out the tracking that sill occurs in most of these institutions, with low prestige in the vocational track. Because they need a large student population and because of the industrial-vocational basis in their technical curriculum, these schools have almost always been located in urban areas. Nicaragua is no exception and the plans are to build a comprehensive secondary school in Managua. This school, along with the placement of almost all other secondary schools in urban centers, has become a cause, if only a minor one, for an increased urbanisation within the country. As E.F. Schumacher pointed out, "Technology cannot eradicate the three-fold disease of mass migration into the cities, followed by mass unemployment, and finally the threat or actuality of mass hunger, Because in the end, food is produced not on the balconies in the cities, but in the vast rural areas.[11]

The schools of Nicaragua have attracted, young people from the rural areas, where they are needed in the farming communities and into the large cities where they become part of the large unemployed or underemployed population. A basic question can be raised, however, as to what aspects of a traditional society, one in which farming, rural life and smallness are valued, are communicated when students are brought into a large, urban, comprehensive secondary school with an industrial-technical bias.

In addition to the urbanisation problem raised by the comprehensive secondary school, a further urban bias is found in enrollment statistics. At the primary school level, although the 1971 census indicated the 53 per cent of the population still lived outside of the cities, only 40 per cent of the primary school enrollment came from those rural areas.[12] Almost all secondary schools are located in urban centers, thus forcing a student from a rural home to go to a city in order to receive further schooling. Although the Nicaraguan government has recently given rural development as its number-one priority, it remains to be seen how successful new program will be in upgrading the rural standard of living.

All too often in the Third World, aid is funneled into bureaucracies located in the capital city, and as has happened in the poverty programmes of the United States, the people benefiting most have been the educated, urbanized, middle classes. One of the mechanisms traditionally used to reach the rural poor has been agricultural education. This is true also of Nicaragua, where what are known as Escuelas Granjas are located in the countryside. In 1974, while giving a speech in Nicaragua on the importance of agricultural education, one of the authors was interrupted by a young man who stood up and told him in no uncertian terms that agricultural education in the absence of meaningful land reform was a waste of time, money, and energy. Some land reform has taken place, but few Third World countries ruled by an elite landholding class are willing to move rapidly in this area. Vocational and agricultural education are all too often a mechanism for maintaining the status quo and improving the lot of the rich, while doing very little for the poor.

Ivan Illich[13] and other authors have pointed out that the schools of the world tend to exacerbate the problems of social class and status, and perpetuate elites rather than break down barriers. Evidence of this can be found in Nicaragua, and also throughout most of the developing world. At the primary level, one finds most social classes represented. By the time one reaches *ciclo básico,* the equivalent of junior high school, and certainly by the time the student comes to the end of senior high or university, the poor, be they urban or rural, are seldom to be found in the schools. Nicaragua is no exception to this pattern in which the schools tend to perpetuate the wealthy of the society. This is not to say that some students do not make it up through the system on their own merit, but for the most part, the elites of the world use the mechanism of a supposed meritocracy to perpetuate themselves in their positions of economic, political, and social power.

In a 1968 study in Thailand, one of the authors attempted to analyze the social class makeup of the Thai universities. While 80 to 90 percent of the people live and work in rural farming communities, less than 8 per cent of the university population was made up of this particular class. University students came from business, government, and military families.[14] In Nicaragua the wealthy send their children to the private parochial schools and to the private university, while the middle class tends to send its children up through the public system to the national university. Most of the rural poor are gone from the system by second or third grade, and the poor in the towns and cities drop out by the end of the primary grades.

Nicaragua serves as an interesting example in the area of teacher training. An American model was adopted in the early 1950s, when advisors went to Nicaragua to structure the secondary level normal schools. Along with the Americanisation of the teacher training which occurred at that time, there has been the inexorable process of upgrading the amount of education the teachers have needed. At one time a secondary school degree was sufficient. Today, the pressures are building for them to have two or four years of college or a *licenciatura,* which is similar to a U.S. master's degree. As teacher-educators, we would be hard put to deny the value of education in upgrading teachers. One must ask, however, where scarce resources should be used. Is it really necessary for all teachers to have a master's, four years of college, or even a secondary normal school degree, or could the money perhaps not be better spent on in-service training to upgrade the quality of instruction, with more emphasis put on literacy and basic adult education programs?

Another evidence of the effort to emulate the American school system can be found in the pressures to expand the number of secondary school years from five to six. This would, of course, put a tremendous strain on an already overburdened economy. In addition, there are pressures to have guidance counselors in all schools and to begin a program of preschool education. The overwhelming problems of health, poverty, and malnutrition facing Nicaragua and other Third World countries make the adoption of an expensive educational system, based on a United States, Russian, French, British, or other developed-nation model, difficult to justify.

Nicaragua is representative of much of the Third World in the large numbers of students and members of the middle and upper classes who go to the United States to study or live. The exact number of Nicaraguans residing in the United States is difficult to estimate. From the size of the Nicaraguan *barrios* in San Francisco, New Orleans and Los Angeles, however, it is known to be many thousands. As with many countries of the Third World, when students have received their training in Western Europe or the United States, they often remain in the developed countries even though their skills are desperately needed back home.

From the standpoint of teaching methodology, the Nicaraguan educational system has also adopted a traditional style. This methodology can be described as a model in which students compete against each other for scarce places both within the educational system and the society. An authoritarian relationship predominates in the schools between principals and teachers, and between teachers and students, as opposed to a more democratic model, and the schools are seen as a mechanism for the creation of a labour force attuned to the needs of the factories of the society. Traditional lecture-recitation-memorisation techniques predominate in the schools, which in their organisation also tend to reflect the hierarchical nature of the society.

In many respects the Nicaraguan educational system is a minor image of thousands of U.S. school districts. The question has yet to be seriously faced as to whether such a system makes much sense in a predominantly poor, rural nation, with massive problems of illiteracy, poverty, disease, and malnutrition.

Ivory Coast

On the African continent is another nation which has adopted a Western educational system. In this case, the Ivory Coast, owing to its colonial history, has opted for a French model. It is one of the "richest" nations of black Africa, with a per capita income of slightly more than $ 380. As with most developing nations, however, the per capita figure is highly misleading in that the wealth is concentrated in Abidjan, among the wealthy Ivory Coast citizens and the large numbers of French advisors, who live and work in the capital. The 80 percent of the people who live in the rural areas have incomes far below the $ 380 figure. In addition, there is high, urban unemployment due to people moving from the rural areas and also from immigration from neighbouring countries.

For a nation which is comparatively wealthy in African terms, the literacy rate is a low 20 per cent even though the government is spending almost one-third of its revenues on the formal educational system. It is not from lack of funding that the Ivory Coast government has been unable to deal with the problems of illiteracy and the shift from rural to urban areas. It has adopted a position of gradualism in its approach to educational reform. This means that the curriculum is still basically French, 30 percent of the students receiving baccalaureate are expatriates, and the educational system is still largely in the hands of French citizens. Ninety-five percent of the nation's industrial capacity is still in French hands.[15]

One experiment which the Ivory Coast government is attempting is the "radical transformation" of the country's primary schools by the use of instructional television. The Ivory Coast was faced, as are many African nations, with large numbers of languages, in this case up to sixty different tribal languages, and thus educational television was instituted in an attempt to teach a national language. The country has rapidly expanded its educational television system with the goal of reaching 720,000 students in 16,500 classes by 1980. The problems with the educational television system, however, are numerous. In the neighbouring country of Niger, the plans for educational television failed to materialize, after it became obvious that a rapid expansion of the primary schools would lead to space problems at the secondary school level. In the initial years of using educational television, the Ivory Coast has experienced many difficulties; first of all is the impact of educational television on the desire of primary school graduates to leave the rural areas and move to the large city. Seventy-five percent of all classrooms experienced television breakdowns, and at any one time, up to 8 percent of the TVs were not functioning. The costs to the government were considerable, with many millions of dollars spent on the initial acquisition of equipment and a continuing expenditure of millions of dollars to maintain it. In addition, the social class bias found through the use of instructional television was not dealt with. Middle and upper class Ivory Coast and French citizens continued to send their children to the elite schools, where they would receive instruction from well-qualified teachers in small classes, while it was the poor who were to be educated through television.

This is not to say that all aspects of educational television in the Ivory Coast have been a failure. It has stimulated curricular and teaching methodological reforms, and through its use large numbers of children who were unable to go to school are now receiving some kind of education. The concepts of education and modernisation given by television in the

Ivory Coast, however, are basically French in milieu and culture. Thus, children are being prepared to reject their own society and adopt foreign ways. Observers of Ivory Coast educational television have remarked that the system is preparing better-educated taxi drivers, manual labourers, and discontented farmers.[16]

Educational Technology

Educational technology has never been the success story that its backers at IBM, General Electric, Sony and a host of other manufacturing firms in this country, Japan, and Europe have hoped that it would be. Pressures have been applied to take this educational salvation to many other countries of the world. Mexico, El Salvador, Turkey, Thailand, and India are just a few of the other countries currently making attempts at providing education of one sort or another through educational television or radio. If one is to believe researchers, the success of these technological systems has been dramatic with great cost savings to the countries involved.

Carnoy and Levin in their article, "Evaluation of Educational Media: Some Issues," in *Instructional Science*, October, 1975, suggest however, that much of the research on the success of educational television may not be as accurate as the researchers indicate. They quote James Q. Wilson, who set forth two laws which he believes apply to all cases of social science evaluation of public policy:[17]

> *First Law:* All policy interventions in social problems produce the intended effect — *if* the research is carried out by those implementing the policy or their friends.
>
> *Second Law:* No policy intervention in social problems produces the intended effect — *if* the research is carried out by independent third parties, especially those skeptical of the policy.

Carnoy and Levin admit to being critics and cynical or

skeptical of the effects of educational technology in the developing world. Their first objection is that the cost of instructional technologies is almost always understated, in that most studies do not include all aspects of the projects such as technical assistance, the inputs of existing government agencies and other institutions, and the use of existing buildings and other resources. Perhaps more importantly, however, they question the standards by which effectiveness of educational television is measured, suggesting that in most cases the researchers use an extremely narrow measurement standard to assess educational outcomes. Although cognitive outcomes may be quite high, the authors point to other research that indicates that noncognitive factors, such as socialisation, appear to be far more important than the cognitive ones. They go on to point out that the use of educational technology tends to force curricula and teaching into a straight jacket.[18]

A further problem, seldom faced by the developing nations, is that with the use of educational technology, there will be a large increase in the numbers of students graduating at the various levels in the educational system. Evidence from Mexico, El Salvador, Samoa, the Ivory Coast, and Korea indicates that technological innovations tend to increase the number of years of schooling in the potential urban labour force, but that vast numbers of these graduates become unemployed and thus put downward pressure on the wages of both skilled and semiskilled labour. Another criticism is the effect that the use of educational technology has on the exposure of children and young people to a diversity of experiences and institutions, and perhaps most importantly the possibilities of misuse of educational mass media by the authoritarian regimes, which currently control much of the world's population.[19]

With little evidence of success in the United States or other developed societies, one would be hard put to predict any great success in the Third World through the use of educational television, and one can only conclude that the basic motivation for its use is the pressure from large multinational corporations and their governments on Third World countries, including pressures on the bilateral and multilateral aid agencies which provide the funding with which these products can be bought.

In a nation such as the Ivory Coast, so thoroughly controlled by an external power, it is understandable why the educational system reflects French culture and technological desires. However, with a large majority of its people illiterate and living outside the money economy, the formal educational system and recent educational television can only be viewed as destructive of a sense of national pride, as perpetuators of social inequality, and as purveyors of Western values and culture.

Cuba

A nation which followed the American-Western model of schooling for some sixty years and later rejected it to develop its own is Cuba. If anything, Cuba has been more deeply involved with the United States than Nicaragua. Much of this involvement has to do with its proximity, only ninety miles off our coast. Its domination of the entrances to the Gulf of Mexico and the principal routes to the Panama Canal have made it of great importance to the United States.

Throughout the nineteenth century, Cuba and the Caribbean were seen as an American sphere of influence. In fact, in 1864, the Polk administration made an informal offer to buy Cuba from Spain. The Treaty of Paris, signed on December 10, 1898, provided that the "civil rights and political status of the island should be determined by the Congress of the United States." It was at this point that the client status of the island to the United States became obvious. The *Platt Amendment,* in 1900, required Cuba to sell or lease lands to the United States for naval stations, limited Cuba's treaty-making power and its capacity to contract debts, and gave the United States the right to intervene and to preserve independence and maintain law and order. These U.S. rights were written into the new Cuban Constitution and on May 20, 1902, Cuba was formally independent.[20] With the Platt Amendment, Theodore Roosevelt wanted to teach the Cuban population to "behave decently." He felt that the best way to help was to Americanize them in education, law, and government.[21] For the next thirty years the Platt Amendment dominated Cuban-American relations and was resented by the Cubans as an extreme example of American paternalism. In May, 1934, a new treaty replaced the permanent treaty, and the Platt Amendment was dropped, except for a provision regarding Guantanamo Naval Base. It was at this time that Fulgencio Batista was installed as provisional president and maintained his rule off and on for the next twenty-four years.[22]

During the two periods of direct U.S. intervention from 1898 to 1902, and from 1906 to 1909, the American-style, Cuban education system was founded. The new school law, based on that of Ohio, created local school boards, called for compulsory school attendance, and set up teacher training schools, textbooks, and curricula based on an Ohio model. Some have suggested that in addition to organisational and structural kinds of changes, American middle-class values were also embedded deeply within the Cuban educational system.[23]

During the Batista regime in Cuba, American investment increased dramatically. Although there was a decrease in the percentage of American ownership within the country, the U.S. total investment rose from $ 624 million in 1950 to $ 955 million in 1959. It is also true that the Cuban ownership also was centered in the hands of an elite and of a middle class, while the vast majority of peasants did not receive the benefits from most of the American investment.[24] By 1959 Cuba had the highest per capita income of any country in Latin America, was an unhealthy imbalance in the spread of the wealth, and intense poverty, unemployment, and other problems still existed.

This American dominance of the culture and the society, along with a twenty-year decline in the amount of education and other benefits for the common man, were some of the causes which led to the Fidel Castro revolution in 1958-59. That revolution wrought significant educational changes. Not all aspects of the Cuban revolution have been admirable, but in education, much of what has occurred can be highly instructive for Third World nations faced with similar problems.

In revolutionary Cuba, education is a major part of the societal attempt to change the country. The revolution had, and still has, four basic goals, (1) to expand and utilize fully the society's productive capacities; (2) to eliminate economic, political, and cultural dependence on the United States; (3) to replace the rigid class structure of capitalist Cuba with a classless and egalitarian society, to eliminate sexism and racism, and to end the urban bias in the economy, culture, and politics; and (4) to transform work into challenging and creative activity for the new socialist man.[25] In addition to these four overall goals of the society, there objectives were stated for the school system: (1) stagnation in education was to be replaced by rapid growth in enrollments, (2) national scientific and cultural dependency was to be eliminated by the expansion of high-level educational, technical, and research facilities, (3) the class structure of Cuban education was to be destroyed and education was to be made available to all, and (4) the social relations of Cuban education were to be transformed to develop a new socialist man.[26]

Cuba, prior to the revolution of 1958-59, had a literacy similar to Nicaragua's. Although between 1899 and 1953 the percentage of illiterates dropped from 43.8 per cent to 23.6 per cent, in absolute numbers the number of illiterates had grown from 690,000 to an estimate of over one million.[27] In 1961, when the Castro regime attempted to register all illiterates in preparation for a massive literacy campaign, over 900,000 were registered. In the one year of the campaign, over 700,000 illiterates were taught to read and the illiteracy rate was brought down to 3.9 percent.[28] This campaign has been seen as one of the most successful of its type in educational history, and yet as one looks around the rest of Latin America and the Third World, one sees very few similar attempts at trying to wipe out illiteracy. Most nations are attempting to deal with the problem in the traditional manner of public schooling.

Such attempts appear to be doomed to failure. The will of the elites, who have seen the successful Cuban example yet refuse to restructure their educational plans to wipe out illiteracy must be questioned.

In addition to the problem of the growing number of illiterates prior to the revolution, the Cuban educational system was going through extreme stagnation from 1938 through 1958, a period in which the number of primary-school-age children never attending school rose from 20 percent to close to 35 percent.[29] In comparison, from 1959 to 1969 the total primary school enrollment more than doubled from 717,000 to over 1,560,000.[30] Perhaps more important than the overall statistics on enrollment have been attempts to balance urban and rural areas in literacy and primary education. This is partially reflected in the dramatic expansion during the ten-year period in adult enrollment, which went from 27,000 in 1958-59 to 425,000 in 1967-68.[31] The educational system of Cuba appears to have been successful in dealing with problems of illiteracy and basic skills for young people and adults, something which cannot be said for most of the Third World, following the traditional American or European patterns of schooling.

Secondary school enrollment also rose dramatically after the revolution, from 63,000 in 1958-59 to 177,000 in 1967-68.[32] Similar figures can be found in technical and higher education. Perhaps more dramatic than the statistics of number of students in higher education since the revolution is the breakdown by departments in which the students study. Before the revolution, 32 percent of the students were in the humanities; following the revolution that number dropped to only 5.8 percent. Agriculture rose from 4.3 percent to 11.9 percent and the sciences rose from 7.9 percent to 11.3 Technological fields grew from 10.3 to 28.4, and medicine went from 22 percent to 24.8 percent.[33] A change of emphasis following the revolution led to education being seen as a service to the people and not just to satisfy the individual needs and interests of the students involved.

Other evidences of the attempt to provide a more egalitarian educational system can be found in the number of state scholarships, which rose from 15,000 in 1958 to 277,999 in 1970.[34] Education is a big business in Cuba. The state education budget rose from 77 million pesos in 1958 to 280 million by 1969. In addition, one-fifth of Cuba's total productive capacity was devoted to schooling in 1968-69, a figure unsurpassed among the major countries of the world. Education rivaled sugar as Cuba's largest productive sector.[35] Cuba has shown that large expenditures on education when tied to productive activity and when part of an egalitarian ethic, need not lead to increased poverty and ignorance. Whereas most nations have seen their schoolroom class sizes rise from twenty to thirty to fifty, sixty or even higher, the Cuban revolution has seen its class size drop at the primary school level from 41.3 in 1958-59 to 29.8 in 1968-69. There have been some increases at other levels, but once again, the Cuban government has attempted to provide good quality at the lowest grades.[36]

In most nations the elite and the newly educated middle class want nothing to do with manual labour. The Cuban revolution has attempted to dignify it. This has been done through a variety of mechanisms, one of which is the *escuela al campo,* or literally "the school goes to the country." In this program students spend summers in the countryside, and during the cane-cutting season, entire schools are moved into the fields. "Interest circles" are found in all schools and are centered around productive kinds of activity, in which the students learn practical things to be used in farming or in other ventures. Through these programs, government propaganda, and the involvement of Premier Castro in the manual occupations, labour has been dignified within the country to an extent found in few other Third World nations. Attempts have been made to tie schooling to factories and farms of the country rather than replicate these activities in technical or agricultural schools, as has been the tradition in most other nations.[37]

Another way in which the Cuban revolution has attempted to deal with education has been to encourage students to study in groups, rather then compete with each other. Teachers are charged with becoming more democratic in their outlook rather than authoritarian, and the system is being changed to provide a more egalitarian milieu in which racial, social and sexual barriers are broken down. In an attempt to change the elite nature of higher education, a process known as the universalisation of the university has taken place. In this program, students are to be integrated into the productive activities of the country and are asked to carry out project in which they put their theories into practice. The Castro regime hopes that in this manner a new elite will not develop, as it has in the Soviet Union, Eastern Europe, and some of the other communist-socialist countries.[38]

Universities or higher education, however, are considered necessary in order to break away from the dependence upon what was previously control of much of the society. Today, one can find Cubans themselves in almost all positions of power and control, something not to be found before the revolution. With the abolition of private schools following the revolution, the elite had no place to send their children. Of course, a very high percentage of the elite left the country and emigrated to the United States and to other parts of Latin America. In one sense, this made the task easier to change the society, and yet also very difficult, for Castro was left without a trained cadre to run the country.

All of this is not to say that the Cuban educational revolution has been a dramatic success in all areas. The problems of elitism can still be found, and there is some question as to the quality of the teachers, following the rapid expansion which occurred after the revolution. There is also a lack of materials, furniture, and equipment in many of the schools, and even though the vast majority of young people are currently receiving a primary education, secondary schools and universities still take only a small percentage of their age groups. Whether Cuba will be able to emphasize primary schooling and basic education and still produce the high level of technical, scientific, and administrative skills needed is still a question to be answered. There is little arguing, however, with the success of the Cuban educational model in dealing with the massive problems of adult illiteracy and primary education within the broader context of a society dedicated to wiping out poverty, disease, and malnutrition.

Tanzania

An African nation which has rejected much of Western-style schooling, in a British model, is Tanzania. For the first six years following its independence in 1961, the country continued in a basic British pattern of education and society. Unlike the Ivory Coast, Tanzania is one of the poorest nations in Africa. It is over 90 percent rural, with large numbers of people not even entering the money economy. It is a nation of about 11.9 million people and has a harsh environment, used primarily for unintensive types of agriculture. About two-thirds of the nation is infested with the tsetse fly, which severely limits its agricultural potential. The nation is 99 per cent African, with small numbers of Arabs, Asians, and Europeans making up the rest of the population. It has about 120 tribes, the largest having less than 10 percent of the total population. Approximately half the people have traditional religious belief systems, one-quarter are Moslem, and another quarter are Christian. The language of Swahili has been the "lingua franca" of the people, although the schools at a higher levels are conducted in English.[39]

Like the Ivory Coast and Nicaragua, Tanzania has a tremendous problem with a literate population of only 10 to 15 percent in Swahili and less than 1 per cent in English. The problems of school attendance are also great, with fewer than 50 percent of the appropriate age groups to be found in elementary school, only 3 per cent at the secondary level, and a small fraction to be found in higher education.[40]

In 1967, President Nyerere, one of the most important intellectuals and leaders of the Third World, made what has come to be called the Arusha Declaration.[41] In that declaration, a strong ideological base was set down for the development of Tanzania, and the nation's only political party, TANU, laid down the direction in which Tanzania was to move over the coming years. The TANU creed states that all human beings are equal and that every individual has the right to dignity, respect, freedom of expression, movement, religious belief, and association. Every citizen has the right to participate in the government at all levels, and the right to receive a just return for his labour. The natural resources of the country belong to all of its citizens. The state must have effective control over the principal means of production, in addition to the right to intervene in the economy to prevent exploitation of individuals or groups and to prevent the accumulation of wealth to an extent inconsistent with the existence of a classless society.[42] The subtitles of the "Arusha Declaration" were "Socialism and Self-Reliance," and those words summarize where the country of Tanzania has attempted to move since 1967. This is obviously a very different direction than that followed currently throughout most of the Third World.

In 1966, President Nyerere could point to increases in the total numbers of students receiving an education: in first grade, from 121,000 to 154,000 between 1961 and 1966, a 27 percent increase; in the last year of secondary school, from 176 to 761, a 332 percent increase.[43] The number of students receiving no education at all or not being enrolled at any particular level, however, was staggering, and thus it became obvious to the president and to the other Tanzanian leaders that the formal educational system could not meet the society's needs. In addition, President Nyerere stated there were four major problems with the system that needed to be changed. First, it was elitist in orientation and benefited mainly the few who were able to climb up through it. Second, the system alienated the people from the countryside and from the society, turning them into 'Europeans." Third, the system was geared towards a perspective that education was acquired from books and that formal education was a criterion for goodness and success. Lastly, the formal educational system was not contributing to the economic output of the society, but was basically a consumption item.[44] These statements, if given by somebody of less stature than the president, would no doubt have led to a revolt on the part of the people. However, Nyerere being the father of his country and having great prestige with most of his people, was able to make such a harsh analysis.

In a 1967 speech entitled "Education for Self-Reliance" Nyerere set forth the basic principles which were to be followed in the Tanzanian society for the years to come. Whereas the education inherited from the British was geared to preparing an intellectual elite, the formal and nonformal education system under the new plans were to become part of a socialist state. Whereas the colonial educational system had tended to emphasize modern, Western values, the new educational system was to emphasize 'Ujamaa,' the Swahili word for familyhood. Nyerere expanded this word to include all the tenets of an egalitarian socialism. The exploitation and control of one man by another and the accumulation of wealth were antisocial acts, while traditional forms of landholding were to be abolished, and familyhood, group, or societal control of the land was to become one of the bases for the new society. The people of Tanzania were to be educated to extend the concept of family beyond tribe, community, or nation, and to look at all men as their brothers.[45] This was a very big order for any educational system, particularly one which reaches such a small percentage of its people, and to say it has been a dramatic success would be an overstatement. However, the reforms were put in practice between 1967 and 1977, and some interesting, even exciting things occurred in Tanzania.

The people, have bene moved into Ujamaa villages through persuasion, not force, for Nyerere adopted a gradualist approach and not a dramatic, violent revolution. The work of creating the new cooperative society is done by the villagers themselves and is not forced on them. This has been done through a decentralisation of the Tanzanian government, so that there are eighteen nearly autonomous regions, which are further decentralised all the way down to the village level. In this way, every Tanzanian citizen participates in the decisions affecting his or her own life. "Self-help, self-reliance and cooperation" is the creed adopted throughout the whole society and in the educational system.[46] In contrast to the Nicaraguan and Ivory Coast examples, the emphasis of the Tanzanian society and educational system had not been on its capital city or upon industry, but upon the rural areas where most of the people live and work in agriculture.

Educational reform, as outlined in "Education for Self-Reliance" has come through three major areas: (1) curricular reform, (2) the reorganisation of the schools, and (3) an increase in the age of those entering primary schools.[47] Recognising that the vast majority of young people would be unable to attend or graduate from primary school the president declared that primary schools must prepare students for life and not just the academics. In an astute recognition, however, that a child of ten, eleven, or twelve, on graduating from primary school, is not capable intellectually, physically or economically, of being an independent productive citizen, Nyerere declared that young people would enter school at a later age. Thus upon completion of their primary education, they would be both old enough and well trained enough to become productive citizens within the society.

A great deal of emphasis has been put on eliminating illiteracy. A successful regional program has been under experimentation for eight years in the Lake Region, and the literacy rate has risen from 14 percent to 67 percent, with over 300,000 people attending over 10,000 classes. Taking seriously the ideals of radical theorist Paolo Friere, the literacy training deals with specific kinds of problems faced by the people. Thus the books talk about how to use pesticides and fertilizers, how not to be cheated by middlemen, and how to develop a cooperative. The materials used are perceived by the rural poor as having direct relevance to their lives. Many hundreds of thousands of adults are learning to read and write in Swahili. All primary school teachers and civil servants must conduct classes, as literacy is seen as a major tool for economic betterment of the rural poor.[48]

In order to break down the elitism so rampant in the educational systems of the Third World, each school is attempting to become self-reliant. Teacher-training schools have their own farms and workshops to raise the funds needed for their institution. Agricultural students at the University of Dar es Salaam no longer become pencil-pushing bureaucrats, but also clean out barns and milk cows. In an attempt to deal with the problems of people moving to the cities and of the rural population being ignored, Rural Training Centers have been created in at least half of Tanzania's districts. Health education, family planning, and agricultural training are all aspects of what occurs in these centers. Village leaders are trained and taught how to plan and conduct meetings, keep books, and form cooperatives. Ministry of Agriculture Training Institutes are also located throughout the country. In these, young people who have graduated from primary school are trained to work in the rural areas, with an emphasis on crops, animal husbandry, irrigation, and land use. They must spend at least two years living in a thatch or mud hut in one of the

Ujamaa villages and help the rural poor improve their lives.[49]

"Learning through living" has become the ideal for education throughout Tanzania. Teachers in special teacher-training institutes no longer study a British curriculum, for the curriculum has been Africanized, with African history and culture replacing British history and culture. Examinations designed by and for Tanzanians are used in deciding who continues for more education. In spite of its goals and obvious efforts towards a just society, Tanzania still has tremendous problems Illiteracy, famine, malnutrition, and lack of work are faced by many of its people. There is great hope and enthusiasm, however, as the country has recognised that a model based upon that of Great Britain, France, the Soviet Union or the United States does not meet the needs of its 90 per cent rural poor, and that only a dramatic restructuring, as has been attempted since 1967, will begin to solve the problems of its society.

A Critique of World Education

With world population doubling in thirty-six years, solutions must soon be found to the related problems of illiteracy, poverty, malnutrition, and starvation. The particular educational model that the powerful nations of the world encourage or permit to exist has life-and-death implications for hundreds of millions of the world's poor.

With a gross national product of a trillion dollars, the United States can, possibly, afford expenditures on education in excess of $ 100 billion annually. With the possible exception of the newly rich oil nations, the Third World countries must carefully shepherd their scarce resources, spending them only on education that benefits all members of their society and not just the elite. In the export of its curricula, teaching materials, technology, textbooks, structure and organisation, idealised educational objectives, and other things being directly copied by other nations, the United States must be careful that it doesn't become an indirect party in keeping the poor of this world illiterate and starving. To speak of spending 5 or 10 percent of the gross national product in a trillion dollar economy or of 15 to 20 percent of a national budget that runs into the hundreds of billions of dollars, is very different from speaking of spending 20 to 50 percent of the national budget for education when only a few million dollars are available for all sectors of a society. Each dollar spent on an educational system that tends to perpetuate elites takes food from starving children. Every dollar spent on massive comprehensive secondary schools and university education prevents other children and adults from being educated at the most basic literacy or primary school levels. Every dollar spent in education is one less dollar that can be spent on economic improvements to provide jobs for the unemployed graduates coming out of primary and secondary schools or universities. In the absence of an egalitarian ideology, education tends to secure the positions and power of the elites, and wastes scarce resources desperately needed in health and agriculture.

That the poor nations of the world cannot afford Western-style schooling should now be obvious to all. Why such schooling is being adopted world-wide may not be quite so obvious. Following earthquakes or other natural disasters, which seem to regularly strike the poor nations of the world, the schools are some of the first structures to be rebuilt with international aid. All too often the motives of powerful nations are not strictly humanitarian. The school is a major socialising agent in all countries of the world, and it has been suggested by some social scientists that it serves an even greater role in the Third World than it does among the developed nations. The socialisation which takes place in the schools leads towards a greater acceptance of urbanisation, mechanisation, a Western-style attitude toward work and achievement. Numerous studies have been made with grants from the various American foundations and funds from USAID to discover the reasons why the Third World nations refuse to or seem incapable of adopting Western attitudes toward work, industry, capital savings, and other aspects of our culture. The schools, with their emphasis upon achievement, future-orientation, and industrial-type work training, are a major socializing influence toward Western style of life. The question is seldom raised as to whether other, more traditional value systems might have some qualities worth maintaining and that the adoption of a Western set of values may not be the best thing for the whole world.

It appears to have been accepted on face value that there are vast benefits to be derived by the Third World in interaction with the developed nations of the West or the Communist-bloc nations. Few have asked what are the costs of that economic or educational interaction. One cost has been the massive brain drain to the United States and Europe. Large numbers of individuals are trained to very high levels within their own country or in the United States, and find themselves caught between the traditional values of their families and homeland and those given to them by Western-style schooling. Confronted with the opportunity to make a better living in the United States or Europe, many jump at the chance.

Not all of the Third World peoples live in abject poverty, despair and disease, nor do all people suffer from a great deprivation of culture or opportunity. Many have enough to eat and live a satisfying existence; yet the mass media and the Western-style educational systems create a sense of deprivation, a desire for an ever greater standard of living, and a dissatisfaction with traditional values and culture. Few nations have been able to resist the cultural, economic, and educational penetration by the United States, Western Europe and the Soviet Union.[50] Few countries have either the leadership or the motivation to take an independent road, but it is precisely this type of independence that much of the Third World possibly needs. It is probably too late for those countries which are rich in mineral resources to prevent constant contact with the developed world. However, those nations with few natural resources and little wealth, those that have recently been called the Fourth World, might find it to their benefit to follow the lead of Tanzania and attempt a policy of noncooperation and non-penetration with and by the developed nations.

Before concluding that such direction is absurd, we should look at "developed" societies with their rising crime rates, mental illness, child brutality, pollution, waste, depletion of natural resources and a host of other problems pointed out by numerous commentators, and ask: Is this the type of society towards which the poor of the world ought to strive? The current model of interaction and involvement by the rich nations with the poor, whether in political, military, economic, or educational terms, has almost always led to the rich getting richer and the increasing poverty of the poor. It is perhaps not too far-fetched, then, to suggest that Western-style economics, politics, values, and education should be rejected by Third and Fourth World nations.

The American, British, French, and Soviet educational systems and their copies in the poor nations of the world are based on a hierarchical, factory, product-oriented, and quality-controlled model of education. Whether such a model has worked for a modernized, technological society will not be debated here. That it has not worked and is not working in the traditional agricultural nations is all too evident. Carnoy suggests that "knowledge itself is colonised."[51] Although we and the Europeans no longer have colonies of our own, there are power elites in most nations who are more than willing to adopt an educational system which continues to perpetuate inequality and protect their positions. The schools become one of the major socializing agents in the shift from a traditional rural, agricultural existence to an urban, factory-oriented one, and these modern institutions are all too often controlled by multinational corporations. Is it any wonder that we support school systems, throughout the world which promote domestic tranquility, profits, and a continued flow of the raw materials and manufactured goods to the United States, Europe, and the Soviet Union and the development of a society of consumers along Western lines?

Knowledge has become curricularised and the school is the only means by which the oppressed of this world are permitted to obtain the sacraments necessary for their own salvation. The poor are given an unequal chance in this colonised, curricularised lottery, which at best will only enslave them in an urban factory setting, little better and possibly worse than their traditional feudal farms. The poverty-stricken of the world seldom rebel, for they suffer from what Friere calls the "culture of silence" and a "pedagogy of oppression."[52] Individuals attempting to break the power of the controlled school systems and institute a pedagogy of liberation find themselves exiled or imprisoned by the power elites of their countries. Nations attempting to break away from the domination of their economies or educational systems by world powers soon find themselves blacklisted and open game for covert and overt pressures. The oppressive aspects of modern schooling have become too clear to many people throughout the world, and unless the United States and other powerful nations become cognizant of the role they play in educational colonialism, we shall become increasingly isolated and lose what international moral integrity we might still have.

The Interdependence of Mankind

The problems listed earlier of population, energy, pollution, war and quality of life indicate the increasing interrelatedness of all nations. Marshall McLuhan heralded the new age in the title of his book *We and Peace in the Global Village.* No longer is mankind separated in time or in space, but we now live in the world of "all at onceness," in which we are not just observers of other men's tragedies and wars but participants. The same theme was struck by Kenneth Boulding who said that mankind no longer lives on an "illimitable plane," where there was always somewhere to go over the horizon and neither man's ignorance nor his armies could be considered a fatal flaw.

Instead, we now find ourselves on a crowded and precarious spaceship which is being destroyed through lack of an appropriate organisation, ethic, and conduct.[53] It is imperative that mankind recognize the nature of the global village and spaceship earth and the demands that such a changing concept puts on societies in general, and the schools in particular.

At one time it was possible for humanity to exist in small, separate, isolated cultures or nations. Such a possibility has been wiped out with the development of modern methods of warfare, our interdependence of raw materials and manufactured goods, and new forms of transportation and instantaneous communication.

Barbara Ward in her book *Spaceship Earth* summarizes the point:

> Most of the energies of our society tend towards unity.... We have become neighbours in terms of inescapable proximity and instant communication. We are neighbours in economic interest and technological direction. We are neighbours in the risk of total destruction.[54]

Traditionally the schools have emphasized the nation-state and the geographical differences between nations. Within the United States we have placed the emphasis upon the melting pot, and it is only recently that our society has moved towards cultural pluralism and an acceptance of diversity on a worldwide scale. Humanity must come to value differences in religion, race, language, culture, economic system, forms of government, and in that acceptance reach an understanding that will lead to a world of peace, freedom, and justice. In that process the role of the schools assumes great importance.

CASE Study : Education in the Third World

Place yourself in the position of the Minister of Education in a Third World Nation. It is your duty to appear before the

Cabinet and make a case for the educational system. In preparing your speech, you realise that you must deal with the following questions: What percentage of students will be enrolled in the formal educational system at the primary, secondary, and higher education levels? What type of infomal educational programs do you propose for those who cannot obtain formal schooling and for the vast numbers of adult illiterates in the country? What mechanisms do you propose to prevent the continuation of the urban migration and make life in the rural villages better for the people? What type of education should be offered at each level in the formal schools? How much education do your teachers need and what should they be paid? Considering that the cost of living in the capital city is similar to that in the United States and Western Europe, you must somehow build schools, pay teachers, and pay for all the other parts of the educational system. What mechanisms do you propose to the Cabinet to save money and yet educate your people fairly and well?

Thought Question

1. Many poor nations see American and other international pressure on the part of the rich nations for birth control as a form of imperialism. Population control follows economic and social justice, it does not precede it, according to this view. If this position is right, and there appears to be some evidence to back it up, what can be done to prevent mass starvation from overpopulation in the years while the poor nations are "catching up" economically?

2. What are ways in which birth-control information can and should be advanced within the schools and the rest of the society?

3. Should people have the right to breed without limit, or should national and/or international controls be instituted?

4. The Green Revolution, which only a few years ago was seen as the solution to humanity's problems of feeding itself,

has sputtered to a halt as a result of values differences, lack of capital, poor water control, inadequate land reform, and inequitable farm wages. What role can the educational systems of the world play in these areas, so that the promise of "miracle grains" can be at least partially realised?

5. With the United States consuming many times its "share" of the world's energy and resources, what can the schools contribute to resolving questions of consumption and environmental pollution? What societal, economic, and political changes might be necessary in the future to deal with problems of overconsumption?

6. In what ways have the schools been part of the "Military-industrial" complex? Can education for peace ever really succeed, given the history of man's violence towards other individuals and nations? What practical steps do you see which can be taken?

7. With the vast amounts of wealth in the world, and the unequal distribution among rich and poor individuals and nations, what can be done to bring about a greater balance? What values support the superiority of the rich over the poor? Can and should the schools attempt to change those values?

8. Many questions of environmental concern also have tremendous economic implications. From your own experience, describe a case involving some problem of environmental concern which affected the lives, jobs, and economic security of a sizable group of people. How was the issue resolved? How might it have better been resolved?

9. Rank-order the "values" which you consider to be the controlling ones in your life. Do any of your conflict with others? Do the conflict with any in the society at large? In what ways do we as individuals regulate our conflicts? In what ways can and should societies regulate their conflicts?

10. In what sense can it be stated that the schools in the

Third World perpetuate elites, promote the status quo, and socialise their citizens into a Westernised value system?

Practical Activities

1. Talk with Peace Corp recruiters when they visit your campus, or inquire at the National Action/Peace Corps office concerning a teaching position in another country.

2. Compare the U.S. system of education with that found in one of the other "developed" nations of the world. What percentage of young people attend high school and college in each society? What are some of the similarities and differences in curriculum and organisation? Which system is more egalitarian or elitist?

3. Study the curriculum of a local school district for evidence of "internationalisation." Look at course titles, units, short courses, textbooks, and the training which teachers have had. Look for evidence of ethnocentrism or a Western bias in the curriculum. In particular, deal with the war/peace emphases in textbooks, teaching materials, and other aspects of the curriculum.

4. Design an educational system for a developing nation which takes into consideration the following realities: a high adult illiteracy rate; extreme poverty; a dictatorial government of the right; other budget priorities besides education; a poorly educated teaching staff; a dependence upon agriculture in the nation's economy; a lack of other communication facilities, i.e., roads, radio, and television.

5. From your observations of the community in which you live, your own background, an analysis of the media (radio, TV, advertising, newspapers, and magazines), and any other relevant materials, what appear to be the dominant values of American society? and are these compatible with the ecological dilemmas and possible catastrophes facing modern man?

BIBLIOGRAPHY

International Education

Becker, James B., and Howard D. Mehlinger, eds., *International Dimensions in the Social Studies.* Washington, D.C.: National Council for the Social Studies, 1968.

Bereday, George Z.F., And Joseph Lauwerys, eds., *Education and International Life.* New York: Harcourt, Brace and World, 1964.

Everett, Samuel, and C.O. Arndt, *Teaching World Affairs in American Schools.* New York: Harper and Row Publishers, 1956.

Shane, Harold G., ed., *The United States and International Education.* Chicago: University of Chicago Press, 1969.

Taylor, Harold, *World as Teacher.* New York: Doubleday and Co., Inc., 1969.

Wilcock, J.B., ed., "Preparing Teachers for Education for International Understanding." New York: UNESCO Publications, 1964.

Comparative Education

Carnoy, Martin, *Education as Cultural Imperialism.* New York: David McKay Company, Inc., 1974.

Comparative Education Review

Coombs, Philip H., *The World Educational Crisis: A System Analysis.*New York: Oxford University Press, 1968:

Friere, Paulo, *Pedagogy of the Oppressed* : New York: The Seabury Press, 1970.

Illich, Ivan, *Deschooling Society.* New York: Harper and Row Publishers, 1971.

REFERENCES

sw1. Population Bulletin, *as quoted in* Africa Now (January-February, 1976), p. 10.

2. Philip H. Combs, *The World Education Crisis: A Systems Analysis* (New York: Oxford University Press, 1968).

3. Jonhson, Research Associates, *Area Handbook for Nicaragua* (Washington, D.C.: U.S. Government Printing Office), pp. 42-49.

4. Nicaraguan Constitution, as quoted in Ministry of Education. *National Plan for Educational Development: 1974—1980* (Managua: Ministry of Education, 1973). p. 28.

5. Ibid., p. 29.

6. Academy for Educational Development, *Nicaraguan Education Sector Assessment* (Managua and Washington, D.C., 1975), p. 113.
7. Ibid., p. 111.
8. Ibid., p. 26
9. Ibid., p. 137.
10. Agency for International Development, *Nicaragua: Statistics of The Educational Sector* (Washington, D.C.: USAID, 1975), p. 3.
11. E.F. Schumacher, "Intermediate Technology," *The Center Magazine* (January-February, 1975).
12. *1971 Nicaraguan Census,* as quoted in Academy for Educational Development, *Nicaraguan Education Sector Assessment,* p. 3.
13. Ivan Illich, *Descholing Society* (New York: Harper and Row, Publishers, 1971).
14. Richard J. Kraft, *Student Background and University Admission* (Bangkok and East Lansing, Michigan: National Education Council and Michigan State University, 1968), p. 20.
15. Peter Muncie. *Torches in the Night* (Washington, D.C.: World Bank). pp. 39-43.
16. Ibid., pp. 47-57.
17. J.Q. Wilson, "On Pettigrew and Armor: and Afterword," *The Public Interest*, pp. 30, 132-34, as quoted by Martin Carnoy and Henry M. Levin in "Evaluation of Educational Media: Some Issues," *Instructional Science,* 4, no. 3-4, p. 387.
18. Carnoy and Levin, "Evaluation of Education Media," p. 388-90.
19. Ibid., p. 404.
20. John Plant, ed., *Cuba and the United States: Long-Range Perspectives* (Washington, D.C.: The Brookings Institution, 1967), pp. 12-13.
21. Ibid., p. 13.
22. Ibid., pp. 22-24.
23. Roland G. Paulston, "Education," in *Revolutionary Change in Cuba,* ed., Carmelo Mesa Lago (Pittsburgh: University of Pittsburgh Press, 1971), pp. 377-78.
24. Plant, *Cuba and the United States*, p. 29.
25. Samuel Bowles, "Cuban Education and The Revolutionary Ideology," *Horvard Educational Review,* 41, no. 4 (November, 1971), p. 474.
26. Ibid., pp. 481-82.
27. Nelson P. Valdes, "The Radical Transformation of Cuban Education," in *Cuba in Revolution,* eds. Rolando E. Bonachea and Nelson P. Valdes (Garden City, N.Y.: Anchor Books, 1972), p. 423.

28. Ibid., p. 428.
29. Bowles, "Cuban Education," p. 480.
30. Ibid., p. 484.
31. Valdes, "The Radical Transformation," p. 430.
32. Ibid., p. 434.
33. Ibid., p.437.
34. Ibid., p. 440.
35. Ibid., p. 339.
36. Bowles, "Cuban Education," p. 487.
37. Ibid., pp. 488-89.
38. Ibid., pp. 489-90.
39. Lewis S. Kurtz, *An African Education: The Social Revolution in Tanzania* (Brooklyn: Pageat Poseidon Ltd., 1972), pp. 12-15.
40. Muncie, *Torches in the Night,* p. 14.
41. Julius K. Nyerere, "The Arusha Declaration," *Freedom and Socialism* (Dar es Salaam—London: Oxford University Press, 1968). pp. 231-50.
42. Kurtz, *An African Education,* pp. 88-89.
43. Ibid., p. 136.
44. Muncie, *Torches in the Night,* p. 14.
45. Julius K. Nyerere, "Education for Self-Reliance," *Freedom and Socialism* (Dar es Salaam-London: Oxford University Press, 1968), pp. 267-90.
46. Muncie, *Torches in the Night,* p. 29.
47. Ibid., p. 15.
48. Ibid., pp. 33-36.
49. Ibid., pp. 15-29.
50. K.J. Holsti, Underdevelopment and the 'Gap' Theory of International Conflict, *"The American Political Science Review,* 69, no. 3, pp. 827-29.
51. Martin Carnoy, *Education as Cultural Imperialism* (New York: David McKay Company; Inc., 1974), p. 3.
52. Paulo Friere, *Pedagogy of the Oppressed* (New York: The Seabury Press, 1970).
53. Kenneth Boulding, "Education for the Spaceship Earth," *Social Education* (November, 1968), as quoted in David C. King, *International Education for Spaceship Earth,* Foreign Policy, Association, 1971, pp. 135-37.
54. Barbara Ward, *Spaceship Earth* (New York: Columbia University Press, 1966). p. 14.

2

The Teaching Profession and its Role

Focusing Questions

In what ways is teaching not fully a profession?

What trends show that teaching is becoming more of a full-fledged profession?

How does merit pay help (hinder) the teaching profession?

What are the essential differences between the NEA and the AFT? Can these differences be reconciled?

What are some other important professional organisations for teachers?

Untill the twentieth century, teachers had relatively little preparation for their job and relatively little voice in determining the conditions of their employment. Teacher training consisted of one or two years and sometimes less at a normal school or teachers college, and teachers had to follow strict rules and regulations concerning their behaviour outside the school. Unorganised and isolated from one another in small schools and school districts, teachers could be summarily dismissed by a board of education. Many were told they could not teach any material that someone in the community might find objectionable.

Times have changed. Today, teachers aspire to be professionals with expert knowledge concerning the content and methods of instruction in their particular fields. In addition, teachers are well organised as a group and have gained greater rights to be judged mainly on the basis of their performance rather than on the basis of their behaviour outside the school and to participate in making decisions about the conditions in which they work. The first part of this chapter describes the ways in which teachers are striving for full professional status, the second discusses how teacher organisations have grown in power and prominence.

IS TEACHING A PROFESSION?

Characteristics of a Profession

Whether teaching can be considered a profession in the fullest sense has been an issue of great concern to educators for many decades. A number of educators have tried to identify the ideal characteristics of professions and, by rating teachers on these, to determine whether teaching is a profession. Here is a list of the characteristics of a full profession, based on the works of noted authorities in the field.[1]

1. A sense of public service; a lifetime commitment to career
2. A defined body of knowledge and skills beyond that grasped by laypersons
3. Application of research and theory to practice (to human problems)
4. A lengthy period of specialised training.
5. Control over licensing standards and/or entry requirements
6. Autonomy in making decisions about selected spheres of work
7. An acceptance of responsibility for judgments make and acts performed related to services rendered; a set of standards of performance

8. A commitment to work and client; an emphasis on service to be rendered
9. Use of administrators to facilitate work of professionals; relative freedom from detailed on-the-job supervision
10. A self-governing organisation comprised of members of the profession
11. Professional associations and/or elite groups to provide recognition for individual achievements
12. A code of ethics to help clarify ambiguous matters or doubtful points related to services rendered
13. A high level of public trust and confidence in individual practitioners
14. High prestige and economic standing

The general consensus is that teaching is not a profession in the fullest sense it does not possess some of the characteristics professions are supposed to possess. In some ways it may be viewed as a "semiprofession" or an "emerging profession" in the process of achieving these characteristics.

Viewed as a Semiprofession

Teaching is a semiprofession, according to Amitai Etzioni, because "the training [of teachers] is shorter, their status less legitimated [low or moderate], their right to privileged communication less established; theirs is less of a specialised knowledge, and they have less autonomy from supervision or societal control than 'the professions.'....[2]" (Several sociologists contend that nursing and social work are also semiprofessions).

Viewed as an Emerging Profession

Teaching should be viewed as an emerging profession, according to Robert Howsam, and thus is higher in status than a semiprofession, near the periphery of full professional status. In this connection, both emerging and full professionals are recognised in courts of law as competent to give expert professional testimony.[3] Considering that teaching is as old as ancient civilizations, however, and goes back to the colonial period in American history, it is hard to imagine that teaching is an *emerging* profession.

If readers are asked whether teaching is marked by the characteristics of a profession, some would probably answer yes, some no, and others would be ambivalent. The general conclusion would follow thte at present teaching is partially but not entirely a full profession, although it is moving in the direction of becoming one. More important, probably *no* profession is marked by all the characteristics listed above.

Knowledge, Control, Autonomy, and Prestige

Of the fourteen characteristics of a profession listed, perhaps the four most important are (1) a defined body of knowledge and skills beyond that grasped by laypersons, (2) control over licensing standards and/or entry requirements, (3) autonomy in making decisions about selected spheres of work, and (4) high prestige and economic standing. The following discussion of these characteristics clearly indicates that the teaching profession does not possess them all. Although no profession has achieved the ideal state, teaching seems to lag behind some others, such as law and medicine.

A DEFINED BODY OF KNOWLEDGE

No Agreed-upon Knowledge

All professions have a monopoly on certain knowledge that separates their members from the general public and allows them to exercise control over the vocation. Members of a profession have mastered a body of knowledge that establishes their expertise and protects the public from quacks, untrained amateurs, and special-interest groups. There is, however, no agreed upon specialised body of knowledge that is "education" or "teaching." Whereas the behavioural sciences, physical sciences, and health fields can be guided by extensive rules of procedure and established methodologies, education lacks a well-defined body, of knowledge that is applicable to the real world of teaching[4] and that has been validated and agreed upon by most authorities.[5]

As a result, too many people, especially the lay public, talk about education as if they were experts—resulting in a great deal of conflicting and sometimes negative conversation. Another result of this ill-defined body of knowledge is that the content of teacher education courses varies from state to state and among teacher training institutions within states.

Teaching out of License

Moreover, it is estimated that many teachers working in the secondary schools are teaching out of license; in other words, teachers of English did not major in English in college, nor are they certified to teach English. This problem is especially acute in the areas of science and mathematics although it has declined with the recent surplus of teachers.

Nonaccredited Training Institutions

Whether teachers possess a defined body of knowledge is also determined by training standards. Despite state regulations requiring a certain number of education courses, minimum requirements and content vary among states. As late as 1946 only fifteen states required a bachelor's degree for elementary teachers; in 1976 only three states required that its teachers hold a master's degree.[6] In 1984 as many as 40 percent of the 1,200 colleges involved in training teachers were not accredited by the national accrediting agency.[7]

To develop and gain acknowledgement of a specialised body of knowledge and to upgrade weak teacher training institutions, teachers must acquire decision-making influence. Teacher organisations have the potential power and leadership to work with interested parties, such as teacher training colleges and school districts, to develop exemplary models. Teacher training institutions that do not cooperate might not be allowed to send their student teachers to work in nearby school systems. and their graduates might not be licensed to teach in the schools.

CONTROL OVER REQUIREMENTS FOR ENTRY AND LICENSING

No Minimum Competencies

Whereas most professions have uniform standards and requirements to ensure minimum competencies, this is not the case in the teaching profession. The problem concerns both the types of individuals who enter teacher education programs and the skills held by those who emerge from the programs and are certified to teach.

Noncertified Teachers

As mentioned in Chapter 1, students who enter teacher training programs have lower aptitude scores than students in most other fields and there are no widely accepted tests used to determine whether the graduate of a teacher training program is adequately prepared to be a teacher. Not only is there wide variation in the certification requirements for teaching in various states; in several states new standards, which were intended to eliminate teacher shortages in selected subject areas or to upgrade the quality of new teachers, have replaced long-established certification procedures. California, New Jersey, and Virginia, for example, are assigning instructional duties on an experimental basis to people who have earned college degrees in subjects but have not taken the education courses prerequisite for a teaching license. New teachers who have not taken education courses can receive on-the-job pedagogical training, which will eventually qualify them for certification. Other states, such as Michigan and West Virginia, are exploring ways to utilise retirees or industrial personnel as part-time teachers to alleviate shortages in mathematics, science, and computer instruction.[8]

Different Licensing Procedures

Whatever they may think about these differing requirements, teachers do not have much say on these matters. The outcome is that teacher mobility is limited from state to state by the different licensing procedures. Most people, including teachers themselves, reject teacher regulation of licensing requirements because teachers are publicly employed. From an educator's point of view, however, professional autonomy would be enhanced if teachers could establish licensing laws or if certification standards were functionally recognised by states. It is in the public interest to place some control of professional standards and requirements in the hands of educators rather than to continue to leave such decisions entirely to laypersons who know little about teaching.

AUTONOMY IN DECIDING ABOUT SPHERES OF WORK

Lay Control Vs. Professional Control

In a profession every number of the group, but not outsiders, is assumed to be qualified to make professional judgments on the nature of the work involved. Professionals usually establish laws of exclusive jurisdiction in a given area of competence; custom and tradition are relied on to maintain effective control over matters relating to work and dealing with clients. Indeed, lay control is considered the natural enemy of professions; it limits the power of the professional and opens the door to outside interference.

Teachers accept the assumption that local and state officials have the right to decide on the subjects, instructional materials, and books to be used. While they sometimes doubt the wisdom of the community in exercising such rights, the legitimacy of these rights is rarely questioned. At best, teachers are permitted minimal input in curriculum decisions, and they are vulnerable when they seek to introduce textbooks or discuss topics considered controversial by pressure groups. Taxpayers are said to "reasonably" claim a share in decision making, since they foot the bill and provide the clients.

Guarding against Client Interference

The physician and lawyer also provide services that their clients pay for, yet no one expects the client or the public to prescribe drugs or write the clauses in a contract. When the client interferes with the decisions of the practicing physician or lawyer, the professional-client relationship ends. This protects clients from being victimised by their own lack of knowledge, while it safeguards the professional from the unreasonable judgments of the lay public. Peter Blau and W. Richard Scott observe that "professional service ... requires that the [professional] maintain independence of judgment and not permit the clients' *wishes* as distinguished from their *interests* to influence his decisions:" The professional has the knowledge and expertise to make judgments, "and the client is not qualified to evaluate the services he needs." Professionals who permit their clients to tell them what to do "fail to provide optimum service."[9]

Teacher Accountability

Teachers, on the other hand, can be told what to do by parents and other citizens, principals, superintendents, and school board members, even in opposition to the teachers' professional judgments. Although collective bargaining has resulted in new arrangements between teachers and administrators, most people still believe that teachers are public servants and are therefore accountable to the people and to the school officials who are hired, elected, or appointed by the people. While it is true teachers must not lose sight of the welfare of their clients or ignore those who are in the position to make decisions for the public, they should not completely surrender the power to determine the nature of the service they render.

State Governing Boards

Professional autonomy does not imply the total absence

of any control over professionals. On the contrary, it means that controls requiring technical competencies are exercised by people who possess such competencies; it calls for the development of control related to the work of members of the profession. This can be enhanced by initiating collective negotiations that define areas in which teachers can make use of their experiences and competencies, by increasing teacher representation on school boards at the local level and teaching licensing and governing boards at the state level, and by helping to elect political candidates who are pro-teacher and pro-education.[10]

HIGH PRESTIGE AND ECONOMIC STANDING

Lower Salaries than other College Graduates

As pointed out in Chapter 1, teachers have registered major gains in salary and status during the past fifty-five years. Although teachers' salaries since 1930 have increased more than those of the average worker in industry, teacher pay remains lower than that of the average college graduate.[11] In addition, teachers still earn far less than lawyers, business executives, and some other professionals with similar levels of formal education. Of course, there is no realistic salary comparison between teachers with a master's or doctor's degree and physicians, lawyers, dentists, or top business executives. Although levels of formal education are nearly similar, earnings of the latter group approach $ 100,000 per year with some earning as much as $ 500,000; these groups also have traditionally high occupational ratings.

Dissatisfaction among Teachers

The fact is that while the prestige and income standards of teachers have risen relative to their past station, they have risen only slightly more than those of the average worker and have declined in comparison to other professions and groups that have similar levels of education. The *status-consistency hypothesis* holds that a group tends to compare its achievements (prestige and salary) with other groups and strives to bring its rewards up to a level with people who have similar jobs, even similar years of education.[12] If this is true, we can expect teachers to make comparisons with other professional groups, to remain dissatisfied, and to express this dissatisfaction through militancy; in fact, this has been one of the major reasons for teacher militancy since the mid-1960s.

Overall, one can conclude that while the status of the teacher has improved, teacher's income and prestige still lag far behind those of many professions. Teaching is still not fully a profession in terms of its economic standing and occupational prestige.

TRENDS TOWARD PROFESSIONALISM

Although teaching probably should not be considered a fully professionalised occupation, its status has been improving. Collective bargaining can enhance teachers' capacity to make decisions about their work in the classroom. In addition, several other major aspects of a long-range trend toward the professionalisation of teaching are apparent.

THE SCOPE OF COLLECTIVE BARGAINING

By 1980, teachers had won the right to have their representatives formally bargain with their employers in most of the United States. The extent and nature of collective bargaining varied from negotiations conducted in the absence of a law allowing or forbidding it to full-scale contract bargaining backed by the right to strike. Knowledgeable observers feel that further development of teachers' collective bargaining power will depend partly on congressional action to extend bargaining rights to all public employees. There is considerable uncertainty, however, regarding the position of teacher organisations on specific proposals for federal legislation, the willingness of Congress to pass additional legislation, and constitutional limitations concerning its power to extend bargaining rights to state employees.[13]

Congressional Action to extend Bargaining Rights

In some ways collective bargaining may be considered a non-professional or even an antiprofessional activity. In the law, medicine, or the ministry, for example, few professionals work in organisations in which terms of employment are determined by collective bargaining. From another point of view, however, collective bargaining can significantly enhance professionalisation of teaching by giving teachers greater authority to determine the conditions of their work and their effectiveness as teachers. The trend in collective bargaining has been to include a growing number of concerns other than the fundamental salary issue. Collective bargaining in the 1980s is often concerned with educational problems and issues, such as class size, grouping of students in classes, instructional materials, testing classroom discipline and management, teacher-supervisory relations, and community relations.[14]

Resolving Conflicts

Collective bargaining as a movement in education now seems to be an integral part of teacher unionism and teacher militancy. Educators on both sides of the negotiating table have gained maturity and experience during this new era in school board-administration-teacher relationships. It is believed that when key players participate intelligently and with legal and professional skill, collective bargaining can resolve conflicts between school boards and teachers; enhance the role, status, and working conditions of teachers; and establish new, positive, and more equitable relationships among various education groups—thereby improving the teaching profession.

PROFESSIONAL PRACTICE COMMISSIONS

Setting Professional Standards

It is not likely that educators will be given complete autonomy in setting standards for professional practice, but teachers have been gaining a greater role in setting professional standards than they formerly had. Thirty-four states have developed teacher standards and practice commissions, among them Alaska. South Dakota, and Utah, in which teachers compose a majority of the commission members and set standards for the preparation of teachers and maintenance of minimal competence in professional practice. These commissions have even placed a few teachers on probation, suspended certificates, and reprimanded teachers for unprofessional or illegal behaviour.

These powers will probably be used more frequently in the future, and educators will thus begin doing what they long have said they wanted to do clean their own house and weed out those who do not meet minimal professional standards—and secure governance of the profession.[15]

TEACHER CENTERS

Another way in which teachers are achieving greater professional status by exercising more control over their own affairs involves the important area of staff development. To stay up to date in their preparation and to acquire new classroom skills, teachers have traditionally participated in various kinds of in-service training. Most of this training has been provided on college campuses, frequently to meet school district requirements for additional college credit for continuing certification. Many observers have viewed this kind of in-service training as a "cafeteria of courses and workshops" with no relationship "to job roles and student needs."[16]

Partially Governed by Teachers

In the past few years, however, a growing percentage of teachers' in-service training opportunities have been provided by teacher centers that are governed partly by teachers themselves. They are intended to make staff development more relevant to teachers' actual training needs and more useful in terms of applicability in the classroom. As used here, the teacher center refers to an in-service training center; it does not focus on preservice training. This movement to establish teacher centers may represent a significant advance toward teachers' participation in making decisions that have important implications for their professional performance.

Teacher centers have existed for years in the form of exchange centers where teachers can obtain ideas about new instructional practices and talk with colleagues about how to apply appropriate methods in their classrooms. Centers of this kind have provided valuable services to teachers but have been dependent on unstable financing and generally have not been able to undertake systematic efforts aimed at improving instructional practice in the schools. Partly for this reason, and partly because many teachers and administrators have felt that colleges and universities have not provided preservice and in-service training adequate to cope with the challenge in contemporary classrooms, teacher centers have spread to many parts of the country—totaling more than two hundred different centers.[17]

Both the National Education Association (NEA) and the American Federation of Teachers (AFT) support the establishment and expansion of the teacher center program, with teachers having a major and sometimes predominant voice in their operation. Once established, a teacher center is supposed to function and evolve in accordance with local in-service needs. Some of the centers serve a single school district, others serve a region or an entire state.

Local In-service Needs

For example, the Kohl Teacher Center in Wilmette, Illinois, has been in operation for more than ten years, is privately funded, annually serves nearly 50 school districts, 800 schools, and 15,000 to 20,000 teachers in Illinois, Wisconsin, and Indiana. It offers a wide variety of services, including recertification courses, graduate level courses for college credit, educational conferences and workshops; it sponsors summer trips for educators, small grants for instructional projects, and awards for excellence in teaching. The New York City Teacher Center, by way of contrast, not only includes the entire city, but in so doing serves teachers who work with approximately 950,000 public school students and a third of a million private school students Governed by a twenty-five-member policy board that represents the teachers' union, board of education members, the supervisors' council, the United Parents Association and other community groups, and the deans of education from the City University, the New York City Teacher Center coordinates the work of nearly thirty higher education institutions in attempting to provide practical in-service training for area teachers.[18]

Funding Teacher Centers

Although most of the funds for teacher centers came from the federal government in the 1970s, we can expect the bulk, if not all, of the funding to be based on state and local monies for the remainder of the 1980s. Most of this funding will be derived from staff development funds, a common terms now used by school administrators and teacher educators promoting in-service needs of teachers.

MEDIATED ENTRY

Supervised Stages of Assistance

Mediated entry refers to the practice of induct persons into a profession through carefully supervised stages that help them learn how to apply professional knowledge successfully in a concrete situation. One good example is in the profession of medicine, in which aspiring physicians serve one or more years as an intern and then as a resident before being considered a full-fledged professional.

Trial and Error in the Classroom

Dan Lortie has studied the teacher's job from a sociological perspective and concluded that in terms of sequenced professional entry, teaching ranks in between occupations characterised by "casual" entry and those that place protracted and difficult demands on would-be members.[19] The lack of more carefully mediated entry has profound consequences, because it means that there is relatively little chance to include empirically derived and rigorously grounded principles and practices of pedagogy. Teachers too frequently report that their main teacher has been experience, and that they learned to teach through trial and error in the classroom. They also report that the beginning years of teaching can be "a period of anxiety and fear, even of trauma."[20] But, then, the beginning period of almost any occupation or profession has its problems and anxieties.

Although efforts have been made to provide for more effective induction of new teachers into the profession, in general past efforts have not been either widespread or systematic enough to ensure their success in practice. Most school districts, for example, now require a probationary period for new teachers, but in too many cases relatively little concrete assistance is provided to help those teaches develop and refine the skills needed for effective performance. Many school districts and a few states require a fifth year of preparation beyond the traditional bachelor's degree and initial certificate, but too often this requirement is implemented in a way that allows new teacher to take a few more courses that may or may not help them improve professionally,[21] As a rule, most new teachers are still largely on their own in their first professional position.

Induction Period

The teaching profession now recognizes the need to develop a period of induction and transition into teaching. The concept of mediated entry is supported by many school district officials, who no longer feel they must immediately accept and put new teachers to work as was done during the teacher shortage of the 1960s and early 1970s. With many applicants vying for a limited number of teaching jobs, school officials can make probationary requirements stronger and more meaningful than they were in the recent past.

Closer Ties Between Professors and Teachers

The trend toward more carefully mediated entry will probably continue—at least as long as the current oversupply of teachers continues; moreover, mediated entry is supported by the NEA and AFT and several teacher education groups. Most important, the notion of mediated entry would focus on the school as the workplace as well as the training place for beginning teachers, like teacher centers, it would address the practical nature of teaching, involve experienced teachers in training beginning teachers, establish closer ties between teacher educators and school people, and insure greater control by the profession over teacher training.

MERIT PAY

Salaries Tied to Performance

Real changes in teacher renumeration are in the offing. Many recent task force reports on education—including *A Nation At Risk,* the report by the Commission on Excellence in Education—are calling for higher teacher salaries based on performance. President Reagan, borrowing from the principles of productivity of free enterprise, has proposed on several occasions that we identify "master teachers" and pay them higher salaries. A growing number of school boards have taken the position that merit pay (a supplement to a teacher's base salary to reward superior performance) is a cost-effective method of motivating teachers and encouraging excellence in teaching.

Politics, Patronage and Pedagogy

Both the NEA and AFT have reservations about merit pay plans, although the AFT is willing to entertain incentive proposals as long as there are sufficient safeguards in the evaluation procedures and so long as monetary awards do not compete with salaries or pay hikes for all teachers.[22] Where master teachers or merit plans have been tried, both organisations contend that teachers did not agree with administrators on the teachers selected for preferential pay. The NEA and AFT question whether objective performance standards can be implemented, and both fear that merit pay will lead to politics and patronage rather than improved pedagogy.[23]

Conflict among Teachers

The concern is that the process will further the aims of the school administration rather than the educational aims of the school. Both organisations feel that ".good" teachers who submit required paperwork a little late or who criticise or have different views than the administration or school board will be penalised: "average" or "poor" teachers who comply with bureaucratic mandates, or who consider themselves discriminated against and threaten to litigate, will be rewarded. Finally, both organisations are afraid the effort to reward a few teachers will take place at the expense of the remaining teachers and that merit pay will threaten the unity of teachers and the collegiality among educators. They maintain that the effort should be to increase all teachers' salaries—not just a few and not to pit teachers against each other.[24]

Consumer Input

Milton Friedman, the well-known economist who believes in a competitive market, increasingly rejects the idea of merit pay for teachers.[25] He argues that merit pay would work only in a truly competitive marketplace, one in which consumers had a variety of genuine choices. There is little competition and diversity among public schools today. Consumers have little to say about where they can send their children. If there were more private schools or alternative schools, there would be more incentive to meet the needs of customers and merit pay would be a realistic proposal. Productive teachers would be in demand, and schools would vie for them.

Merit Plans Spread

Regardless of all these practical and theoretical reservations, the *idea* of merit pay — and its various derivatives — is spreading to many school districts and even entire states. The states of Illinois, New York, and Ohio are considering state-funded pay incentives. Tennessee, North Carolina, and Virginia have introduced the career ladder as a means of rewarding teachers and increasing their responsibilities. It is viewed by some as an alternative to (and by others as an extension of) merit pay. The career ladder combines rewards for good teaching with improved in-service education for all teachers.[26] Both the AFT and NEA support career ladders for teachers, and it is likely that other states will move in this direction, also. Meanwhile, in Alaska, the idea of merit pay is being considered for schools, not teachers. Entire schools could be rewarded for outstanding team efforts, and the morale of the teaching staff would not be damaged as it might be if a few teachers in each building were singled out for extra pay.

Incentive Plan

Then, there is the Houston school district incentive plan, begun in 1979 and well known because of the district's size and visibility. Six categories qualify for incentive pay: (1) Service in a high-priority school; (2) teaching a special subject where staff shortages exist; (3) teacher attendance that exceeds minimum requirements; (4) professional growth or in-service training appropriate to one's current teaching assignment or in an area where critical shortages exist; (5) service in a school where the average academic gain of students, as measured by standardised tests, is greater than statistical predictions and (6) service at a unique or experimental school site.[27]

Increased Teacher Morale

It is important to note that the categories for merit are for the most part based on objective criteria, not subjective evaluations. During the first year, two-thirds of all Houston teachers collected stipends totaling some $ 11 million. The average stipend was $ 936; the range was $ 300 to $ 3,500. School officials claim that (1) standardised test scores in the district have improved for three consecutive years, since the plan began; (2) teacher absenteeism (a costly item for most big-city school districts) and teacher turnover have dropped, especially in inner-city schools; (3) teacher shortages in areas like science, mathematics, special education, and bilingual education have been reduced sharply; and (4) teacher morale has increased.[28]

Right to Appeal

The teaching profession can benefit from merit pay in terms of money and prestige so long as certain guidelines or principles are followed: (1) teachers must be evaluated objectively on clear and agreed-upon standards; (2) teacher raters, those who evaluate teachers, must receive training in the use of objective measures; (3) teachers must be afforded appeal procedures, but those procedures cannot be time consuming; (4) teachers should receive assistance to meet the standards for merit; (5) public disclosure of merit awards should be minimised, since it often humiliates nonrecipients before students, parents, and colleagues; and (6) the expense of incentive pay should not be offset by lowered annual salaries.[29]

In general, the administration, school board, public, and teachers must be willing to accept the fact that teaching is a position of professional importance. To accept this assumption means to believe that school administrators (and teachers themselves) can make competent judgments about the worth of teaching and the individual performance of teachers; it means that if we replace traditional pay scales, based on experience and education, with some form of merit plan, master teachers might have the opportunity to earn $ 50,000 or more by the late 1980s.

$ 50,000 Teacher Salaries

The fact that teacher salaries have been capped historically at a low figure, and that we have avoided making distinctions based on performance, has hurt the profession. Granted there are risks in merit pay plans, but there are risks in any endeavour. By raising the lid on teaching salaries and by making distinctions based on merit, we will improve the teaching profession; subsequently, we will raise the prestige of teachers, attract brighter students into the profession, and keep good teachers from leaving classrooms for more competitive salaries in other fields

TEACHER ORGANISATIONS

Restrictions on Teachers

A critical factor in the development of teaching as a profession has been the growth of professional organisations for teachers. Although today's working conditions still need to be improved, they sharply contrast with the restrictions teachers once endured. Here are the details of what is reputed to be a Wisconsin teacher's contract for 1922, calling for a salary of $ 75 a month.

Miss —— agrees:

1. Not to get married. This contract becomes null and void immediately if the teacher marries.
2. Not to keep company with men.
3. To be home between the hours of 8 P.M. and 6 A.M. unless in attendance at a school function.
4. Not to loiter downtown in ice-cream parlors.
5. Not to leave town at any time without the permission of the chairman of the Trustees.
6. Not to smoke cigarettes.
7. Not to drink beer, wine, or whiskey.

8. Not to ride in a carriage or automobile with any man except her brother or father.
9. Not to dress in bright colours.
10. Not to dye her hair.
11. Not to wear less than two petticoats.
12. Not to wear dresses shorter than two inches above the ankles.
13. To keep the schoolroom clean:
    a. To sweep the classroom floor at least once daily.
    b. To scrub the classroom floor at least once weekly.
    c. To clean the blackboard at least once daily.
    d. To start the fire at 7 A.M. so that the room will be warm at 8 A.M. when the children arrive.
14. Not to wear face powder, mascara or to paint the lips.[30]

Consider these requirements in the context of the times: the status of women, the image of teachers, and what Small Town, U.S.A. was like. Those were the days of the Model T Ford, the protest manarches of suffragettes, the growing pains of labour, the "muckrakers," and Simpleclair Lewis's *Main Street* and *Babbitt*.

NEA and AFT are Rivals

Obviously, the conditions described above no longer exist, and to a large extent the growth of teacher organisations and teacher militancy have played a role in improving the conditions of teaching. In these endeavour, the National Education Association and the American Federation of Teachers are the two most important organisations. These two organisations usually are considered rivals, competing for members, recognition, and power. Although some educators believe that perpetuation of this division is a healthy form of professional competition, others view it as detrimental to the teaching profession—a splitting of power and a waste of resources.

NATIONAL EDUCATION ASSOCIATION (NEA)

1.7 Million Members

The National Education Association, which was founded in 1857 by forty-three educators, is a complex, multifaceted organisation involved in many areas of education on local, state, and national levels. The NEA, unlike the AFT, includes both teachers and administrators. As shown in Table 2.1, membership grew tenfold from 1900 to 1920 and another tenfold by 1940. Membership totaled 450,000 in 1950 and nearly 1.7 million in 1984.[31]

Suburban and Rural Members

Since 1980 membership has leveled off, primarily because of the minimal change in the total supply of teachers. Among the members in 1984 approximately 25,000 were students, 40,000 were retired members, 50,000 were auxiliary staff (school secretaries, teacher aides, cafeteria workers, bus drivers, and custodians), 55,000 were college professors, 200,000 were professional support staff (guidance counselors, librarians, and administrators), and nearly 1.3 million were classroom teachers.[32] This figure comprises more than half of the nation's 2.4 million teachers. By 1990, membership is expected to increase slightly because there should be a small rise in the supply of teachers.

4,000 Members in Every Congressional District

Disproportionately suburban and rural, the membership is served by a large network of affiliates in every state, Puerto Rucco, and the District of Columbia and by an Overseas Educational Association. There are more than 7,000 local affiliate groups. In sheer members, the NEA represents the second largest lobbying force in the country, outnumbering all other public employee organisations. Among unions it trails only the Teamsters. Its combined annual budget is over $ 350 million, and it averages about 4,000 members in every congressional district. The state affiliates are usually among the most influential education lobbies at the state levels.[33]

TABLE 2.1

Membership of the NEA and AFT by Decades

Year	*NEA Membership*	*AFT Membership*
1857[a]	43	
1870	170	
1880	354	
1890	5,474	
1900	2,322	
1910	6,909	
1916[a]		1,500
1920	22,850	10,000
1930	216,188	7,000
1940	203,429	30,000
1950	453,797	41,000
1960	713,994	59,000
1970	1,100,000	205,000
1980	1,650,000	550,000
1985[b]	1,700,000	600,000
1990[b]	1,800,000	700,000

[a]Year organisation was founded.

[b]Estimated Membership.

Source: "AFT Membership Growing Again," *Annual Report of the American Federation of Teachers, 1982-83* (Washington, D.C.: AFT 1983), p. 43; Allan C. Ornstein, *Education and Social Inquiry* (Itasca, III.: Peacock, 1978), pp. 311, 329; and "Your NEA," *Today's Education* (1983-84), pp. 78-79.

Today's Education

The Representative Assembly, consisting of some 7,240 delegates who are elected by members in state and local affiliates, meets annually to set NEA policy. The board of directors, consisting of 116 directors, and the executive committee (consisting of the NEA president, vice president, secretary-treasurer, and six other members), are both elected by the Representative Assembly and act for the NEA between assembly meetings.[34]

A wide range of professional services is offered by the NEA. The Research Division, organised in 1922, conducts annual research studies on the status of the profession; it also publishers the *NEA Research Bulletin* and several research memos and opinion surveys on an annual basis. The major publication of the NEA is *Today's Education,* now an annual publication, with a supplementary monthly newspaper. In addition, the national councils for the various subjects—mathematics, science, social studies, modern language, speech, home economics, business education, art, and so on—also publish professional journals. (These councils are loosely affiliated with the NEA). Most of the fifty state affiliates publish a monthly magazine as well.

AMERICAN FEDERATION OF TEACHERS (AFT)

590,000 Members

The AFT was formed in 1916. It is affiliated with the AFL-CIO and is open to classroom teachers only. Membership in 1984 was 590,000, organised in some 2,200 locals in large and medium-sized cities. As shown in Table 2.1 membership limped along in the 1920s and 1930s as a result of antilabour sentiments and a feeling in some quarters that labour organisations were led by radicals. Most of the AFT membership increase has taken place within the last twenty-five years. Among its 590,000 members in 1984 were some 25,000 paraprofessionals, 60,000 municipal workers and nurses who are not teachers. 75,000 college professors, and 430,000 teachers.[35] By 1990, the AFT membership is expected to reach 700,000, with most of the increase coming from the ranks of classroom teachers, college professors, and municipal workers.

The national governing body of the AFT is the Annual Convention, representing local affiliates according to a proportional formula. The Executive Council (consisting of the AFT president and thirty-four vice presidents) assumes the leadership between the annual conventions. Unlike the NEA affiliates, the AFT locals tend to be millitant in philosophy and more eager to bargain collectively over economic matters and working conditions, although the NEA state affiliates have become more aggressive since 1968.

American Teacher

The AFT has not in the past, been involved with research and publication to the extent of the NEA, but the union does publish a professional magazine, *Changing Education,* a *Consortium Yearbook,* and a monthly newspaper, *American Teacher.* In addition, the local affiliates put out a monthly newsletter. Unlike the NEA, the AFT members have always been required to join the local state (twenty-two in all), and national organisations simultaneously. Only recently has the NEA encouraged unitary membership. The NEA dues policy emphasizes local support, whereas the AFT channels a large portion of local funds to the national level. Most contracts negotiated with schools by the AFT local affiliate require an automatic dues deduction and agency free (whether or not the teachers belong to the union). Only a few local NEA contracts insist on this provision, although one might expect a move in this direction because of the obvious advantages to the organisation.

Automatic Dues Deduction

The AFT remained quite small until criticism of the schools mounted at the end of the 1950s. The membership breakthrough came when AFT leaders decided to concentrate on the New York City school system. In 1961 the union group defeated the organisation supporting the NEA, and the United Federation of Teachers (UFT) was chosen to represent New York City teachers. Following its victory, the UFT engaged in a number of strikes in New York City over the next decade—for improved working conditions, salary increases, health benefits, pensions, and teacher rights. Success in New York City led to a series of victories over the NEA in several other large cities for the right, represent teachers. The AFT became the dominant teacher organisation in many large urban centers where unions have traditionally flourished, where militant tactics such as collective bargaining and strikes have been common, and where teachers in general perceived a need for a powerful organisation to represent them. In rural and suburban areas, where union tactics have typically received less support, the NEA remains dominant.

PAST DIFFERENCES BETWEEN THE NEA AND AFT

Professionalism *vs.* Unionism

Without question there has been intense organisational rivalry between the NEA and the AFT for years. These two organisations have competed for members and for exclusive local rights to represent teachers. The NEA has historically viewed itself as a professional association, not a union. It shunned collective bargaining, strikes, and other militant tactics. It vehemently criticized the AFT for its labor affiliation and maintained that this relationship was detrimental to the professional image. For its part, the AFT criticized the NEA's more conciliatory tactics as unrealistic and argued that union affiliation provided political and economic clout; it also criticized the NEA for permitting administrators in the organisation.

Becoming More Militant

Teacher strikes. Until the mid-1960s, the NEA relied on sanctions as the most aggressive measure against a school board. It condemned the AFT for its strike tactics, which the NEA considered illegal and unprofessional. In 1968 the NEA did an about-face, largely for two reasons: the AFT's successful use of strikes and the growing demand by its own members that it assume greater responsibility for improving their occupational status.

Increased NEA Strikes

For the last two decades, then, the NEA has viewed the strike as a legitimate option. Along with mediation, fact finding, binding arbitration, and political action, the strike is considered a viable process for obtaining better salaries, smaller classes, and other bread-and-butter concerns.[36] Indeed, the strategies or options the NEA now advocates coincide with the tactics of organized labor, and there is little difference with the AFT on these strategies. Now both are considered to be aggressive unions that strike freely and negotiate with roughly equal success for the benefit of teachers. Today the NEA is quick to point out that there are more NEA-related strikes than AFT-related strikes. (This is due to the fact that there are more than three times as many local affiliates—7,000 versus 2,000—and three times the number of members—1.7 million versus 590,000—in the NEA than the AFT.).

The AFT has always taken a strong position on the right and need to strike in order to improve salaries, benefits, and working conditions of teachers. Albert Shanker, the president of the AFT, has also viewed the strike as a tactic "to eliminate all vestiges of paternalism" that school boards have "in their dealings with teachers."[37]

Early Teacher Strikes

Prior to 1966 teachers' strikes were sporadic and infrequent. From 1940 to 1966, a total of 108 such stoppages occurred (or about 4 per year). These early strikes were spearheaded by the AFT. especially the local affiliates in New York. Michigan. Minneapolis, and Rhode Island.

The Year 1966 saw a dramatic upswing in the number of teachers' strikes Thirty stoppages were recorded during that year alone, followed by 76 in 1967 and 88 in 1968. Whereas the major issues prior to 1966 involved salaries and working conditions, this new period also involved the right to organise collectively.

More than 200 Annual Strikes

From 1969, (after the NEA had sanctioned the strike tactic) through 1980, the number of strikes increased significantly. During this twelve-year period, the number of strikes exceeded 100 almost every year and snow-balled to over 200 in 1975 and 1980. During this new period, a fourth issue involving strikes surfaced—job security.

Decline in Teacher Strikes

The 1980s is seeing a noticeable decline in the number of teacher strikes; there have been fewer than 100 annual strikes between 1981 and 1983.[38] The AFT has toned down its original militant position and is now encouraging fact finding, mediation, and binding arbitration—much like the NEA, which sees a strike as only one of several options available when an impasse is reached. Both the NEA and AFT are developing other organising strategies, among them forming coalitions with business and civic groups, participating in public hearings regarding school budgets, and enhancing their political clout at the state and local levels.

Why the decline in strikes? Today unions of all kinds are losing many strikes, and government is more rigid and less willing to listen to union demands. President Reagan's confrontation with striking air traffic controllers in 1981, and their subsequent loss of jobs, gave antilabor sentiment a big boost. The taxpayer revolt of recent years has made it financially necessary—and in some cases politically popular—to confront public employees at state, county, and local levels.

Dismissing Striking Employees

Across the country, government officials are now willing to have a show down with striking employees, to curtail and cut back contract provisions won by unions in the past, to suspend and dismiss striking employees, to refuse to budge on many issues, and to say no to pay increases. Indeed, government workers (including teachers) are finding that government work isn't necessarily permanent—a hard pill to swallow since it was assumed prior to the 1980s that working for the government (or working as a teacher) assured lifelong job security.[39]

Unemployed Teachers

The mood of taxpayers, who fund our schools, is vividly illustrated by California's proportion 13 and Massachusetts' Proposition 2½, which impose property tax limitations that reduce monies available to municipalities and school districts. It is further demonstrated by the increasing number of teacher layoffs, some 100,000 per year since 1980, and by the fact that there are often hundreds of unemployed teachers willing to fill vacancies (just as there are hundreds of people willing to fill vacancies for air traffic controllers, police officers, firefighters, and transit workers).

As municipal officials get tougher in bargaining with public workers and tax-cut fervor increases, the NEA and AFT will be forced to once more reassess the goals and tactics of striking. As school districts demand that teachers agree to contract concessions, the two unions will be fighting to protect members' jobs and previous benefits.

Administrative Membership. In the past, the AFT criticised the NEA for encouraging administrators to join. It argued that the NEA was "management oriented." So long as administrators were in the organisation and wielded power, the NEA could not make adequate progress toward securing a professional level of income and status for teachers. The NEA countered that the organisation was concerned with the interests of teachers, and that it was good professional practice to include both teachers and administrators. Attacks and counterattacks at both organisations are found in the literature of the 1950s and 1960s. A number of teacher negotiation statutes and state administrative agency decisions have settled the issue over administrative membership basically along the lines advocated by the AFT. In many cases, state legislation permits and even mandates the inclusion of administrative personnel in a teacher bargaining unit. But the NEA local affiliates have come to realise that this creates too many practical problems for all parties concerned.

School principals and superintendents in many parts of the country have pulled out of the local and/or state NEA affiliates. The issue of administrative membership is seen as a conflict of interest during grievances or lawsuits, contract negotiations, arbitration, work stoppages,and strikes. In some school districts, the issue is seen as pertaining to local affiliates; it is argued that administrators can retain membership in the state and national NEA on an individual basis. In other places, it is accepted that administrative personnel should not be regular members of the local and state units, but that they should continue as members of the national NEA.

Administrators Organise

Compounding the problem today is the fact that school administrators, mostly in the big cities, have organised into separate unions and bargaining associations with more than 70 local units and 11,000 school administrators and supervisors as of 1984. Most of these people are middle-ranked administrators who engage in collective bargaining with their own bosses (the school board and superintendent). Although the AFT has refused to become affiliated with them, its parent organisation, the AFL-CIO, has granted these administrative units a charter, referred to as the American Federation of School Administrators.[40]

CURRENT DIFFERENCES BETWEEN THE NEA AND AFT

A number of important differences in philosophy and strategy still exist between the two organisations; these differences have contributed to continued tension and conflict and prevent a potential merger of the two organisations.

AFL-CIO Affiliation

1. *Conflict over labour affiliation*. The AFTs affiliation with the AFL-CIO remains an important difference. The NEA has always considered itself a professional organisation as opposed to any kind of labour affiliation; this stance coincides with its predominantly conservative and suburban-rural membership, a group that is traditionally antilabour and identifies city strikes and job dislocations with the politics and tactics of labour.[41]

Membership of Professors

2. *The battle of Professors*. Recent rivalry between the NEA and AFT has intensified over enrolling professors into their organisations. The desire among professors to organise is linked to financial stringencies and hiring and tenure problems plaguing the colleges and universities; henceforth, we can expect large membership gains within the NEA and AFT—and also greater rivalry.

College and university teachers have been somewhat slow to seek organised labour's support, but the picture seems to be changing. A survey found that in 1978 three-fourths of all professors a majority at every type of institution of higher learning, said that they would vote for collective bargaining and a prounion agent if an election were held at their institution. As many as 76 per cent of the respondents credited collective bargaining with bringing higher salaries and improved benefits to professors.[42]

Despite the higher percentage of professors who now endorse collective bargaining and unionisation, a considerably smaller percentage have actually voted to be represented by such agents. Perhaps the reasons for the gap are that the professors cannot agree on what organisations should represent them and that there is rivalry not only among the organisations but also among professors themselves. In addition, inertia must be overcome if college professors are to join militant organisations.

Still another problem is that the National Labour Relations Board ruled in two separate rulings in 1984 that professors at Boston University and Polytechnic Institute of New York are "managers" and "supervisors" (with authority over the hiring process) and thus do not have the right to bargain collectively under federal labour law. This ruling followed the Supreme Court's decision in 1980 involving Yeshiva University that restricted efforts to organise faculty members at *private* institutions of higher learning. Although we can expect the board's ruling to be appealed, we can also assume that NEA-AFT attempts to organise professors in the future will be focused on *public* higher education institutions.

Municipal Workers and Nurses

3. *Organising noneducational workers.* The AFT has announced a major campaign to broaden its membership to include state and county white collar municipal employees, school custodians, health-care workers, and nurses. On the whole, rank-and-file members, support the idea and are willing to funnel a substantial amount of money into organising these workers.

The biggest organisational attempt has occurred within the health-care field, affecting a potential 4.2 million workers including 750,000 registered nurses. The AFT has developed a new division called the Federation of Nurses and Health Professionals to unionise these people.[43] The AFT has also been successful in its efforts to improve the salaries, working conditions, and job security of state and county social, recreational, and clerical workers.[44]

Organising Non-educators

The NEA dismisses the idea of unionising non-educational workers as a further dilution of the AFTs interests in teachers, an attempt to shore up sagging membership that cannot compete with the NEA's, and an illustration that the AFT is willing to organise any group that is willing to join. The AFT, on the other hand, sees much potential political and economic advantage in broadening its membership.

Raiding Members

4. *The fight over existing members.* Declining student enrollments, the recent recession, and school budget cuts fan the animosity between the unions. Neither one of these organisations faces a growth market, so they are beginning to raid each other's ranks more often. The two unions have been fighting over members for the last twenty-five years, but now the rivalry is more intense, the quarreling is more costly, and the stakes involve existing turf. The fight has changed its focus because about 85 per cent of public school teachers now belong to one of the two organisations. Also, it is increasingly difficult to win big contract concessions from schools so that teachers are more willing to listen to the other side and to switch unions.

Different Attire and Atmosphere

5. *Different styles of leadership.* Deep differences in organisational make-up and style still divide the two groups. It shows, up in differences in the way the local and national offices in Washington, D.C., are run. The AFT offices are staffed by a handful of informally dressed people (70 in Washington) and the workplace is buzzing with noise and activity. The NEA offices are dominated by staff (500 in Washington) who tend to be formally dressed and more deliberative and quiet.[45]

Shanker's Visibility

Then there is Albert Shanker, president of the AFT, who has a distinctive leadership philosophy and style. The AFT tends to be Shanker's one-man show. As AFT president for more than ten years, he has traveled extensively (both nationally and internationally) for purposes of organising and building stronger ties with political and labour groups. He is frequently the main speaker at conventions; he gives testimony and advice to government agencies, Congress, and the presidents; and he writes a regular column in the *New York Times.* Without doubt, he is a very controversial, outspoken, and visible person.

Low-profile NEA President

In contrast, the NEA leadership is diffuse and lacks well-known leaders who can deliver votes on controversial issues. The president is elected for two years and is eligible for only one additional term. This creates a somewhat weak presiding officer and makes it difficult for a strong, well-known NEA leader to emerge. Few people in education, much less the public, know the NEA president by name.

All these differences leave scars and intensify the two unions' rivalry. For these reasons, both groups will continue to spend big dollars fighting each other, pressuring legislators, and developing their own political base of parent, business, and other interest groups.

AREAS OF AGREEMENT

Political Activism

Both the NEA and AFT recognise the need to elect proteacher and proeducation political representatives at the local, state, and federal levels. Both organisations now spend millions of dollars annually and encourage their teachers to volunteer time in election contests. They have been successful in this approach, and most of the candidates whom they have supported in recent years have won election.[46] Behind these successes lies the fact that in states where the NEA and AFT decide to support selected candidates, they usually throw their muscle behind the same candidates — illustrating that their political views are compatible.

Guaranteeing Collective Negotiation

The combined political strength of the NEA and AFT is considerable. The organisations drew wide attention in 1982 and 1983 by adopting a joint resolution, their first, assailing proposed tax credits for private school tuition. Their coordinated lobbying helped stall the bill in Congress. And the AFT, laying aside its past opposition to the creation of the Department of Education, joined the NEA to thwart President Reagan's plan to abolish the agency.

Both the NEA and AFT advocate a federal law guaranteeing collective bargaining. As of 1984, as many as thirty-five states had laws providing some form of collective bargaining, although they varied considerably.[47] No doubt more states will adopt collective negotiation laws, but the NEA and AFT would prefer a uniform federal law to safeguard their right to strike and more important, to guarantee their benefits on retirement, sick leave, seniority and tenure, holidays, work days and work year, leave benefits (personal, military, maternity, and the like), and other protections and benefits now provided to public sector employees by statute.

In an era of teacher retrenchment, the NEA and AFT are also in basic agreement on securing unemployment benefits for teachers (only eight states currently provide them), enlarging the demand for teachers by extending free public education to all children and youth from prekindergarten to grade 14, convincing the public of the proved value of smaller classes, increasing tax-free fringe benefits, raising teacher pay and implementing cost-of-living adjustments, increasing teacher retirement benefits, and stepping up teacher militancy to resist possible cutbacks.

Questions concerning tenure laws, accountability, school budget cutbacks, as well as teacher unemployment, may force teachers to conclude that the best way to combat the dangers facing them is to end the organisational rivalry and move toward greater unity—and ultimately toward merger. To be sure, there are immense political and economic advantages to be gained by such a merger. As many as 2.3 million teachers, paraprofessionals, professors, and miscellaneous educators from state and federal departments and non-profit and foundation organisations would provide enormous potential power unavailable to the two separate organisations. Many of the nearly 1 million teachers and professors who presently belong to neither organisation would probably join the united "super" teacher organisation.

GENERAL PROFESSIONAL ORGANISATIONS FOR TEACHERS

In addition to the NEA and AFT, there are more than three hundred other national teacher organisations.[48]

SPECIALISED PROFESSIONAL ORGANISATIONS

Subject-related Teacher Organisations

At the working level of the classroom, the professional organisation of greatest benefit to a teacher (and education student) is usually one that focuses on his or her major field. Each such subject-centered professional association provides a meeting ground for teachers of similar interests. The activities of these professional organisations customarily consist of regional and national meetings and publication of a professional journal, usually monthly or quarterly, that provides current teaching tips and describes accepted curriculum practices. Below are fifteen major teaching organisations that focus on specific subject matter.

1. American Alliance for Health, Physical Education, Recreation and Dance
2. American Council on the Teaching of foreign Languages
3. American Industrial Arts Association
4. American School Health Association

5. American Vocational Association
6. Association for Education in Journalism
7. International Reading Association
8. Modern Language Association
9. Music Teachers National Association
10. National Art Education Association
11. National Business Education Association
12. National Council for the Social Studies
13. National Council of Teachers of English
14. National Council of Teachers of Mathematics
15. National Science Teachers Association

Student-related Teacher Organisations

For those readers who identify with a particular type of student—say by age or grade level, or by cognitive, physical, or ethnic characteristic—the teaching organisations listed below should be of interest. These professional organisations, also national in scope, focus on the needs and rights of special students and are organised to ensure that these children and youth are served by well-prepared school personnel. These associations attempt to advance the teaching profession by improving teaching techniques for specialised groups of students. The associations also hold regional and national meetings and publish monthly or quarterly journals.

1. American Association for Gifted Children
2. American Association of Workers for the Blind
3. American Association for Asian Studies
4. American Montessori Society
5. American Speech-Language Hearing Association
6. Association for Childhood Education International
7. Association for Children with Learning Disabilities
8. Convention of American Instructors of the Deaf
9. Council for Exceptional Children
10. National Association for Bilingual Children

11. National Association for Creative Children and Adults
12. National Association for the Education of Young Children
13. National Rehabilitation Association
14. National Scholarship Service and Fund for Negro Students
15. Rural Education Association

Still another type of organisation that merits comment is the professional organisation whose members cut across various subjects and student types. These organisations tend to highlight innovative teaching practices in general. describe new trends and policies impacting on the entire field of education, comprise a wide range of membership, and work for the advancement of the teaching profession in general.

RELIGIOUS EDUCATION ORGANISATIONS

Catholic Teacher Organisations

As of 1984, there were approximately 280,000 nonpublic school teachers in grades K-12, of which 75,000 belonged to one of eighty religious education associations. The largest of these religious teacher organisations is the National Association of Catholic School Teachers (NACST), founded in 1978 and comprising in 1984 over 3,000 teachers—mainly from large cities. The organisation is expected to grow in membership, since the great majority of Catholic teachers are not organised on a national or local level.[49] The largest and oldest Catholic education organisation is the National Catholic Education Association, founded in 1904 and comprising 15,000 institutions. Most administrators, as principals or superintendents of their respective schools, join the organisation. It is estimated that no more than one thousand teachers are members.[50]

In the meantime, the 9,500 Catholic schools, which

constitute approximately 46 percent of all private schools and two-thirds of all private teachers, now permit their teachers to bargain in matters dealing with salary, job security, advancement, and grievances. Furthermore, they have established procedural recommendations for collective bargaining. Although concern has been expressed about Catholic teachers belonging to the NEA or AFT, no more than a few thousand belong to either organisation.[51]

PARENT-TEACHER ASSOCIATIONS (PTAs)

A forum for parents and teachers to work together to plan and to resolve educational problems on the local, state, and national levels is provided by Parent-teacher associations. Teachers usually take an active part in these associations and work with parents on curriculum and instructional programs, student policy, and school-community relations.

5.2 Million Members

Founded in 1897, the PTA — the most prominent of the groups — is a loose confederation of fifty branches and 25,000 local units, with over 5.2 million members (mostly mothers) in 1984. Its branches include all fifty states, the District of Columbia, and the European Congress of American Parents, Teachers, and Students, No local unit is exactly like any other, although all local PTA members belong to the national PTA. Every PTA unit devises its own pattern of organisation and service to fit its school and neighbourhood. Membership in the PTA is open to anyone interested in promoting the welfare of children and youth, working with teachers and schools, and willing to support the goals of the PTA.[54]

The *PTA Today* and *What's Happening in Washington* are the official monthly magazines of the association. Many teacher and administrative associations, including the NEA and AFT, maintain a working relationship with the PTA on important issues; in fact, the NEA is loosely affiliated with the PTA.

Local School Influence

In some school districts, however, parents and teachers have preferred not to affiliate with the state or national PTA organisation because of political differences and because they want to keep local monies in the community. The Parent-Teacher Organisation (PTO) and Parent-Teacher Student Organisation (PTSO) have replaced the PTA in some communities.[53]

National Impact

Although the PTA claims to wield considerable power in shaping local school-community relations and local school policy, its actual influence at the local level is often determined by the philosophy and attitudes of the superintendent, principal, and teachers. Actually the PTA tends to have more influence on the national, than on the local, level. As the nation's largest child-advocacy organisation, the national PTA is constantly assessing children's welfare so that it can respond to changes in our society and in the needs of children. For a number of years, the national PTA has lobbied to reduce violence on television and to improve the quality of children's television programing. The national PTA is also very active in programs related to reading, urban education, special education, sex education, child nutrition and health education, and drug abuse prevention as well as in improving school discipline and combating censorship of school and library materials.

Organisations for Prospective Teachers

Students who are thinking of or are committed to a career as a teacher may join a number of professional organisations. These organisations help answer many questions; develop an understanding of the profession; stimulate ideals of professional ethics, standards, and training; provide an opportunity to meet other education students and educators at local and national meetings; and publish materials that help members keep up with current trends in the profession. Education-related organisations open to students include the following:

Free Insurance for Students

1. *Student National Education Association.* Founded in 1937, the Student NEA was originally called Future Teachers of America and admitted high school and college students. Currently there are about 25,000 Student NEA members (a drop of 50,000 between 1975 and 1984) in about thirty-five college chapters. Members receive *Today's Education* and the annual *NEA Handbook* and are entitled to request free research reports. They also obtain automatically free liability protection when they student teach.

The student NEA strives to develop an understanding of the education profession; its major purpose is to encourage young men and women to enter teaching and join the NEA. The AFT has not established student organisations for prospective teachers, although local chapters are exerting pressures to organise them. The AFT takes the position that with the current oversupply of teachers, there is no pressing need to move in this direction.

Educational Horizons

2. *Honorary Education Associations*. Professional and honorary groups in education include Phi Lambda Theta, Phi Delta Kappa, and Kappa Delta Pi. Phi Lambda Theta has initiated more than 100,000 individuals since its inception in 1910 and has grown from seven chapters to more than a hundred chapters (mostly campus based) in thirty-one states. Originally open to undergraduate and graduate female students and faculty members who met the necessary qualifications, it began to admit men in 1974. Current membership is 16,000. General qualifications include superior scholastic achievement (B + or higher), evidence of high professional standards, and leadership potential. Phi Lamda Theta publishes a quarterly entitled *Educational Horizons,* as well as a newsletter.

Phi Delta Kappan

Phi Delta Kappa, founded in 1906, now includes 585 local and 7 regional chapters in the United States and Canada, as well as 8 international chapters. About half are campus based. As of 1984, there were approximately 140,000 members, with no distinctions made among graduate students, teachers, and administrators. Originally open only to men, it opened its membership to women in 1974. Membership requirements include high scholastic achievement, completion of a minimum of fifteen semester hours of graduate work in education, commitment to a life career of educational services, and residence status in an approved institution at the time of election. The purpose of the organisation is to promote quality education, with particular emphasis on publicly supported education. Members receive *Phi Delta Kappan,* a highly respected professional journal published ten times a year, and the fraternity newsletter. Other publications are available at reduced rates.

Kappa Delta Pi, founded in 1911, has always been open to men and women. Total membership is 430,000, of which 60,000 are considered active. Approximately 20,000 members are students. The purpose of the association is to recognise outstanding contributions to education. To this end, it invites to membership persons who exhibit worthy educational ideals sound scholarship, and commendable personal qualities. The association is international in scope and comprises several hundred alumni and active chapters. Kappa Delta Pi publishes two well-known journals, *Educational Forum,* a quarterly, and *Kappa Delta Pi,* a monthly, as well as a limited number of books on education as part of the Kappa Delta Pi Research Publications series.

Review of Educational Research

3. *American Educational Research Association.* The American Educational Research Association (AERA), founded in 1915, is a national organisation of educators and social scientists

who have a vital interest in research in education and application of research to education practice. It is considered by many to be the most prestigious research organisation in education. AERA is constituted in ten divisions and more than seventy special interest groups. Membership in 1984 totaled 14,000, of which 2,500 were students. Members are entitled to three periodicals: the *Educational Researcher,* a monthly news and feature magazine, and *American Educational Research Journal* and *Review of Educational Research,* both quarterlies. Members also receive discounts for AERA-sponsored publications and research training sessions at the annual meeting. The annual meeting is held in a different city each year and attracts a wide array of researchers and educators from across the country; several thousand original papers on a broad spectrum of topics are presented at these meetings.

Students interested in joining any of these organisations can ask their professors for appropriate information, since many of them are members. If you visit your college library, you can track down the respective journals for each organisation. The first or second page of each issue will list the membership address and membership dues; some journals will also indicate lower membership rates for students.

Summing Up

1. It is generally agreed that teaching is not as yet a full profession, although it is moving towards becoming one.
2. Many trends in education are increasing the status of teacher professionalism. Professional practice commissions, for example, enable teachers to participate in setting criteria for entering the profession. Teacher centers and mediated entry enable them to play a major role in professional training and development. Merit pay provides an opportunity for increased salaries and professional responsibilities.

3. During the past few decades teachers have become more militant and have gained increased status as professionals. Teacher organisations have played a crucial role in this quest for greater power and professionalism.
4. The NEA and AFT now represent the large majority of classroom teachers; these organisations have improved teachers' salaries and working conditions and have gained them a greater voice in decisions that involve teaching and learning in the schools.
5. There are other professional organisations that teachers can join that work to improve education. Some of these, like Phi Delta Kappa and the American Educational Research Association, are open to students of education.

Discussion Questions

1. Is teaching a profession? Defend your answer.
2. Does a teacher surplus tend to make teaching more or less a full-fledged profession? Why or why not?
3. What trends are giving teaching more status as a full-fledged profession than it has had in the past?
4. What are some similarities and differences between the NEA and the AFT? Is a merger desirable? Defend your answer.
5. What professional organisations other than the NEA or AFT might you join? Why?

Suggested Readings

Hosford, Philip L. ed. *Using What We Know About Teaching*, 1984, ASCD Year-book Alexandria, VA: Association for Supervision and Curriculum Development, 1984.

The book examines how knowledge is utilised and applied in the teaching profession and compares the diffusion of knowledge in the teaching profession with what goes on in other professions.

Howsam, Robert B., et al. *Educating a Profession*, Washington D.C.: American Association of Colleges for Teacher Education, 1976.

A recent overview concerning the problems and prospects of enhancing the profession of teachers as well as future policies of the profession.

Lortie, Dan C. *Schoolteacher: A Sociological Study.* Chicago: University of Chicago Press. 1975.

An interesting book with observations on and interpretations of the nature of teaching and the social dynamics of the classroom and school.

Ornstein, Allan C., and Harry L. Miller. *Looking into Teaching.* Boston: Houghton Mifflin, 1980.

An examination of crucial issues and ideas related to the teaching profession, including what is taught, who teaches, how teachers are prepared, what constitutes the work of teachers, and what organisations teachers join.

Smith, B.O. *A Design for a School of Pedagogy,* Washington, D.C.: Government Printing Office, 1980.

An examination of various strategies for improving teacher education and teacher professionalism.

Woodring, Paul. *The Persistent Problems of Education.* Bloomington, Ind: Phi Delta Kappa, 1983.

The author describes uby certain problems in education persist from generation to generation, including what should be taught in schools, how teachers should be educated, and how teachers can improve their professional status.

REFERENCES

1. Ronald G. Corwin, *Sociology of Education* (New York: Appleton-Century-Crofts, 1965); Robert Havighurst and Daniel Levine, *Society and Education,* 5th ed., (Boston : Allyn and Bacon, 1979); and Robert B Howsam et al., *Educating a Profession* (Washington, D.C.: American Association of Colleges for Teacher Education. 1976).
2. Amitai Etzioni, *The Semiprofessions and Their Organisations Teachers. Nurses and Social Workers* (New York: Free Press, 1969). p. v.
3. Howsam et al., *Educating a Profession.*
4. Dan C. Lortie, *Schoolteacher: A Sociological Study* (Chicago: University of Chicago Press. 1975) : B O. Smith. *A Design for a School Pedagogy* (Washington. D.C.: Government Printing Office, 1980).
5. Henrick D. Gideonse. "The Necessary Revolution in Teacher Education," *Phi Delta Kappan* (September 1982). pp. 15-18: Paul

Woodring, *The Persistent Problems of Education*(Bloomington, Ind. Phi Delta Kappa, 1983).

6. Corwin *Sociology of Education.* Allan C. Ornstein. "Characteristics of a Profession. "*Illinois School Journal* (Winter 1976-77). pp. 12-21.
7. *30th Annual List of Accredited Programs. 1983-84* (National Council for Accreditation of Teacher Education, 1984). Telephone conversation with Gloria Cheray. Assistant Director of the National Council for Accreditation of Teacher Evaluation, April 6, 1984.
8. Jim Gallagher, "On the Job Teacher Training Makes Grade." *Chicago Tribune* December 25, 1983, Sect. 1, p. 4.
9. Peter Balu and W. Richard Scott. *Formal Organisations* (San Francisco : Chandler, 1965), pp. 51-52.
10. James Browne, "Power Politics for Teachers, Modern Style," *Phi Delta Kappan* (October 1980), pp. 158-64: Leonard L. Gregory. "Unintended Consequences of Public School Negotiations. *School Business Affairs* (January 1979). pp. 26-27: and Susan M. Johnson. "Teacher Union in Schools." *Harrard Educational Review* (August 1983), pp. 309-326.
11. Victor R. Lindquist and Frank S. Endicott. *Employment Trends for College Graduates.* Thirty-Eighth Annual Survey (Evanston, III: Northwestern University, 1984).
12. Ronald G. Corwin, *Militant Professionalism: A Study of Militant Conflict in High Schools* (New York: Appleton-Century-Crofts, 1970).
13. Richard Wynn. *Collective Bargaining* (Bloomington. Ind. Phi Delta Kappa 1983); Telephone conversation with Donald Walker. Collective Bargaining Department. NEA, February 13, 1984.
14. Marc Gaswirth and Garry Whalen, *Collective Negotiations* (Trenton: New Jersey School Boards Association, 1983); Stephen J. Knezevich. *Administration of Public Education* 4th ed. (New York, Harper and Row, 1984).
15. *Standards and Certification Bodies in the Teaching Profession* (Washington, D.C. NEA, 1983).
16. Arnold M. Gallegos, "Politics and Realities of Staff Development," *Educational Leadership* (January-February 1980), p. 21 Bruce Joyce, "The Ecology of Staff Development" (Paper presented at the Annual Meeting of the American Educational Research Association, Boston, April 1980).
17. Roy A Edelfelt, "Critical Issues in Developing Teacher Centers," *Phi Delta Kappan* (February 1982), pp. 390-394; Sally Mertens, "Teacher Centers : Support for Professional Practice," *Journal of*

Teacher Education (March-April 1982), pp. 7-12.

18. Telephone conversation with Myra Cooper, Director of the New York City Teacher Center, January 9, 1984, Leon Intrater, Associate Director of the Kohl Teacher Center, Wilmette, Illinois, January 9, 1984.
19. Lortie, *Schoolteacher.*
20. Frederik J. McDonald and Patricia Elias "The Transition into Teaching. The Problems of Beginning Teachers and Programs to Solve Them" (Paper prepared for the Educational Testing Service Berkeley, Calif, 1983), pp. 4-5.
21. G. Thomas Fox, "Challenging How Teachers Are Educated: A Source for Dialogue and Action" (Paper published by the ERIC Clearing house on Teacher Education. February 1983).
22. The Teaching Professsion: Taking A New Look," *Annual Report of the American Federation of Teachers, 1982-83* (Washington, D.C.: AFT, 1983),p. 22.
23. "Merit Pay for Teachers: Worth Another Try," *American School Board Journal* (May 1983). pp. 8-13; Nancey R, Needham, "Descheduling Teacher Salaries." *Today's Education* (1982-83), pp. 103-107.
24. Ibid. Also see Robert S. Soar and Ruth M. Soar, "Teacher Merit Pay: Can Research Help" *Journal of Human Behaviour and Learning* (no. 1, 1984), pp. 3-13.
25. Milton Friedman. "Busting the Monopoly." *Newsweek,* December 5, 1983. p. 96.
26. Chris Pipho, "An End to the State Revolt—Maybe, " *Phi Delta Kappan* (January 1984), pp. 309-310.
27. John Dahl. "America's New Bonus Babies: Teachers," *New York Times.* Education Survey, sect. 12, January 8, 1984, p. 23; Elaine Say and Leslie Miller, "The Second Mile Plan: Incentive Pay for Houston Teachers," *Phi Delta Kappan* (December 1982), pp. 270-271.
28. *Ibid.*
29. Larry W Barber and Karen Klein. "Merit Pay and Teacher Evaluation." *Phi Delta Kappan* (December 1983) pp. 247-251. Brian Burke. "Merit Pay for Teachers," *Phi Delta Kappan* (December 1982), pp. 265-266 and Soar and Soar, "Teacher Merit Pay: Can Research Help?"
30. *Chicago Tribune,* September 28, 1975, sect. 1, p. 3.
31. *NEA Handbook 1983-84* (Washington, D.C., National Education Association 1984), table 1, p. 134. Telephone conversation with Simeon Taylor. Department of Membership. NEA, April 12, 1984.

32. Ibid.
33. Anthony M. Cresswell and Michael J. Murphy *Teachers Education and Collective Bargaining* (Berkeley, Calif: McCutchan, 1980), Allan C. Ornstein and Hangary 1 Miller, *Looking into Teaching* (Chicago. Rand McNally, 1980) "Your NEA "*Today's Education.,* 1983-84), pp. 78-79.
34. *NEA Handbook 1983-84.*
35. *Annual Report of the American Federation of Teachers, 1983-84.* (Wshington D.C. AFT. 1984; Telephone conversation with Robert Porter, Secretary Treasurer, American Federation of Teachers, April 16, 1984.
36. National Education Association Annual Meeting. Philadelphia, July 1983, Resolution E-17, NEA Resolutions," *Today's Education* (1983-84). p. 145.
37. Albert Shanker "Why Teacher Are Angry," *American School Board Journal* (January 1975). p. 23.
38. *Work Stoppages Involving Teachers 1940-62* (Washington, D.C.; U.S. Department of Labour 1963). Table 1, p. 2 *Work Stoppages in Government. 1958-68* (Washington. D.C.; U.S. Department of Labour. 1970), table 9, p. 13. *Government Work Stoppages 1960, 1969 and 1970* (Washington. D.C.; U.S. Department of Labour 1971), table 9 p. 6. From 1971 to 1980, annual reports from the U.S. Department of Labour *Work Stoppages in Government* are used as sources for 1981 to 1983. Robert Porter Secretary Treasurer of the AFT, and Will Meyer of the Collective Bargaining Department of the NEA supplied the appropriate information for their respective organisations. April 16, 1984; Pat Strongin of the Bureau in National Affairs supplied information for all teachers, April 23, 1984.
39. See William M. Bulkeley, "Getting the Ax: Government Workers Find That Job Security Can suddenly Vanish," *Wall Street Journal* July 29, 1981 pp. 1. 17; Martin Feldstein, "The Job of Controlling Public Sector Pay," *Wall Street Journal* October 1, 1981, p. 13; and Barbara Mahany and Patricia Tennison , "Suburban School District Face Teacher Strike Peril." *Chicago Tribune* August 21, 1983. Sect. 2, pp. 1-3.
40. *American Federation of School Administration Affiliated Locals* (New York; AFSA, 1984); *American Federation of School Administrators: Who are We?* (New York AFSA, 1984). Also see Bruce S. Cooper and Kent F. Murmann, "Managerial Identification and Unionisation of School Administrators. *Administrator's Notebook* (January 1982), pp. 1-4.
41. Marshal O. Donley. *The Future of Teacher Power in America* (Bloomington, Ind Phi Delta Kappa, 1977).

42. Evertt Ladd and Seymour M. Lipset. "Faculty Support for Unionisation," *Education Digest* (May 1978), pp. 56-58.
43. "Health Care, Looking Ahead." *Annual Report of the American Federation of Teachers 1982-83.* pp. 28-30.
44. "Public Employees: Preparing for Change," *Annual Report of the American Federation of Teachers 1982-83.* pp. 26-27.
45. Joann S. Lublin. "Two Rival Teachers' Unions Quarrel Even More." *Wall Street Journal,* November 22, 1983, p. 58.
46. Stanley E. Elam. "The NEA, Political Powerhouse or Paper Tiger?" *Phi Delta Kappan* (November 1981). pp. 169-174.
47. *Government Employee Regulations Report* (Washington D.C.: Bureau of National Affairs. (1984).
48. See *Directory of Education Associations 1980-81)* (Washington, D.C.: U.S. Department of Education 1981).
49. *Projections of Education Statistics to 1990-91* (Washington, D.C.: National Center for Education Statistics, 1982). Table 20 p. 84; Telephone conversation with Rita Schwartz, Secretary-Treasurer, National Association of Catholic School Teachers, April 13, 1984.
50. *United States Catholic Elementary and Secondary Schools, 1983-84* (Washington, D.C.: National Catholic Education Association, 1984); telephone conversation with Bruno Manno, Director of Research and Statistics, National Catholic Education Association, April 13, 1984.
51. *Digest of Education Statistics, 1982* (Washington, D.C.: National Center for Education Statistic 1983), figure 5, p. 48; table 40, p. 49; telephone conversation with Rita Schwartz, Secretary, Treasurer, National Association of Catholic School Teachers. April 13, 1984; and telephone conversation with Simeon Taylor, Department of Membership, NEA, April 12, 1984.
52. *Partners in Education : Teachers in the PTA* (Chicago: The National PTA, (1983).
53.. *The National PTA Handbook 1983-1985* (Chicago: The National PTA, 1983).

3

Public Education

FOCUSING QUESTIONS

How do governments—local, state, and federal—influence education?

How does the local school board work with the district superintendent in formulating school policy?

Why have schools consolidated, decentralized, and retrenched in recent years?

What are the different roles and responsibilities of the governor, state legislature, state board of education, state department of education, and chief state school officer in determining school policy?

How has the federal role in education changed in recent years?

What are some of the nongovernmental influences on school administration?

Education in the United States is organized on various governmental levels—local, intermediate, state, and federal. Knowing about the formal organization of schools and how they are governed is important to people who work in schools. Teachers—or prospective teachers—who know how schools are organized and how they are influenced at different levels of government will be in a better position to make wise choices and realistic decisions about schools and to take political action. In this chapter we will examine the various governmental levels and how they impact on education. We will also explore a number of other important influences on the administration of schools.

No National System of Education

A national system of education does not exist in this country in the same sense that it does in Great Britain, France, or the Soviet Union. Education here is considered a state and/or local function; we have fifty different state systems and many differences among local school systems even within the same state.

State Responsibility for Public Education

The U.S. Constitution makes no mention of public education, but the Tenth Amendment to the Constitution reserves to the states all powers not specifically delegated to the federal government or prohibited to the states by the Constitution. This amendment is the basis for allocating to the states primary legal responsibility for public education in the United States. However, responsibility for the practical day-to-day operation of school systems has been delegated by the states to local districts. So we begin our discussion of how schools are governed and administered at the local level.

LOCAL RESPONSIBILITIES AND ACTIVITIES

Limited Corporation

Every public school in the United States is part of a local school district. The district is created by the state. Subject to the restrictions of the state constitution, the state legislature can modify a local district's jurisdiction, change its boundaries and powers, or even eliminate it altogether. The local district encompasses a relatively small geographical area and operates the schools for children within a specific community. It is the avenue through which local citizens act in establishing districtwide policies in education. However, because a school district operates to carry out a state function—not a local function—local policies must be consistent with policies set forth in the state school code. The local district can be compared to a limited corporation whose powers are granted by state laws: it has only those powers expressly granted to it and those discretionary powers essential to its operation.

LOCAL SCHOOL BOARDS

Delegated Powers from the State

The local boards of education have been delegated powers and duties by the state for the purpose of assuring that their schools are operated properly. The school boards have limited power and can exercise only those prerogatives specifically delegated to them by the state legislature. Nevertheless, by law and custom, school boards have assumed significant decision-making responsibility. School boards have the power for the most part to raise money though taxes with a debt limitation. They exercise power over personnel and school property. Some states leave curriculum and student policy pretty much in the hands of the school board, but others, by law, impose specific requirements. In general, the school board must conform to state guidelines to qualify for state aid, as well as conform to federal guidelines where U.S. government monies are involved.

Most School Boards Elected

Methods of selecting board members are prescribed by state law. The two basic methods are election and appointment. Election is thought to make for greater accountability to the public, but some people argue that appointment leads to greater competence and less politics. Election is the most common practice. In 1981, 86 percent of school board members nationwide were elected in nonpartisan elections, 10 percent were elected in partisan elections, and 4 percent were appointed.

Appointment is more common in large urban districts than in suburban or small-town districts: 11 percent of urban board members in 1981 were appointed. A few states specify a standard number of board members, still others specify a permissible range, and a few have no requirements. Most school boards fall within a three-to-nine member range, with the largest known school board having nineteen members.

Characteristics of Board Members

Based on a recent nationwide survey of school board members, a significant trend in recent years is the increase in the number of women on school boards, from 28 percent in 1982 to 37 percent in 1983. Minority representation has remained stable at 6 percent. (Most interesting, southern states show a higher minority representation on school boards: 14 percent black and 5 percent Hispanic.) School board members tend to be older than the general population (73 percent are over forty); more educated (65 percent have had four or more years of college); wealthier (53 percent have family incomes of $40,000 or more, 4 percent earn more than $100,000 annually); and more likely to be professionals or managers (55 percent.)

The largest school systems (those enrolling 50,000 or more students) tend to have most heterogeneous boards. A 1981 survey indicates that minority members constitute 29 percent of the school board composition; women make up 36 percent.

Types of Board Meetings

There are three general types of board meetings: regular, special, and executive. The first two are usually open meetings and the public is invited. Open board meetings obviously enhance school-community relations and allow parents to understand the problems of education as well as to air their concerns. The use of closed board meetings to reach major policy is generally disdained but is occasionally used by central school boards in some large cities if conflict and tension arise. Many school districts, however, have mandated open meetings except under certain specified, and rather limited conditions.

THE SCHOOL SUPERINTENDENT AND CENTRAL OFFICE STAFF

Executive Officer of School System

Subject to Board Approval

One of the most important responsibilities a school board has is to appoint a competent superintendent of schools. The superintendent is the executive officer of the school system, whereas the board is the legislative policy-making body. Since the school board consists of laypeople who are not experts in school affairs, it is their responsibility to see that the work of the school is properly performed by professional personnel. The board of education often delegates many of their own legal powers to the superintendent and staff. The superintendent's policies, of course, are subject to board approval.

One of the major functions of the school superintendent is to gather and present data so that school board members can make intelligent policy decisions. Increasing reliance on the superintendent and staff is evident as school systems grow in size. The superintendent advises the school board and keeps members abreast of problems, generally, the school board will refuse to enact legislation or make policy without the recommendation of the school superintendent. However, it is common knowledge that when there is continuous disagreement or a major conflict over policy between the school board and the superintendent, the latter is usually replaced. The average time in office of superintendents is only approximately three to four years.

Duties of the Superintendent

The superintendent's powers are broad and his or her duties are many and varied. Besides being an adviser to the board of education, he or she is usually responsible for certain functions. They include the following :

1. Serves as supervisor and organizer of professional and nonteaching (for example, janitors and engineers) personnel
2. Makes recommendations regarding the employment, promotion, and dismissal of personnel
3. Ensures compliance with directives of higher authority
4. Prepares the school budget for board review and administers the adopted budget
5. Serves as leader of long-range planning
6. Develops and evaluates curriculum and instructional program
7. Determines internal organization of the school district
8. Makes recommendations regarding school building needs and maintenance

In addition, the superintendent is responsible for the day-to-day operation of the schools within the district and serves as the major public spokesperson for the schools.

To fulfil these responsibilities the superintendent is assisted by a central office staff, as well as by support personnel, consultants, and citizen groups. The larger the school district, the greater the number of central administrators and professional staff needed to assist the superintendent .

THE PRINCIPAL AND THE SCHOOL

Small *vs.* Large Schools

Usually, each school has a single administrative officer—a principal—who is responsible for the operation of the school. In small schools this person may teach part-time as well. In a large school, in addition to the principal, there may be one or more assistant or vice principals. The administrative hierarchy may also consist of a number of department chairpersons, a discipline officer (for example, dean of boys, dean of girls), a director of guidance, and so on.

Although functions vary by locality and size, the principal is primarily responsible for administering all aspects of a school's operations. It is common practice for the principal to work with some type of community group for the improvement of the school. In the past, this function was often performed by a parent-teacher association and various advisory school-community committees that had little influence or real power. Since the 1960s, however, many people have demanded greater input into the operation of the schools, particularly in the cities. As teachers have become more militant, principals are being more careful to follow contract provisions and to include teacher representatives in policy-making decisions for the school unit.

Although principals juggle many different roles, there is overwhelming agreement that their major task is to provide instructional leadership (improving teacher techniques, developing appropriate curricula, and affording optimal learning situations for students). Authorities also recommend that principals spend from 50 to 75 percent of their time on improving instruction. The trouble is, as principals point out, their numerous organizational and managerial tasks take up an inordinate amount of time, and in many cases prevent them from exerting instructional leadership.

Instructional Leader

Nevertheless, the principal is at his or her best in the role of instructional leader when (1) teachers can openly share concerns with the principal, (2) there is open communication among teachers and between teachers and the principal, (3) teachers feel they can count on the support and expertise of the principal, (4) the principal values and encourages the professional growth of teachers, and (5) teachers are recognized or rewarded for competent performance by the principal.

SIZE OF SCHOOL DISTRICTS

What is the ideal size for a school district? In terms of minimum size, how many students must be enrolled to justify offering the diversified programs, services, and personnel needed to meet modern educational requirements? A 1934 study of city and county school systems concluded that a minimum of 10,000 to 12,000 students was needed to justify specialized and adequate staff size, as well as a varied program, in relation to reasonable costs of the educational program. At the time, those numbers were criticized severely by many educators who believed that a district of that size was unattainable and impractical for most parts of the country.

Ideal School District Size

Regarding maximum size, a research team headed by Paul Mort and Francis Cornell developed a method for measuring the effectiveness of a school system based on an adaptability index. The index was correlated with school characteristics such as financial policies, curriculum innovation, community and staff participation, location, and size. These studies considered the maximally effective school district to comprise 100,000 students. This estimate was supported by other researchers, but later was disputed by advocates of decentralization who put the figure between 12,000 and 40,000. Another study has concluded that the optimal size for a school district is between 10,000 and 50,000 pupils.

Small Rural School Districts

Historically, 10,000 students is a large number for a school district. Our schools, we must remember, are an outgrowth of one-room school houses and school districts in rural America. With the exception of a few urban areas, even as late as the turn of the twentieth century, most school districts consisted of three, four, or five schools and a few hundred students. As late as 1930, nearly 50 percent of American school districts had fewer than 300 students.

TABLE 3.1

Distribution of Public School Systems by Size of District, 1980-1981

Size of District (Number of Pupils)	*Public School Districts*		*Public School Students*	
	Number	*Percentage*	*Number*	*Percentage*
Total operating districts	15,625	100.0	42,851,396	100.0
25,000 or more	183	1.2	11,907,985	27.8
10,000-24,999	511	3.3	7,434,630	17.3
5,000-9,999	1,106	7.1	7,705,372	18.0
2,500-4,999	2,065	13.2	7,181,460	16.8
1,000-2,499	3,457	22.1	5,665,386	13.2
600-999	1,820	11.7	1,437,725	3.4
300-599	2,316	14.8	1,014,640	2.4
Less than 300	4,161	26.6	504,198	1.2

Source: Digest of Education Statistics, 1983-84 (Washington, D.C.: National Center for Education Statistics, 1984), table 50, p.62.

Large School Districts

By 1980, nearly half of public school students were in school districts containing 10,000 or more students. There were only 183 school districts with 25,000 or more students, but they accounted for 11.9 million students or 28 percent of the nation's public school enrollment. Table 3.1 shows how school systems are distributed according to enrollment size.

Most of the largest school systems (50,000 or more students) are located in California, Florida, Texas, Ohio, and Maryland. In most cases, the larger school systems are located in or near cities, the largest being the New York City system with approximately 960,000 students as of 1980, followed by Los Angeles with 545,000 students and Chicago with 475,000 students. (Two other large school systems, Puerto Rico and Hawaii, span an entire territory and state, respectively). The medium-sized and smaller school systems have followed metropolitan sprawl and tend to be located in the outer ring of the suburbs or in rural areas.

Declining Number of School Districts

Consolidation Trends. The number of school districts in the United States continues to decline. In 1930, there were more than 130,000 school districts. By 1950 the number had shrunk to 83,718; by 1980 to 15,625. The declining number of school districts in ten-year intervals from 1930 to 1980, with projections for 1990.

Benefits of Consolidation

The reduced number of school districts is a result of *consolidation,* the combination of a number of smaller school districts into one or two larger ones. Consolidation is thought to bring about more effective schools by increasing the tax base, quality of professional personnel, breadth of educational program, special services, and transportation facilities and by reducing overall educational costs per student.

A great many of the reorganized school districts are still too small to provide a comprehensive educational program and adequate specialized personnel to meet the needs of all the students. While the trend toward consolidation continues in the rural and small school districts (although at a slower pace today than in the past), there is a recent countertrend in large urban school districts to decentralize and divide into smaller school districts.

White Flight

Decentralization. Changes in the urban population after 1950 became noticeable as more and more low-income and minority residents pushed middle-class and white populations to the suburbs. The white flight movement became apparent in the 1950s and 1960s and to a lesser extent in the 1970s. As a result, schools in the cities became multiethnic and many schools in the suburbs became more homogeneous in terms of income and race. By the 1960s, the frustration of diverse ethnic groups, especially blacks, found a common "solution" in the call for decentralization, accompanied by greater community involvement in the schools. By definition, *decentralisation* divides the school system into smaller units, but the focus of power and authority in a single central administration and board of education remains intact. There is usually little controversy over decentralization, so long as jobs are not consolidated or expanded on the basis of racial or ethnic patterns; even professional educators today see a need to reduce school bureaucracy and accept decentralization because it allows the professional educators to retain power. At the same time, school critics and minority spokespersons see decentralization as a first step toward increasing community involvement in the schools; they believe that decentralization will give the people greater access to the schools.

Smaller Units

A nationwide survey on decentralization of school systems with 50,000 or more students was conducted in 1980. Of the sixty-nine school systems in this category, 64 percent reported that they were decentralized.

Seventeen reasons were given for decentralization in a recent study. The top eight reasons, in order of priority and representing 79 percent of the responses, were (1) to enhance school-community relations, (2) to provide greater community input at the local level, (3) to provide local schools with more field and resource personnel, (4) to provide efficient maintenance and support for local schools, (5) to reduce administrative span of control, (6) to provide greater linkages between local schools and the central school board, (7) to redirect spending for local school needs, and (8) to provide greater curriculum continuity, from kindergarten through grade twelve. These results closely correspond with the findings of other studies.

Reasons for Decentralisation

Oddly enough, little evidence has been found to support these generalizations about decentralization. Very few of the school systems have conducted evaluations of their new organizational models or tested the assumptions, goals, and recommendations related to decentralization. There is little hard evidence that school decentralization improves education.

COMMUNITY INVOLVEMENT

Advisory Committees

Increasing pressure from minority groups, accompanied by growing pressure for reform from educators, has played a part in forcing school authorities in many large school systems to seek additional ways to increase community involvement in the schools. What has emerged are the following, not mutually exclusive, community alternatives for governing metropolitan schools; community participation, community control, and community education.

Sharing of Decision-making Authority

Community participation connotes the formation of advisory committees or groups beyond the usual parent-teacher associations. These committees may operate at various levels within the system—the local school or central level. The main function of these groups is to make recommendations (not policy) and to serve as a liaison between the schools and community. *Community control* connotes a legal provision for an elected community school board functioning under specific guidelines and in conjunction with the central school board. It means a sharing of decision-making authority and power between the local and central school boards; it also means that the powers of the professionals and central school board members are abridged and transferred to community groups. *Community education* changes the focus of school-community relations from the schools to a broader perspective (that is, education) and includes several cooperative educational extensions of the community. The idea envisions the schools as only one of many educational agencies within the community, and the notion of education is extended in both directions: from prekindergarten to the retired and elderly. School people, under this arrangement, share educational responsibilities with various community institutions.

Broadened View of Education

Community Participation and Control. In New York City and Detroit a form of community control has evolved in which elected local school boards function in conjunction with the central school board. A far more frequent school-community arrangement has been some form of increased community participation with the appointment of advisory committees at either the neighborhood school or central board level. These committees are usually appointed by school officials; only in a few cases are the advisory groups elected by the community. Nevertheless, the committees are advisory, as their names suggest, and whenever guidelines are established, the school boards usually reaffirm their own authority and expectations that the advisory committees abide by the rules and regulations of the system.

SUPPORT FOR COMMUNITY PARTICIPATION

Areas of Community Involvement

For the most part, school officials have encouraged community participation but have resisted any movement toward community control of schools. A survey of the 399 school systems that enrolled more than 15,000 students in 1975 showed that superintendents were much more positive about community participation (defined as input that involved giving advice on school policy) than about community control (defined as determining school policy). They envisioned that community control entailed the forfeiture of their perceived or actual decision-making power; furthermore, they perceived community participation as beneficial and in line with traditional school-community relations and community control as disruptive. They felt it carried the potential for overt hostitility between different school-community factions. Researchers at the Institute for Responsive Education surveyed hundreds of examples of community participation and found nine general areas in which many citizen groups were providing advice and assistance to educators: (1) identification of goals, priorities, and needs; (2) budget analysis; (3 and 4) selection and evaluation of teachers and principals; (5) development of curricula; (6) extracurricular programs; (7 and 8) community support and financing for schools; and (9) recruitment of volunteers.

In another study of 1,270 parents and 3,700 teachers, it was found that the great majority of parents do not have time, or the inclination, to participate in school matters. Their involvement is limited to helping their children with homework or reading to their children (at the lower grades). More than 70 percent never helped teachers in the classroom or never participated in school functions. Only 4 percent of the parents surveyed were active, that is spending more than twenty-five days per year at the school or on school business. In short, community participation and community control are not relevant issues to the vast majority of parents—suggesting that school-community problems or policies may be confined to a few educators and a few community activists.

Limited Parental Input

New Coalition

Controversies involving community control, and even community participation, have lain more or less dormant for the past few years, but they may come to prominence again if a serious community effort is made to reform or change public schools. When school officials are forced to confront the problem of making classrooms and schools more effective, they may look for ways to locate more authority and responsibility for solving instructional problems at the local level where the problems are manifested. Considering this prospect, David Selden has pointed out that for urban schools "any successful scheme of parent or community participation ... must take into account [that] most American cities are ... becoming mainly black, Hispanic, and Oriental," and this shift has implications for the political structure of schools (as well as the country). It seems that both schools and society "can best be served by forming a new coalition, based on mutual respect, between teachers and leaders of the new urban power structures."

Many Educational Agencies

Community Education. Important trends suggest that we are entering a new stage of school-community relations. In the 1980s the school has come to be seen as one, but only one, of the educational agencies within the community. Museums, libraries, parks, businesses, private foundations, labor unions, religious institutions, health care centers, and self-help groups, among others, perform important educational functions. The school serves as a partner—or possibly as a coordinating institution—in developing various community educational, social, recreational, and cultural activities.

Lifelong Education

Because the school is part of a community educational system, it avoids fragmenting and duplicating services provided by other community agencies. The delivery system is open to all consumers: students, parents, childless adults, and aging populations. The notion of lifelong education, and the education of diverse learners of various age groups, is an integral part of the notion of community education. In Flint, Michigan, for example, there are some fifty schools offering a host of educational, recreational, family, and community services to local citizens—including a wide range of preschool programs for three- and four-year-olds and their parents, as well as adult sports and drama, exercise, recreational, and vocational programs.

Needs of Diverse Groups

As part of the community education plan, schools share their personnel (such as teachers, counselors, and specialists) and facilities (such as portions of the building, yard, or stadium, and buses) with other community agencies; open their physical plant to a larger segment of the community; and offer programs and services to meet the growing needs of diverse population groups (such as working mothers, business people, and retirees). This sharing process takes place not only after school hours, on weekends or holidays, but also during school hours and school days—wherever underutilized space (say a conference room, auditorium, or pool), equipment, or personnel may be shared for a portion of the day. In return, the schools may expect to share in the facilities, equipment, and personnel of other community agencies—and may expect increased private and public support for their programs and people. This is especially important in a period of retrenchment and school budget cutbacks.

A New Option

Each of the three community-involvement models has its proponents. Most educators advocate community participation because it allows them to retain power; moreover, they envision it as a method for encouraging parental support and participation in school matters. An increasing number of liberal and minority leaders, however, favor community control as a vehicle for transferring power to the community, or at least to people who claim to represent the community. The third option—community education—is relatively new and only a few reform-minded educators speak of or write about this as an alternative form of community involvement.

In reality, there is little controversy over the first alternative, because most people, both defenders and critics of the schools, accept this community model. Many professional educators see a need for it because it increases community involvement while leaving their decision-making power intact; many critics accept it because they view it as a first step toward community control. The controversy concerns control: which group—elected public officials and professional educators, or community groups—will have the power and authority to run the schools. The issues are highly political and are related to issues of self-interest, group ideology, and the power of the purse strings. The third option, community education, arouses little concern or conflict since so few people have crystallized the concept, but it is likely to gain increasing support in the next few years as community groups seek to use underutilised schools for their own needs and interests and as educators seek new allies in their attempt to increase sources of school funding.

INTERMEDIATE UNITS

The term *intermediate unit* or *educational service agency (ESA)* refers to an office or agency in a middle position between the state department of education and local school districts. The intermediate unit is usually a legal and political extension of the state department of education, generally created by the state legislature. (A few intermediate units, those sponsored by local school districts, can only be viewed as an extension of the school districts.) As many as thirty-nine states had some form of intermediate units as of 1984. The average intermediate unit comprised twenty to thirty school districts and covered about fifty square miles. The number of intermediate units in a state ranged from two in Alaska, Idaho, and Missouri to fifty-eight in California and Michigan.

Provision of Support Services

The intermediate unit or educational service agency provides coordination and supplementary services to local school districts and serves as a link between local and state educational authorities in most states. This pattern creates a legally constituted government relationship involving limited regulatory powers and providing support services to school districts. In a few states, however, the intermediate school district is formed by local school districts (not by the state) in a given area or region to provide common services: such districts lack legal, political, and financial support from the state.

Intermediate units are being called on more frequently to regulate and enforce state mandates. In recent years, the intermediate unit has also provided school districts with a wide range of consulting services and resource personnel in such general areas of education as curriculum, instruction, evaluation, and in-service training. Intermediate units have also provided services in more specialized areas, such as education of the handicapped, gifted, and talented; bilingual education; prekindergarten education; vocational education; and data processing and computer education. in 1980, 25 million students in 12,000 local school districts were receiving some kind of service from established intermediate units or educational service agencies. That year these agencies spent $1.7 billion for the purpose of improving public education.

Reliance on Grant Money

Especially during the 1970s, many intermediate agencies actively sought outside funding as a way of expanding their services. In some cases, local educators became jealous of their growth, especially when district budgets were shrinking. Local educators felt that resources going to the intermediate units could have gone directly to their schools. Also, heavy reliance on short-term grants not only reduced the continuity in services and programs, it put these agencies in a difficult bind when cutbacks in educational funding became widespread.

Many of these problems can be reduced, even eliminated

by state action that defines more clearly the scope and functions of these intermediate units. Careful attention to the divergent expectations of all the parties who are interested in the work of intermediate units can ensure a constructive state-intermediate-local relationship. It is important that these intermediate units receive their money from the state and that it be allocated by the state legislature, not from other sources. Such funding will reduce tensions between them and local school districts. It is also important that the intermediate agencies serve the needs of the school districts and that local educators perceive those services as useful.

Another Bureaucratic Layer?

A number of other questions also arise. Since some states seem to get along without intermediate units, why can't the other states do the same? Are we not just creating another bureaucratic layer in the educational enterprise of the states? Is it possible that the functions of the intermediate units are not truly needed, that they are more relevant in rural America or where school districts are more diffuse?

On the other hand, we can argue that many small or financially strapped school districts today need the services of intermediate units: moreover, these services can be provided economically by serving several districts. To those who would have us consolidate these small or poor school districts, the supporters of intermediate units might reply that such arrangements diminish local control of schools and local identification of communities; intermediate agencies can provide support services to these school districts without any loss of local power.

School Cooperation

One might argue that if school districts wish to remain independent they could develop a pian of cooperation without the intermediate unit. Actually a number of school districts have formed cooperative agencies without state regulations or mandates. One wonders, however, how many of these cooperative arrangements are properly staffed or financed or can continue without an outside party (state agency) ensuring financial support and a network of communication, research, and evaluation.

New Metropolitan Relationship

Finally, we cannot ignore the growth of metropolitan areas and their implications for educational organization. Many of the large city school districts are declining in student population, are growing more racially segregated, and are financially strapped. Although suburban communities are no longer the exclusive domain of white, middle-class people, they have grown in size. Many are still experiencing moderate increases in student populations; moreover, these school districts tend to be predominantly white and financially more stable than their adjacent city school districts. Reformers emphasize the need for a city-suburban or metropolitan relationship in education. In the future, the intermediate unit may become a more common metropolitan arrangement, imposed by the courts or state legislatures for purposes of school desegregation or fiscal prudence and to provide many functions and services. In fact, metropolitan arrangements are being organized in St. Louis and Milwaukee for purposes of desegregation, and the intermediate unit is expected to play a role with this new city-suburban school plan.

STATE RESPONSIBILITIES AND ACTIVITIES

Legal Responsibility for Education

Every state, by constitution, statute, and practice, assumes that education is a function of the state, and federal and state court decisions have supported this interpretation. Each state has legal responsibility for the support and maintenance of the public schools within its borders. Local school boards, as we have seen, are considered creatures of the state that have been devised for the purpose of running a system of schools.

Being responsible for the schools, the state enacts legislation; determines school taxes and financial aid to local school districts; sets minimum standards for the training, recruitment, and salaries of personnel; decides on the curriculum (some states establish "approved" textbook lists, too); makes provisions for accrediting schools; and provides special services (such as student transportation and free textbooks).

Mandatory and Permissive Laws

State school codes are a collection of laws that establish ways and means of operating schools and conducting education in the state. The state, of course, cannot enact legislation that is contrary to, or conflicts with, the federal Constitution. State statutes can be divided into two groups: *mandatory laws* that establish the minimum program of education and *permissive laws* that define the functions that are delegated to the school district under appropriate conditions.

Although state constitutions and statutes may simply direct state legislators to provide for the establishment and maintenance of a uniform system of schools, provisions in many states are quite detailed concerning methods of operation. The typical state and local organisation and relationship of education, and their respective hierarchy of responsibilities.

THE GOVERNOR AND STATE LEGISLATURE

Although the powers of governors vary widely, their authority on educational matters is spelled out in law. Usually a governor is charged with making educational budget recommendations to the legislature. In many states the governor has legal access to any accumulated balances in the state treasury, and these monies can be used for school purposes.

Powers of the Governor

The governor can appoint or remove school personnel at the state level. These powers often carry restrictions, such as approval by the legislature. In a majority of states the governor can appoint members of the state board of education and, in a few states, the chief state school officer. A governor can kill educational measures through his or her two veto powers or threaten to use the veto to discourage the legislature from enacting educational laws he or she opposes.

Powers of the State Legislature

In most states, the legislature is primarily responsible for establishing and maintaining the public schools and has broad powers to enact laws pertaining to education. These powers are not unlimited; there are restrictions in the form of federal and state constitutions and court decisions. But within these parameters, the legislature has the full power to decide basic school policy questions in the state.

The state legislature usually determines how the state boards of education will be selected, what will be their responsibilities, how the chief state officer will be selected, what will be the duties of this office, what the functions of the state department of education will be, what types of local and regional school districts there will be, and what will be the methods of selection and powers of local school boards. The legislature usually decides on the nature of state taxes for schools, the level of financial support for education, and the taxing power for schools to be allocated on a local or municipal level. The legislature may determine what may or may not be taught, how many years of compulsory education will be required, the length of the school day and school year, and whether or not there will be community colleges and adult and vocational schools. The legislature may also determine staff and student policies and testing and evaluation procedures, authorise school programs, set standards for building construction, and provide various auxiliary services (for example, student transportation and school lunches). Where the legislature does not enact these policies, they are usually the responsibility of the state board of education.

Laws Affecting Nonpublic Schools

The nonpublic or private schools within a state are not exempt from the action of the legislature. General laws apply to private schools, including parochial schools. These laws pertain to health standards, building codes, welfare of children, student codes, and so on. Legislative bodies in many states have passed laws to benefit private schools and, at public expense, provide aid in such areas as student transportation, health services, dual enrollment or shared-time plans, school lunch services, purchasing of books and supplies, student testing services, teacher salary supplements, student tuition, and student loans. Although the courts have generally held that the legislature has the right to pass laws providing for the supervision of nonpublic schools, rarely has a state legislature enacted comprehensive regulatory requirements—and where such laws do exist on the books they are not strictly enforced.

For either the governor or members of the legislature to formulate educational policy without consulting representative educators or the state education agency, and possibly representatives of private industry and pressure groups, seems to many to be an arbitrary and indefensible act. Both the governor and the legislature have available staff members and agencies to help them analyze and interpret data and can obtain additional information on matters of educational concern as needed.

STATE BOARD OF EDUCATION

Two Separate State-boards

The state board of education is usually the most influential and important state education agency. Almost all states have some sort of state board of education, which is dependent on the state legislature for appropriations and authority and serves an advisory function for the legislature. (New York's Board of Regents is perhaps the strongest and most respected state board of education.) In addition, most states have a separate governing board for state colleges and universities; thus there are often two separate state boards, one for elementary and secondary education and another for higher education.

With the exception of Wisconsin, all states have boards of education. As of 1982, thirty-four were appointed by the governor of the state, thirteen were elected by popular vote (this method has increased during the last twenty years), and two were *ex officio* state boards. The number of members of state boards ranges from three in the state of Mississippi to twenty-seven in Texas, with a nine-member board occurring most frequently. (An odd number of members eliminates tie votes).

Characteristics of State School Board Members

While state boards were originally dominated by white males, their composition has changed dramatically in the past two decades. A survey of board members conducted in 1967 showed that only 18 percent were women and 3 percent were minority. A 1982 survey reveals the growing participation by women and minorities. As many as 34 percent of board members are women, and 16 percent are minorities. This trend toward greater heterogeneity is important, widening the perspectives of board members and insuring that boards reflect a wide range of social and educational concerns. Most board members tend to be older (88 percent are forty or older) and well educated. Currently 99 percent have at least some postsecondary education, compared to 86 percent in 1967; 57 percent have a degree beyond the bachelors. The voluntary nature of service on a state board means, however, the members must have the time and resources to participate. As a result most board members who are in the workforce describe their occupation as "managerial" (25 percent) or "professional" (50 percent); and those not in the paid workforce are either retired (11 percent) or homemakers (12 percent) with a history of voluntary service.

Duties of State Boards of Education

The precise duties and functions of state boards of education vary, but generally the boards are charged with the following functions.

1. Adopting and enforcing policies, rules, and regulations necessary to implement legislative acts related to education.
2. Establishing qualifications and appointing personnel to the state department of education.
3. Setting standards for teacher and administrative certificates.
4. Establishing standards for accrediting schools.
5. Managing state funds earmarked for education.
6. Keeping records and collecting data needed for reporting and evaluating.
7. Adopting long-range plans for the development and improvement of schools.
8. Creating advisory bodies as required by law.
9. Acting as a judicial body in hearing disputes arising from state policies.
10. Representing the state in determining policies on all matters pertaining to education that involve relationships with other agencies (including the federal government).
11. Advising the governor or legislature on educational matters.
12. In some states, appointing the chief state school officer, setting minimum salary schedules for teachers and administrators, and adopting policies for the operation of institutions of higher learning.

STATE DEPARTMENT OF EDUCATION

Another major state education agency is the state department of education, which usually operates under the direction of the state board of education and is administered by the chief state school officer.

Functions of State Departments of Education

Traditionally, the primary function of state departments of education was to collect and disseminate statistics about the status of education within the state. Since the 1950s, they have enlarged their services and functions to include (1) accrediting schools, (2) certifying teachers, (3) apportioning funds, (4) overseeing student transportation and safety, (5) monitoring state regulations, and (6) conducting research, evaluating programs, and issuing reports. In the 1960s and 1970s, they expanded their functions to include (1) monitoring compliance with federal regulations and (2) identifying and improving programs to meet the needs of special students (in particular, disadvantaged bilingual and handicapped students who were targeted for these programs).

During this twenty-year period, the state departments had to grapple with controversial issues such as desegregation, compensatory education, student rights and unrest, school finance reform and fiscal crisis, aid to minority groups, declining enrollments, collective bargaining, accountability, and competency testing. During the 1960s and 1970s, the federal government, the courts, and active interest groups joined the fray and wrestled with many educational or school issues—forcing governors and legislators to increase the staff budget and functions of state departments of education.

Professional Staff

State departments of education, once innocuous and invisible, doubled and tripled in size and assumed major new responsibility in administering complex programs (and policies). By 1982, only six states (Delaware, Idaho, Nevada, South Dakota, North Dakota, and Wyoming) had professional staffs of fewer than 100, and six states (California, Connecticut, Michigan, New Jersey, New York, and Texas) had staffs of more than 1,000. Although some divisional administrators of these departments change with changes of political party control or with a change in the chief officer, the professional staff—such as the statisticians, secondary administrators, clerks, and secretaries—are usually civil service employees. By and large, staff members of the state departments of education are recruited from public school personnel and from local schools and colleges.

The leadership role of the state departments of education is expected to grow in the 1980s. The 1981 Education Consolidation and Improvement Act (ECIA) presents states with a broad number of options for spending federal monies allocated to the states. Not only did ECIA give the states more responsibility for determining how and where to spend federal money for education, but it also reduced federal funding—and thus put more importance on state funding. This trend is expected to continue into the mid-1980s, a part of the new federalism impacting on education.

Reduced federal funding has put added pressure on state departments to spend educational money wisely, to administer the state programs effectively, and to think about where they are going to get extra money to make up for the deficits created by the federal shortfall. In addition, controversial issues in education will not go away, and public groups are becoming more and more aggressive and astute in making their demands felt at the state level. In short, state departments of education must now provide real leadership and technical assistance to local school districts as well as to state boards to education, state legislators, and governors.

THE CHIEF STATE SCHOOL OFFICER

Chief Executive

The chief state school officer (sometimes known as the state superintendent or commissioner of education) serves as the head of the state department of education and is also the chief executive of the state school board. He or she is usually a professional educator.

The office is filled in one of three ways: in 1982, five states filled the position through appointment by the governor; twenty-seven states through appointment by the state board of education, and eighteen states by popular election. The duties of the chief state school officer and the relationship between that position and the state board and state department vary from state to state. They usually depend on whether the official was appointed or voted into office. Where appointed, greater dependence is likely, where elected, the chief officer tends to have more independence.

Functions of the Chief State School Officer

Because of differences in method of selection, and in the legal relationship between the state board of education and the chief state officer, the responsibilities of the chief state officer vary widely. However, the major responsibilities associated with the office are likely to include certain functions.

1. Serving as the chief administrator of the state department of education and of the state board of education.
2. Selecting personnel for the state department of education.
3. Recommending improvements in educational legislation and educational budgets.
4. Ensuring compliance with state educational laws and regulations.
5. Explaining and interpreting the state's school laws.
6. Deciding impartially controversies involving the administration of the schools within the state.
7. Arranging for studies, committees, and task forces as deemed necessary to identify problems and recommend solutions.

8. Reporting on the status of education within the state to the governor, legislature, state board of education, and the public.

STATE COURTS

State courts are subject to constitutional restrictions and may be overruled by federal district courts or the U.S. Supreme Court. Even though state courts may serve to set a precedent, decisions rendered in one state are not binding in another. Moreover, there are instances (in matters dealing with teacher tenure, teacher strikes, and student rights, for example) in which a decision in one state appears to be in conflict with a decision in another state. In spite of areas of apparent conflict, on major issues relating to control to schools there has been consistency among the state courts.

Education as State Function

State courts have repeatedly held that public education is a function of the state and that the ultimate control of school affairs is vested in the law-making power of the state. The state courts have also made it clear that the state controls the schools for the fulfilment of the public good, not for the benefit of the individual. The state courts have also taken the position that a local school has no inherent powers of government, and its boundaries may be changed or its district abolished at the will of the state legislature, unless prohibited by the state constitution. State courts have upheld the power of the legislatures to levy taxes for school purposes, to confer upon other governmental units (municipalities, counties, towns, or school districts) such taxing power, and to allocate monies to schools.

THE FEDERAL ROLE IN EDUCATION

The role of the federal government can be considered in four parts: (1) the federal agencies that promote educational policies and programs, (2) the growing trend that moves most educational decisions from Congress to the President's Office, (3) federal financing of education, and (4) the Supreme court's decisions concerning education. Here we will focus on the first two parts.

FEDERAL EDUCATIONAL AGENCIES

Although many different federal agencies (about eleven departments and fifteen other agencies or units) are involved in some type of educational program or activity, the U.S. Department of Education is the major agency through which the federal government demonstrates its commitment to education.

The Department of Education. When the Department of Education was founded in 1867, its commissioner had a staff of three clerks and a total of $18,600 to spend. From these humble beginnings the department has grown to about 4,800 employees and annual expenditures of more than $15.5 billion in 1984. The department presently administers over 120 separate programs. Its budget has remained fairly constant in recent years, avoiding many of the reductions in federal education expenditures of the early 1980s.

The original purpose of the department was to collect and disseminate statistics and facts and to promote the cause of education throughout the country. Even though it was known as the Department of Education, the commissioner was not a member of the president's cabinet. In fact, the department was attached to the Department of the Interior in 1868 and given the status and name of a bureau.

Department of Health, Education and Welfare

In 1929, the title Office of Education was adopted, and ten years later the office was transferred to the Federal Security Agency. Then, in 1953, the Office of Education as transferred again, this time to the newly formed Department of Health, Education and Welfare. The Office of Education continued to perform its original functions, and additional responsibilities and program activities were added by various acts of Congress or by order of the president. In particular, it assumed new responsibilities of (1) administering grant funds and contracting with state departments of education, school districts, and colleges and universities; (2) engaging in educational innovation and research; and (3) providing leadership, consultative, and clearing-house services related to education.

ENLARGED RESPONSIBILITIES

Cabinet Level Status

In 1979, after much congressional debate and controversy, a Department of Education was signed into law by President Carter, who declared that education was the "biggest single national investment" and that the creation of the department was the "best move for the quality of life in America for the future." A secretary of education was named, with full cabinet-level status, and the department officially opened in mid-1980.

The establishment of a Department of Education with full cabinet status had long been a goal of a number of professional organizations (especially the NEA). In theory, there now exists a person (the secretary of education) with widespread visibility and influence, who can exert persuasion and pressure in political and educational circles and who is in charge of educational policy and the promotion of programs to carry out those policies.

National Institute for Education (NIE). Established in 1972, its first budget, a modest $142 million for fiscal year 1973, turned out to be its largest. Initially organized within the Department of Health, Education and Welfare, it became part of the Department of Education in 1980. Its primary focus is on research and development in education, but it has had numerous problems getting off the ground. The early years for the NIE were difficult, for many senators and representatives were disappointed by the agency's lack of direction and action and by the general feeling that educational research has produced little of real value and that it has failed to improve schooling.

Loss of Confidence in NIE

Its budgets have been repeatedly slashed below its requests. The NIE has lost the confidence not only of Congress and the Reagan administration but also of many educators and educational organizations. Many of its problems with the educational community involve lack of communication between researchers and practitioners, unfair competition for limited funds, and partisan agreements among favored institutions of higher learning and individuals.

Future Directions

It is hoped that the recent national concern over education will spill over to research in education and give an assist to the NIE. Manuel Justiz, the current NIE director, believes that the 1980s will emerge as a new period of stability and opportunity for the NIE to (1) provide leadership in educational research and development, (2) promote excellence and equality in education, and (3) translate research into practical benefits. It is the hope of many educators, especially of the research community, that his visions are on target.

THE NEW FEDERALISM IN EDUCATION

Shift in Federal Policy

For most of the last two centuries federal support of education has increased steadily, albeit slowly. For the last two decades, there were dramatic increases in federal commitment to education. For many liberal and egalitarian groups, this increased federal activity was a welcome step.

As we enter the 1980s, there has been a dramatic shift in federal policy. Driven by a belief that the federal government is too intrusive, President Reagan has reduced federal involvement, in terms of money, activities, and regulations—in education as well as in other sectors of society.

The new federalism, according to Jack Schuster, can be viewed in terms of three policy moves by the executive branch of government: (1) deregulation, the reduction of federal bureaucratic rules and regulations; (2) consolidation, the reduction of government proliferation of agencies and programs; and (3) cutbacks, the move to reduce social and educational spending.

Reduced Federal Role in Education

David Clark and his collegues have analysed the Reagan administration in terms of five policy shifts—or what they term the "five Ds": (1) diminution, reduction of federal expenditures in education; (2) deregulation, revocation of federal enforcement rules and regulations; (3) decentralization, the belief that the ills of education are related to federal intrusion into what should be a state or local responsibility; (4) disestablishment, limiting the powers of the Department of Education and other federal agencies; and (5) deemphasis, the sum of the preceding aspects or the narrowing of the focus and scope of the federal role in education.

Reduced Federal Funding

Diffused and Decentralised Influence

What is evolving, then, are three basic and broad trends in federal educational policies for the 1980s. First, there has been a shift in priorities from human and social or educational concerns to business and military interests. It shows up in the Reagan administration's lack of formal policy regarding education and in the belief that the federal government should be involved less, not more, in the education of the nation's children and youth. Second, there is a reduction in federal funds for education; greater monetary and program responsibilities are being shifted to state (and local) agencies. Urban schools will probably suffer more than other schools because many states will distribute funds to local schools on a per child basis rather than on the basis of need. Moreover, nearly 16 percent of big-city school revenues came from Washington, as compared with the national average of 8 percent. Third, there is the growing demise of egalitarianism as a national policy. It is evidenced in a reduction of programs for big-city schools, especially those for minority and low income groups, and in an increase in federal programs that coincide with national need—say in areas of math and science education. Although the federal government's influence in schools has never been primary, it is expected to become more diffuse and decentralized than it has been in the past.

NONGOVERNMENTAL INFLUENCES ON PUBLIC SCHOOLS

Pressures on School Boards

In addition to the agencies and offices that have been established by law to govern and administer public schools, there are also a number of other groups that influence decisions about the administration and operation of schools. Some of the groups seek to influence schools by shaping public opinion and the opinions of national policy makers. Others seek to put more direct pressure on school boards and state legislatures to achieve their goals. All share the belief that in a democracy public schools should be responsive to the views and goals of the community at large.

Increased Interest in Schools

Here is a brief summary of the important political influences and interest groups that have a significant effect on public education.

1. *Political parties.* Both Republicans and Democrats at the national state and local level have exhibited growing interest in schools and have drawn educational institutions into complex social, political, and economic controversies.

2. *National and state commissions.* Commissions are influential because of their agenda, prominent members, and the publicity they often receive. There are many commissions devoted to various aspects of education, but the most influential ones tend to focus on problems or goals of education. Since the 1980s, these commissions have recommended upgrading schools and curricula, improving teacher quality, and raising student and school productivity.

3. *Pressure and lobbying groups.* Pressure groups in the United States number in the thousands. Many have as their primary interest something other than education, but they are willing to take strong stands on specific educational issues. Pressure groups that represent the extremes of the political spectrum, left or right, for example, are the most controversial. They are often willing to risk engulfing the schools in deep political or social conflict to advance their causes.

Promoting Members' Interests

4. *Professional groups.* Closely related to pressure groups are hundreds of professional and educational organizations that seek to promote the interests of their members. Among the influential groups are the National Education Association, American Federation of Teachers, Educational Commission of the States, National Association of State Boards of Education, National Schools Boards Association, National Chief State School Officers, American Association of School Administrators, and National Parent-Teacher Association. These groups exert a major influence on schools and teachers, and on educational policies in general, and they also help to establish professional standards and behavior that impact on education.

Selectivity in Funding

5. *Private foundations.* While there are many different private foundations, with different goals and causes, some of the most influential ones in education are the Ford Foundation,

Spencer Foundation, Kettering Foundation, Charles Stewart Mott Foundation, Carnegie Corporation, and Rockefeller General Education Board. These foundations, along with many others, tend to be sensitive to changing social and educational issues and selective in their funding patterns. Because of their large endowments and selectivity in funding, they are quite influential. Many fund programs are innovative and promote change, while others generally support social justice and equality of opportunity. In many cases, they assist in the funding of special task forces and committees, as well as research and publications, which have considerable impact on schools. During the Reagan administration, private foundations have been asked to make up for some of the federal cutbacks in educational funding; their response has been mixed and has reflected their own fiscal health and investment portfolios.

Impact on Secondary Schools

6. *Colleges and universities.* These institutions have a direct impact on the secondary schools in terms of program requirements, curriculum content, and college admissions—and an indirect effect on the elementary schools. The colleges' greatest influence has obviously been on that segment of the secondary school program to which high status has been attached, namely the college preparatory program (sometimes called the academic track).

Major Curriculum Source

7. *Textbook publishers and authors.* The influence of textbook companies remains strong—they are the major curriculum source for schools. To a lesser degree, individual authors influence schools and teachers, however, the content and tone of the narrative, the type of exercises and activities, even the pictures (if any) are primarily based on the criteria and decisions of the publishing companies.

8. *Testing companies and services.* Although many large

textbook companies have a testing department and publish tests, the most noted testing companies are the nonprofit Educational Testing Service and the College Entrance Examination Board. The latter two organizations are national in scope and exert considerable influence on the curriculum throughout the country.

National Center for Education Statistics

9. *Opinion poll agencies.* Some opinion poll groups are independent organizations. Others are affiliated with colleges or universities, political organizations, or professional organizations. For many years, the NEA's research department, which surveyed teachers and schools about various professional issues, was very influential. Prior to the formation of the National Center for Education Statistics, it was the most important source of research on the status of the teaching profession. Today, the Center, which is now part of the U.S. Department of Education, collects and disseminates much more statistical information than does the NEA Research Division, but it does not, by itself, engage in opinion polls.

The Gallup organization is another source of public opinion about education, although it collects and reports results of attitudes about other issues and institutions as well. Since 1969 *Phi Delta Kappan* has published a nationwide survey conducted by the Gallup organization. The primary focus of the poll is public attitude, but beginning in 1973 a sample of professional educators was included among the respondents. The survey has been established as a major source of information on opinion in education matters, representing a nationwide sample based on approximately 2,000 adults each year and a cross-section of local school opinion. The survey is read by education leaders and administrators throughout the nation and by policy makers at all levels of government.

10. *Educational consultants.* These consultants work on a private for profit basis; they serve as resource personnel,

develop or evaluate programs, speak at professional or public meetings, and / or give testimony in court trials and legislative hearings. While they may work at various levels—local, state, regional, and national—those with the greatest influence provide knowledge and service to people who make legislative policy or judicial decisions.

Objectivity *vs.* Advocacy

11. *Research community.* Most researchers in education are members of the American Educational Research Association. Related to but often different from consultants, researchers have gained recent influence among policy makers and even media people who are concerned with important questions regarding education. An essential difference between a consultant and researcher is that the former may serve appropriately in the role of advocate, but the researcher—at least in the traditional sense—should be objective and present information without regard to political consequences. When the researcher limits or slants information, presents a point of view on paper or in public, promotes a position in some political or social debate, or gives advocacy testimony, that person is surrendering his or her role as researcher and has become a consultant (or advocate). That individual's research is value-laden, and the researcher is no longer impartial.

12. *Citizen groups.* There are many different citizen groups, literally thousands, acting at various national, state and local levels, whose policies and goals are as divergent as the groups themselves. While some citizen groups are independent and well-established organizations, the great majority come and go. Most are sponsored by an organization—some existing legislative committee, pressure group, or foundation. Most citizen groups in education make the public aware of its rights to participate in school affairs and its obligations to participate constructively; other groups are motivated by strong political and social convictions. Among the independent and influential citizen groups are the Council for Basic Education,

Common Cause, and the now defunct National Citizen Council for Better Schools (founded by Omar Bradley, Harry S. Truman, and James B. Conant among others). Most groups, however, don't last long enough to have major impact for an extended period. They are frequently issue oriented or organized around a political or social crisis that passes in time. Perhaps the most controversial citizen groups today are affiliated with censorship organizations, taxpayer organizations, and minority organizations. In the 1960s, community and antipoverty groups were particularly active, having evolved as part of the War on Poverty. Although most of these particular community groups no longer exist, many states and cities have encouraged local community groups to convene over controversial issues such as school finance, accountability, desegregation, student discipline, and competency tests for teachers.

Summing Up

1. The enterprise of education is organized on various government levels—local, intermediate (in most states), state, and federal. Knowing about the formal organization of schools and the government relationship in which they operate is important to people who work in schools or who are studying to become teachers.
2. Schools are organized into school districts, and there are today approximately 15,000 public school systems—operating under a widely accepted system of laws, regulations, and customs.
3. While most small and rural school districts have consolidated their schools since 1930, decentralization has been underway in large urban areas since the 1960s.
4. Three forms of community involvement are impacting on schools: community control, community participation, and community education. The first is the most controversial of the three alternatives.

5. Most states have an intermediate agency, which supports and has limited regulatory powers over local school districts.
6. With the exception of Wisconsin, all states have state boards of education. State departments of education operate under the direction of the state boards and are headed by the chief state school officer.
7. The federal role in education has dramatically increased for most of the past two centuries. The 1980s, however, witnessed reduced federal involvement in education.

Discussion Questions

1. How can teachers effect changes at the federal, state, and local levels of education?
2. What are the advantages and disadvantages of an elected or appointed state board of education? A local board of education?
3. Why have school districts consolidated? Why have they decentralized? What are the advantages and disadvantages of each trend?
4. Enumerate the ways in which community control, community participation, and community education differ. Which trend do you prefer? Why?
5. What are the arguments for and against the new federalism as it applies to education?

Suggested Readings

Davies, Don, *Communities and Their Schools.* New York: McGraw-Hill, 1981. *A fresh look into the current movement toward greater community participation and control of local schools.*

Golembiewski, Robert T., and Aaron Wildavsky. *The Costs of Federalism.* New Brunswick, N.J.: Transaction Books, 1984.
An analysis of the new role of federal and state governments in various sectors of society, including education

Kimbrough, Ralph B., and Michael Y. Nunnery, *Educational Administration*, 2nd ed. New York: Macmillan, 1983.

A broad overview of educational administration and the administrative hierarchy in American schools with emphasis on the role of the superintendent of schools and the local board of education.

Knezevich, Stephen J. *Administration of Public Education*, 4th ed. New York: Harper & Row, 1984.

A well-documented examination of past and current trends dealing with public school administration.

Morphet, Edgar I., Roe L., Johns, and Theodore I., Reller, *Educational Organization and Administration*, 4th ed. Englewood Cliffs, N.J.: Prentice-Hall, 1982.

An important work on the organization of American Schools, which includes a detailed discussion of the role of federal, state, and local governments in the administration of public education.

4

Curriculum and Instruction

Focusing Questions

How does curriculum content reflect changes in society?

What forces affect curriculum change?

What are some of the ways in which curriculum may be organised?

How might your work as a teacher be different in a school that utilises team teaching? flexible scheduling? computerised instruction?

What are some of the instructional innovations that characterise the era of school reform?

What are some trends that seem likely to affect curriculum and instruction?

Americans—perhaps more than citizens of any other country—have demanded the utmost from their schools. We ask the schools to teach children to think, to socialise them, to alleviate poverty and inequality, to reduce crime, to perpetuate our cultural heritage, and to produce intelligent, patriotic citizens. Inevitably, American schools have been unable to meet all of these obligations. Nonetheless, the American public continues to demand much from its schools, and it is the *curriculum*—the planned experiences provided through instruction—that is the focal point of these demands. Consequently, the curriculum is continuously modified as the goals and objectives of the schools are revised, as student populations change, as issues are debated, as interest groups are activated, and as society changes. Keep these concepts in mind as this chapter sweeps through time to note the shifts in curriculum and to put our curricular heritage in perspective.

Curriculum Involves Instruction

As we examine curriculum, we will also examine instructional activities that relate to curriculum. To some extent they are intertwined. Teaching a curriculum involves instruction, which is the process of a curriculum—its methods and materials. Although some educators argue for a separation, based on theoretical and traditional grounds, other educators recognise that in reality the two realms of knowledge need to be synthesised. As a result, some schools of education offer separate courses in curriculum and instruction, while others combine some of them.

HISTORICAL INFLUENCES

A Changing Society Requires Curriculum Changes

Part 2 examined the historical development of the American schools. Here we will briefly summarise the historical factors that shaped curriculum. A changing society demands changes in education, which, in turn, require changes in the curriculum. That is to say, as the role of schools changes, the aims and objectives are modified and so is the curriculum. By analysing the historical trends in curriculum, we may better understand the themes that pervade curriculum today.

Early Emphasis on Religion and the Three Rs

As noted, three different regional attitudes toward the functions of education arose during colonial times. In the New England colonies education was considered to be the responsibility of the commonwealth. The middle Atlantic colonies saw education as a function of the local community, or more precisely, the local religious denominational group. In the southern colonies, responsibility for education was left to the family. With the exception of the rich, who could afford private education, parental neglect of children's education was evident in the South. In general, the major purpose of education during the colonial years was to meet the needs of religion; learning the catechism and various prayers was a part of the reading program. As the schools evolved, the three Rs were stressed, and the practical values of reading, writing, and doing simple mathematical sums were associated with the new occupations and apprenticeship programs.

Instruction was usually inadequate; it consisted mostly of rote recitations and oral readings. Attitudes toward children were steeped in Calvinist traditions. Children were born in sin, and it was the function of the teacher (and other adults to beat the sin out of them. The famous *New England Primer* was the most widely used book in colonial schools for more than a hundred years; all the editions contained the alphabet, some sounds, and syllables. The content was of a religious nature. It has been estimated that more than 3 million copies the *Primer* were sold. In 1740 Thomas Dilworth published *A New Guide the English Tongue,* which contained a mixture of grammar, spelling, and religious material. It was followed a few years later by the *Schoolmaster's Assistant,* a widely used mathematics text. Noah Webster's spellers for appeared in 1783; they were continuously revised and set the standard in spelling until midway through the nineteenth century.

Academy Replaces the Latin Grammar School

Only a small percentage of colonial youth took advantage of secondary schooling, the Latin grammar school continued to be the main instrument of schooling of the privileged class in the early colonial period, while the academy was designed to offer a more practical curriculum for future tradesmen and workers. The academy eventually became a dual-purpose institution, preparing students both for the world of work and for college; since academies offered the classical curriculum, they drove the old Latin school out of existence. The new academies, however, did offer a larger variety of courses and the result was great variation in secondary school curricula.

From the time of the American Revolution until approximately 1850, great uniformity prevailed and very little change in the elementary school curriculum occurred. Reading, spelling, writing, and arithmetic continued to be stressed in the elementary schools, along with good manners and morals. The *McGuffey Readers,* first published in 1836, were used in most elementary school districts throughout the nineteenth century. But as curricula changed more and more subjects were included.

Common Schools and Free Public High Schools

In the meantime the common schools, which evolved in Boston in the 1820s, became popular, particularly on the frontier; and in 1874 the concept of free public schooling was extended to the high school level. Thereafter the academy dwindled in importance. Although many of the new high school students had no intention of going to college, the high school curriculum concentrated on academic and college preparatory subjects, thus illustrating the pervasive influence of the ideals of mental discipline.

Progressivism in Schools and Society

As the scientific and industrial revolution shaped the United States from the second half of the nineteenth century to the present, a companion movement for social reform of schools evolved. Much of the impetus for change came from the *progressive movement* in education; it was part of a larger political reform movement, which focused on many sectors of society—labor, housing, health, social-welfare, as well as education. There was increased recognition of the relationship between schools and society—and of the need to reform both.

The purposes of schools gradually were broadened to meet the new demands. Social problems relating to unemployment, poverty, urbanisation, and the Americanisation of immigrants who did not speak English came to be responsibilities of the schools. The curriculum was broadened to meet the diverse needs of all children and youth. Courses in citizenship, family living, home economics and health education, and a number of vocational courses were offered. School curriculum and teaching methods shifted from a complete disregard for the learner, accompanied by respect for the subject matter only, to a strong regard for the child's interests, motives, and abilities.

On a general level there was gradual movement away from traditional subjects and teaching techniques toward utility in subject matter and toward student interests and self-expression, but changes were gradual and peripheral. Robert and Helen Lynd's description of Middletown schools illustrates the normal, regimented world of schooling in the mid-1920s.

Regimented Classrooms

> Immovable seats in orderly rows fix the sphere of activity of each child. For all, from the timid six-year-old entering for the first time to the most assured high school senior, the general routine is much the same. Bells divide the day into periods. For the six-year-olds the periods are short (fifteen to twenty-five-minutes) and varied; in some they leave their seats, play games, and act out make-believe stories, although in "recitation periods" all movement is prohibited. As they grow older the taboo upon physical activity becomes stricter, until by the third or fourth year practically all movement is forbidden except the marching from one set of seats to another between periods, a brief interval of prescribed exercise daily, and periods of manual training or home economics once or twice a week. There are "study periods" in which children learn "lessons" from

"textbooks" prescribed by the state and "recitation periods" in which they tell an adult teacher what the book has said. With high school come some differences; more "vocational" and "laboratory" work varies the periods. But here again the lesson-textbook-recitation method is the chief characteristic of education.

Progressivism Left its Mark

In many ways the description of the Middletown schools indicates that progressive education did not carry over in mass scale beyond the universities and their campus laboratory schools. The same sort of mechanical bureaucracy that infected Middletown characterised most of the schools in Boston, Chicago, and New York. While there were shining examples like the Dalton, Massachusetts, and Winnetka, Illinois, schools, some school systems still used *McGuffey* into the 1930s. Yet, this progressivism did leave remark, helping to increase educational opportunity for all students in a number of ways: (1) school organisation shifted from eight-year elementary schools and four-year high schools to three-year junior high and senior high schools to give greater attention to the requirements of pubescent children; (2) the curriculum was reorganised and extended to areas such as vocational education, agriculture, home economics, physical education, and the arts; (3) extracurricular activities expanded; (4) students were grouped with greater flexibility to meet varying needs; (5) students and teachers tended to be more active and more informal in their relationships with one another; (6) innumerable materials and media were introduced into the classrooms; and (7) certification of teachers required more education.

New Science, New Math

The Cold war and Sputnik in the 1950s curtailed the progressive movement in education and produced a demand for academic rigor—a concentration on the three Rs, accompanied by drill and seatwork, at the elementary level, and the essential, core subjects of science, math, English modern languages, and history at the secondary level. New science, new math and the early introduction of foreign language were products of the fifties. Concepts and courses previously postponed until the upper elementary grades as junior high school were introduced at the primary grade level. These were serious and competitive times in schools and society. The opinions of researchers, scientists, and academic specialists prevailed in the area of curriculum; there was little time for play or frills or for meeting the social and psychological needs of the child; it was a return to the mental discipline approach and to testing and tracking students. The smartest survived and were pushed forward.

Social Reformers

This academic, subject-centered approach to education produced a reaction in the mid-1960s, and for the next fifteen years, educational psychologists and social reformers introduced several new courses, including elective and remedial courses, as well as new approaches to learning. This was the era of "radical reform," "relevancy," and "humanistic education", cognitive learning was put on the back burner—affective learning and attempts to meet the needs of the whole child came to the fore.

Curriculum is Maturing

As the 1980s unfold, international competition has resurfaced—it has the cry for tougher standards and educational productivity. The academic curriculum is being expanded. The field of curriculum is maturing—moving beyond schools and including programs in business, industry, the military, government, and health. Curriculum today incorporates many disciplines, among them philosophy, psychology, sociology, and politics. Curriculum is developing an international character and is moving into the area of computers and instructional technology.

Curriculum Change as an Evolutionary Process

Looking back at the schools since the colonial period, curriculum change can be viewed as an evolutionary process of offering courses in more and more subjects, followed by an attempt to develop scientific and conceptual principles. In brief, the seventeenth and eighteenth-century schools emphasised the three Rs at the elementary school level and Greek. Latin, and higher mathematics at the secondary school level. The nineteenth century witnessed additional course offerings, especially in history, science, and mathematics. The twentieth century saw the development of a general and diversified curriculum to fit the needs of a diversified student population, as well as the development of curriculum as a field of study.

CURRICULUM ORGANISATION

The shifts and changes in curriculum organisation that resulted from; the increased complexity of the American schools over the past one hundred years can be viewed from the perspectives of two basic schools of thought. One emphasizes the subject, the other emphasizes the learner in the first case, the curriculum is viewed as a body of content—or subject matter—leading to certain achievement outcomes or products. The second case views curriculum in terms of the needs and attitudes of the student; the concern is with process—in other words, with the climate of the classroom or school.

Extremes on a Continuum

Actually, both views represent the two extremes of a continuum, and most practitioners (and researchers) rely on some curriculum blend within this continuum. While most teachers tend to emphasise one school of thought over the other, they still incorporate both choices in the classroom. Very few of us employ pure cognitive (subject-matter) or pure psychological (student needs and interests) approaches in the teaching-learning process.

SUBJECT-CENTERED CURRICULUM

Subject matter is both the oldest and the most recent framework for curriculum organisation. It is also the most common-primarily because it is convenient. In fact, the departmental structure of secondary schools and colleges tends to prevent us from thinking about the curriculum in any other way. Curricular changes usually occur at the departmental level. Courses are added, omitted, or modified, but faculty members rarely engage in comprehensive, systematic curriculum development and evaluation. Even in the elementary schools, where self-contained classrooms force the teachers to be generalists, curricula are usually organised by subjects.

Proponents defend the subject-centered curriculum on four grounds:

1. Subjects are a logical way to organise and interpret learning.
2. Such organisation makes it easier for people to remember information for future use.
3. Teachers (in secondary schools, at least) are trained as subject-matter specialists.
4. Textbooks and other teaching materials are usually organised by subject.

PROS AND CONS OF SUBJECT MATTER

Critics, however, claim that the subject-centered curriculum is fragmented, a mass of facts and concepts learned in isolation. They see this kind of curriculum as demphasizing life experiences and failing to consider adequately the needs *are* interests of students. The emphasis, such critics argue, is on the teaching of knowledge, the recall of facts. Thus the teacher dominates the lesson, showing little student input. Let us look at six variations on the subject-centered curriculum.

Subject-Area Curriculum. The subject area is the oldest and most widely used form of curriculum organisation. It has its roots in the seven liberal arts of classical Greece and Rome: grammar, rhetoric, dialectic, arithmetic, geometry, astronomy, and music. Modern subject-area curricula trace their origins to the work of William Harris, superintendent of the St. Louis school system in the 1870s. Steeped in the classical tradition, Harris established a subject orientation that has virtually dominated U.S. curricula from his day to the present.

Common, Special, and Elective Content

The modern *subject-area curriculum* treats each subject as a specialised and largely autonomous body of verified knowledge. These subjects can be organised into three content categories, however. *Common content* refers to subjects considered essential for all students; these subjects usually include the three Rs at the elementary level and English, history, science, and mathematics at the secondary level. *Special content* refers to subjects that develop knowledge and skills for particular vocations or professions, for example, business mathematics and physics. Finally, *elective content* affords the student optional offerings. Some electives are restricted to certain students, say, advanced auto mechanics for vocational students or fourth-year French for students enrolled in a college-preparatory program. Other electives, such as photography and human relations, are open to all students.

Latin, Logic, and the Classics

Perennialist Curriculum. Two conservative philosophies of education are basically subject-centered: *perennialism and essentialism.* Perennialists believe that a curriculum should consist primarily of the three Rs, Latin, and logic the elementary level, to which is added the study of the classics at the secondary level. The assumption, according to Robert Hutchins, is that the best of the past—the so-called permanent studies, or classics—is equally valid for the present.

Perennialists believe that the main purpose of education is the cultivation of the intellect, along with emphasis on certain timeless values about work, morality, and family living. They believe that only certain studies have this power. They reject consideration of students' personal needs and interests or the treatment of contemporary problems in the curriculum on the ground that such concerns detract from the school's mission of cultivating the mind.

Five Major Disciplines

Essentialist Curriculum. Essentialists believe that the curriculum must consist of the three Rs at the elementary level and at the high school level of five major disciplines: English (grammar, literature, and writing), mathematics, the sciences, history, and foreign language. They believe these subject areas constitute the best way of systematising and keeping up with the explosion of knowledge.

Essentialism shares with perennialism the notion that the curriculum should focus on rigorous intellectual training a training possible only through the study of certain subjects. Although the perennialist sees no need for nonacademic subjects, the essentialist is often willing to add such studies to the curriculum provided they receive low priority. Modern-day essentialists are willing to provide minimal play and puzzle activities at the primary grade level, so long as these activities are cognitively oriented, but workbook and drill-like activities still prevail—along with the three Rs. For the perennialists, there is no time to play.

Both perennialists and essentialists advocate educational meritocracy. They favor high academic standards and a rigorous system of grading and testing to help schools sort students by ability. The goal is to educate each person to the limits of his or her potential. Today, many parochial schools and academically oriented public schools stress various aspects of the perennialist and essentialist curricula.

Unifying Concepts and Principles

Subject Structure Curriculum. During the 1950s and 1960s, the National Science Foundation and the federal government devoted sizable sums to the improvement of science and mathematics curricula at the elementary and secondary levels. New curriculum models were formulated according to the structure of each subject or discipline. The subject structure curriculum rejects memorisation, factual information, and rote learning—characteristic of most subject-centered curricula—and stresses those unifying concepts, rules, and principles that define and limit a subject and control the methods of research and inquiry. Structure brings together and organises a body of knowledge, while it dictates appropriate ways of thinking about the subject and of generating new data. Other subjects quickly followed the lead of mathematics and the sciences.

Those who advocated this kind of focus on structure nonetheless rejected the idea that knowledge is fixed or permanent. They regarded teaching and learning as continuing inquiry, but they confined such inquiry within the established boundaries of subjects, ignoring or rejecting the fact that many problems cut across disciplines. Instead, they emphasised the students' cognitive abilities. They taught students the structure of a subject and its methods of inquiry so that students would learn how to learn. They tended, however, to dismiss learners' social and psychological needs. As Philip Phenix wrote: "There is no place in the curriculum for ideas which are regarded as suitable for teaching because of the supposed nature, needs, and interests of the learner, but which do not belong within the regular structure of the discipline."

New Methods of Inquiry

The emphasis on structure led each discipline to develop its own unifying concepts, principles, and methods of inquiry. Learning by the inquiry method in chemistry differed from learning by the inquiry method in physics, for example.

Moreover, curriculum planners could not agree on how to teach the structure of the social sciences and the fine arts. Science and mathematics programs continue even today to provide the best examples of teaching according to the structure of a subject.

Setting for the Basics

Back-to-Basics Curriculum. A strong back-to-basics movement has surfaced today among parents and educators, called forth by the general relaxation of academic standards in the 1960s and 1970s and by declining student standardised test scores in reading, writing, and computation. Automatic promotion of marginal students, the dizzy array of elective courses, and text-books designed more to entertain than to educate are frequently cited as reasons behind the decline in basic skills. Even the mass media have attacked the "soft-sell approach" to education. The concerns voiced today parallel those voiced after Sputnik. The call today is less for academic excellence and rigor, however, than for a return to basics or minimum standards. Annual Gallup polls have asked the public to suggest ways for improving education; since 1976 "devoting more attention to teaching the basics" and "improving curriculum standards" have ranked no lower than fifth in the list of responses.

By 1983, all of the states had implemented statewide testing programs for various grade levels, and in twenty-seven states the tests were mandated. In ten states (Alabama, California, Florida, Hawaii, Louisiana. Nevada, New York, North Carolina, Tennessee, and Virginia) the test was required for high school graduation.

Demand for Solid Subjects

Although the back-to-basics movement means different things to different people, it usually connotes an essentialist curriculum with heavy emphasis on reading, writing, and mathematics. So-called solid subjects—English, history, science, and mathematics—are taught in all grades. History means U.S. and European history and perhaps Asian and African history but does not include Afro-American history or ethnic studies. English means traditional grammar, not linguistics or nonstandard English; it means Shakespeare and Wordsworth, not *Catcher in the Rye* or *Lolita.* Creative writing is frowned upon. Science means biology, chemistry, and physics—not ecology. Mathematics means old math, not new math. Furthermore, these subjects are required. Proponents of the basics consider elective courses in such areas as scuba diving, transcendental meditation, and hiking to be nonsense. Some even consider humanities or integrated social science courses too "soft." They may grudgingly admit music and art into the program—but only for half credit.

Devaluation of Diplomas

Proponents of the movement believe that too many illiterate students pass from grade to grade and eventually graduate, that high school and college diplomas are meaningless as measures of graduates' abilities, that minimum standards must be set, that the basics (reading, writing, math) are essential for employment, and that students must learn survival skills to function effectively in society. Some of these advocates are college educators who would do away with open admissions or related entrance requirements and grade inflation; they would simply insist that their institutions require students to meet reasonable standards in the academic disciplines—that students be able to understand their homework assignments, write acceptable essays, and perform numerical computations accurately.

Criticism of Back-to-Basics

Critics point out that the decline in standardised test scores—a grave concern of the back-to-basics enthusiasts—may be linked less to curriculum than to higher student/teacher ratios, a decrease in the number of low-achieving students who drop out of school, the competing influence of television, and the more permissive attitudes of society. They worry that a focus on basics will suppress the students' creativity and shortchange other domains of learning, encouraging instead conformity and dependence on authority. Others expect the back-to-basics movement to fail because teaching and learning cannot be defined and limited precisely and because testing has too many inherent problems.

While the debate is raging, the movement is spreading quickly in response to public pressure. State legislators and state boards of education seem convinced of the merit of minimum standards. But there remain unanswered questions. If we are to adopt a back-to-basics approach to education, what standards should be considered minimum? Who determines these standards? What do we do with students who fail to meet these standards? Are we simply punishing the victims for the schools' inability to educate them? How will the courts deal with the fact that proportionally more minority than white students fail the competency tests in nearly every case? What is the issue—minimum competency or equal educational opportunity? And, when all is said and done, are we not educationally speaking, reinventing the wheel?

Upgrading the Curriculum

Higher Standards Curriculum. There is a demand today for tougher academics. The demand for higher achievement (not just minimum competency) for all children (not just college-bound students) focuses on the cognitive and academic areas. The ability to think, reason, and solve problems, to take serious subjects such as calculus, physics, and advanced foreign language are stressed. Proponents believe that we must upgrade our definition of minimum competencies to include advanced skills and knowledge, including computer and communication competencies, that will be required for tomorrow's technological world. They believe we must increase the time and quality of instruction, and reestablish the prestige of our teachers and schools. The health and vitality of our economy and international position are linked to the strength of our educational institutions.

It is easy to argue for greater emphasis and tougher standards in mathematics, science, and foreign language—even for computer literacy. But if students take more courses in these subject areas, observers point out, they will have fewer opportunities to study such areas as culture and the arts, thus raising the question of curriculum balance. It is possible that students not going to college will be overlooked or pushed into poorly equipped classrooms and second-rate programs. Appropriate mathematics, science, and other classes for vocational and non-college bound students should be developed. Although students should be required to speak fluently at least one foreign language, we must not forget our immigrant and limited-English-speaking students who must learn formal English.

Increasing requirements and offering additional courses in the subject areas we have mentioned will have an impact on the supply of teachers, too. New teachers of math, science, and foreign language will be needed—exacerbating the existing shortage of qualified teachers in these subject areas. Moreover, math and science teachers are increasingly seeking employment outside of education.

Raising Standards Costs Money

Raising standards will cost money. Teacher salaries, for example, will have to be raised to attract—and retain—teachers in math, science, and foreign language. We will have to improve, and in some cases build, science laboratory facilities. Schools will need to introduce new instructional materials, including updated textbooks, computers, and language laboratories. In addition, research suggests that it is effective to begin instruction in these subject areas in the elementary grades. Given an era of federal retrenchment in education, state and local deficits, and school cutbacks, the agenda for excellence in curriculum policy may have to sit on the back burner—while educators and society settle for the basics.

STUDENT-CENTERED CURRICULUM

If the subject-centered curriculum focuses on cognitive aspects of learning, the *student-centered curriculum* emphasizes students' interests and needs—the affective aspects of learning. The student-centered approach, at its extreme, is rooted in the philosophy of Jean Jacques Rousseau, who encouraged childhood self-expression. Implicit in Rousseau's philosophy is the necessity of leaving the child to his or her own devices; he considered creativity and freedom essential for children's growth. Moreover, he thought children would be happier if they were free of teacher domination, the demands of subject matter, and adult-imposed curriculum goals.

Progressivism and Student Interests

Progressive education gave impetus to the student-centered curriculum. Progressive educators believed that, when the interests and needs of learners were incorporated into the curriculum, intrinsic motivation resulted. This does not mean to imply that the student-oriented curriculum is dictated by the whims of the learner. Rather, advocates believe that learning is more successful if the interests and needs of the learner are taken into account. One flaw of student-centered curriculum, however, is that it sometimes overlooks important cognitive content.

A Balanced Curriculum

John Dewey, one of the chief advocates of the student-centered curriculum, attempted to establish a curriculum that balances subject matter with students' interests and needs. As early as 1902, he pointed out the fallacies of either extreme. The learner was neither "a docile recipient of facts" nor "the starting point, the center, and the end" of school activity. More than thirty years later, Dewey was still criticising over-permissive educators who provided little education for students under the guise of meeting those students' expressive and impulsive needs. Dewey sought instead to use youngsters' developing interests to enhance the cognitive learning process. (In the 1980s, one hears the call for nearly the same synthesis; some advocates of educational excellence are asking educational psychologists and student-centered educators to combine students' interests with academic rigor, cognitive concepts with concepts of the learner.)

There are at least six variations of the student-centered curriculum.

Permissive Atmosphere in Kindergartens

Child-Centered Curriculum. The movement from the traditional subject-dominated curriculum toward a program emphasising student interests and needs began in 1762 with the publication of Rousseau's *Émile,* in which Rousseau maintained that the purpose of education is to teach people to live. Early in the next century the Swiss educator. Johann Pestalozzi, began to stress human emotions and kindness in teaching young children. Friedrich Froebel introduced the kindergarten in Germany in 1837. He emphasised a permissive atmosphere and the use of songs, stories, and games as instructional materials. Early in the twentieth century Maria Montessori, working with the slum children of Rome, developed a set of didactic materials and learning exercises that successfully combined work with play. Many of her principles became popular in the United States during the 1960s as part of the compensatory preschool movement.

Experimental Schools

Early progressive educators in the United States adopted the notion of child-centered schools, starting with Dewey's organic school (which he described in *Schools of Tomorrow*) and including many private and experimental schools—the best known of which were Columbia University's Lincoln

School, Ohio State's Laboratory School, the University of Missouri Elementary School, the Pratt Play School in New York City, the Parker School in Chicago, and the Fairhope School in Alabama. These schools had a common feature: their curricula stressed the needs and interests of the students. Some stressed individualisation; others grouped students by ability or interests.

Child-centered education is represented today by programs for such special groups as the academically talented, the disadvantaged, dropouts (actual and potential), the handicapped, and minority and ethnic groups. Many of these programs are carried on in *free schools or alternative schools* organised by parents and teachers who are dissatisfied with the public schools. These schools are typified by a great deal of freedom for students and noisy classrooms that sometimes appear untidy and disorganised. The teaching-learning process is unstructured. Most of these new schools are considered radical and anti-establishment, even though many of their ideas are rooted in the child-centered doctrines of progressivism.

Summerhill, a school founded in 1921 by A.S. Neill and still in existence today, is perhaps the best-known free school. Neill's philosophy was to replace authority with freedom. He was not concerned with formal learning; he did not believe in textbooks or examinations. He did believe that those who want to study *will* study and those who prefer not to study will *not*, regardless of how teachers teach. Neill's dual criteria for success were the ability to work joyfully and the ability to live a happy life.

Recent Radicals

Although Neill, Edgar Friedenberg, Paul Goodman, and John Holt all belong to an earlier generation of school reformers, younger radicals have emerged. They include George Dennison, James Herndon, Ivan Illich, Herbert Kohl, and

Jonathan Kozol. These educators stress, the need for, and in many cases have established, child-centered free schools or alternative schools.

Critics condemn these schools as places where little cognitive learning takes place. They decry a lack of discipline and order. They feel that the reformers' attacks on establishment teachers and schools are overgeneralised and unfair. They do not find the radicals' idea of schooling to be feasible for mass education. Proponents counter that children do learn in these schools, which—instead of stressing conformity—are made to fit the child.

Purposeful Activities

Activity-Centered Curriculum. This movement, which grew out of the private child-centered schools, has strongly affected the public elementary school curriculum. William Kilpatrick, one of Dewey's students, was its leader. Kilpatrick differed with Dewey's child-centered view; he believed that the interests and needs of children could not be anticipated, making a preplanned curriculum impossible. He attacked the school curriculum as unrelated to the problems of real life and advocated purposeful activities that were as lifelike as possible and that were tied to a child's needs and interests.

During the 1920s and 1930s, many elementary schools adopted some of the ideas of the activity movement, perhaps best summarised and first put into practice by Ellsworth Collings, a doctoral student of Kilpatrick's. From this movement a host of teaching strategies emerged, including lessons based on life experiences, group games, dramatizations, story projects, field trips, social enterprises, and interest centers. All of these activities involved problem solving and active student participation; they emphasised socialization and the formation of stronger school-community ties.

Recent curriculum reformers have translated ideas from this movement into community and career-based activities intended to prepare students for adult citizenship and work and into courses emphasising social problems. They have also urged college credit for life experiences. Secondary and college students often earn credit today by working in welfare agencies, early childhood programs, government, institutions, hospitals, and homes for the aged.

Fish-Catching, Horse-Clubbing, and Tiger-Scaring

Relevant Curriculum. Unquestionably, the curriculum must reflect social change. This point is well illustrated in *The Saber-Tooth Curriculum,* a satiric book on education, written in 1939 by Harold Benjamin under the pseudonym Abner J. Peddiwell. He describes a society in which the schools continued to teach fish-catching (because it would develop agility), horse-clubbing (to develop strength), and tiger-scaring (to develop courage) long after the streams had dried up and the horses and tigers had disappeared. The wise men of the society argued that "the essence of true education is timeless...something that endures through changing conditions like a solid rock standing squarely and firmly in the middle of a raging torrent." Benjamin's message was simple: the curriculum was no longer relevant.

Relevant to Students

The 1960s and 1970s saw a renewed concern for a relevant curriculum, but with a somewhat different emphasis. There was less concern that the curriculum reflect changing social conditions and more concern that the curriculum be relevant to students. This shift was part of the Dewey legacy: learners must be motivated and interested in the learning task, and the classroom should build on their real-life experiences.

Credit for Life Experiences

The demand for relevance came from both students and educators. In fact, the student disruptions of the last two decades were related to this demand. Proponents who advocate this approach today see as needs: (1) the individualisation of instruction through such teaching methods as independent inquiry and special projects; (2) the revision of existing courses and development of new ones on such topics of student concern as environmental protection, drug addiction, urban problems, and cultural pluralism; (3) the provision of educational alternatives (such as electives, minicourses, open classrooms) that allow more freedom of choice; and (4) the extension of the curriculum beyond the school's walls through such innovations as work-study programs, credit for life experiences, and external degree programs.

Efforts to relate subject matter to student interests have been largely adhoc, and many were fragmented and temporary, a source of concern to advocates of relevance. In other cases, changes made in the name of relevance have in fact watered down the curriculum.

Hidden Curriculum. The notion of a *hidden curriculum* implies that values of the student peer group are often ignored when formal school curricula are planned. Some educators have focused on the hidden curriculum—the informal, covert, obscure dynamics of the classroom and school—that affects what is learned. Along with other factors (such as social class, family, home life, intelligence, and personality), students' achievement and behavior seem to be related to their status and roles in school; it is suggested that peer association, friendship selection, and student cliques control much of adolescent performance both inside and outside of school. These social interactions are related to students' personal characteristics, abilities, interests, and age—and correlate with achievement scores, extracurricular activities, student-teacher interactions, and even career choices. Sometimes these hidden, informal social interactions conflict with the formal curriculum and with classroom and school rules.

Students as Cunning Strategists

The hidden curriculum includes the strategies adopted

by students to outwit and outguess their teachers. According to John Holt and other educators. "successful" students become cunning strategists in a game of beating the system. Experience has taught them that trickery and even occasional dishonesty pay off. The implication is that teachers must become more sensitive to students' needs and feelings in order to minimise counterproductive behavior. A school that encourages personal freedom and cooperative group learning—instead of competitive individualisation, lesson recitation, "right" answers, and textbook/teacher authority—is more conducive to learning because the atmosphere is free of trickery and dishonesty. Or so the argument goes.

RITUALS, RULES, AND REGULARITIES

Students Lost in the "Cracks"

There is another type of hidden curriculum, the culture of the school—its rituals, rules, and regularities. Since the classic work of Willard Waller, who explored normal school procedures—promptness, neatness, docility, adult authority and control, and so on—the hidden social and psychological dynamics of the school have been examined with a good deal of exactitude and zeal. Philip Jackson, in *Life in Classrooms*, examines how elementary students sit, listen, wait, and raise their hands; how they sharpen their pencils, stand in line, and file out of school. Bel Kaufman, in a best-selling fictionalised account of a high school, *Up the Down Staircase*,describes how the system imposes a stillness and silence on teachers and students who prefer lively and active classrooms; how bells, schedules, and interruptions over the loudspeaker, and petty rules and administrative memos, hinder the teaching and learning process. More recently. Philip Cusick and Sara Lightfoot have analysed how some students are lost in the "cracks," getting by with grades of C. and how there is a quiet indifference and a sense of conformity in many working-class schools. In all of these studies, there are the common themes of praise and criticism, rewards and punishment for purposes of modifying student behavior—for control and conformity—a hidden agenda.

Phony, Antiseptic Curriculum

Another interpretation of the hidden curriculum suggests that some intentional school behavior is not formally recognised in the curriculum or discussed in the classroom because of its sensitive or because teachers do not consider it important. At the same time, students sometimes see what is taught as phony, antiseptic, or unrelated to the real world. For example, some ethnic or minority groups are discussed in a derogatory manner in some homes. This raises several questions. Should curriculum specialists or teachers try to suppress the hidden curriculum in order to further the purposes of the school? Or should they try to incorporate it into school life? At what age is the student nature enough to discuss such sensitive topics as racial and ethnic stereotypes? A student-oriented school, some educators contend, would try to reduce the disparity between the student's world outside of school and that within.

Subject Matter and Personal Growth

Humanistic Curriculum. Like many other modern curriculum developments, humanistic education began as a reaction to what was viewed as an overemphasis on cognitive learning in the late fifties and early sixties. Terry Borton, a Philadelphia schoolteacher, was one of the first to write about this movement. He contended that education had only two major purposes: subject mastery and personal growth. Nearly every school's statement of objectives includes both purposes, but Borton, and later others, asserted that objectives related to personal growth, feelings, and the happy life were included only for show. Almost everyone knows, the argument went, how little schools have done to promote learning related to personal insights and the affective domain. Some educators believe the time has come for schools to put into practice their goals for children's social and personal growth.

Docility and Conformity

In his best-selling book, *Crisis in the Classroom,* Charles Silberman also advocates the humanising of U.S. schools. He charges that schools are repressive, teaching students docility and conformity. He believes that schools must be reformed, even at the price of deemphasizing cognitive learning. He suggests that elementary schools adopt the methods of the British infant schools. At the secondary level, he favors independent study, peer tutoring, and community and work experiences.

The humanistic model of education grew out of the human potential movement in psychology. Within education it is rooted in the work of Arthur Jersild, who linked good teaching with knowledge of self and students, and in the work of Arthur Combs and Donald Snygg, who explored the impact of self-concept and motivation on achievement. Combs and Snygg considered self-concept to be the most important determinant of behavior.

"Self Actualising People"

A humanistic curriculum emphasises affective rather than cognitive outcomes. Such a curriculum draws heavily on the work of Abraham Maslow and of Carl Rogers. Its goal is to produce "self-actualising people," in Maslow's words, or "total human beings" as Rogers puts it. The works of both psychologists are larded with such terms as *choosing, striving, enhancing,* and *experiencing*—as well as *independence, self-determination, integration,* and *personal relationships.*

Higher Domains of Consciouness

Advocates of humanistic education contend that the present school curriculum has failed miserably by humanistic standards, that teachers and schools are determined to stress cognitive behaviors and to control students *not* for students' good but for the good of adults. Humanists emphasise more than affective processes; they seek higher domains of consciousness, aesthetics, and morality. But they believe today's schools are unconcerned with higher planes of understanding, enhancement of the mind, or self-knowledge, which leads students, they believe, to turn to such out-of-school activities as drugs, yoga, transcendental meditation, group encounters, T-groups, and psychotherapy.

Humanists would attempt to form more meaningful relationships between students and teachers; they would foster student independence and self-direction and promote greater acceptance of self and others. The teacher's role would be to help learners cope with their psychological needs and problems, to facilitate self-understanding among students, and to help student develop fully.

System of Values

Values-Centered Curriculum. A curriculum that stresses values is related to affective learning and personal growth. The affective domain, discussed in the previous chapter, has as its most advanced level of feelings and emotions the values area in which the act of valuing, organising values, and behaving according to value commitments are emphasized. It is this system of values, according to which people behave individually and in common, that educators today have attempted to clarify.

Value Confusion

Conflicts in values are inevitable in a society as diverse and complex as ours. As social and economic conditions change, and they do very rapidly in our modern society, so do people and ideas they value. The values a person holds depend on many factors, including environment, education, and personality. People often suffer from value confusion—the symptoms of which are apathy, uncertainty, inconsistency, overconforming or overdissenting. Value clarification is designed to overcome value confusion and to help persons become positive and purposeful.

According to Louis Raths and his associates, who have developed one of the most popular books on the subject, the process of valuing follows seven requirements: "choosing freely, choosing from alternatives, choosing after thoughtful consideration, prizing and cherishing, affirming, acting upon choices, and repeating...as a pattern in life."

Teaching Valuing

There are five distinct ways to teach valuing. The first is *inculcation,* in which accepted values are taught with the support of common law. Next is *moral development,* highlighting moral and ethical principles and their application. Third is *analysis* of issues and situations involving values. Fourth is *clarification,* the method Raths emphasizes. The fifth is *action learning,* by which values are tried and tested in real-life situations. In addition, the humanistic approaches used by Abraham Maslow and Carl Rogers may be described as *evocation,* a calling forth from the individual of personal values and the ability to make choices and think creatively.

Lack of Attention to Cognitive Learning

A drawback to humanistic and value-clarification theories is the lack of attention to cognitive learning. When asked to judge the effectiveness of their curriculum, both humanists and value educators generally rely on testimonials and subjective assessments. They may also present students' paintings, poems, interviews, and reports or talk about improvement in student behavior and attitudes. They present very little empirical evidence or student achievement scores, however, to support their stance. Moreover, the humanists disagree on how they should teach self-actualisation, self-determination, human striving, and the like; value educators do not concur on the values they teach or how to teach them. Until these issues are resolved, we shall continue to flounder in the areas of affective learning.

CURRICULUM CONTRASTS: AN OVERVIEW

Subject Matter and Student Needs

Recapping the subject-centered and student-centered curricula, each represents an extreme on a continuum that is rooted in the past and present practices of curriculum organisation. Most schooling in the United States falls somewhere between the two—effecting a tenuous balance between subject matter and student needs, between cognitive outcomes and psychological factors.

Regardless of a teacher's personal bias or approach, decisions on what is taught and how curriculum is organised are usually influenced by the philosophical orientation of the school at which he or she is teaching. More traditional schools that subscribe to a perennialist or essentialist philosophy generally advocate a subject-centered curriculum. Schools that are oriented more toward progressive or reconstructionist education tend to use a student-centered curriculum. (Overview 4.1 summarises the various subject-centered and student-centered curricula and their corresponding philosophies, content emphases, and instructional emphases.) Regardless of one's views or one's aims or objectives, one need not take an extreme position on the subject matter—student interests continuum. We would expect some type of blend, although many educators would emphasise one organisational approach (subject or student emphasis) over another.

Actually, the relative emphasis on subject matter or student interests is essentially a question of philosophical orientation, and to a lesser extent, learning theory. From these philosophical and theoretical concerns, we must eventually move to the area of curriculum development; this is a technical concern and involves systematic reflection and planning.

OVERVIEW 4.1

Curriculum Organisation Approaches

Curriculum Approach	*Corresponding Philosophy*	*Content Emphasis*	*Instructional Emphasis*
Subject-Centered			
Subject-area curriculum	Perennialism, essentialism	Three Rs; academic, vocational, and elective subjects	Knowledge, concepts and principles; specialised knowledge
Perennialist curriculum	Perennialism	Three Rs; liberal arts; classics; timeless values; academic rigor	Rote memorisation; specialised knowledge; mental discipline
Essential curriculum	Essentialism	Three Rs; liberal arts and science; academic disciplines; academic excellence	Concepts and principles; problem solving; essential skills
Subject structure curriculum	Essentialism	Science, math, and foreign language; academic disciplines; academic excellence	Concepts and principles; problem solving; intuitive thinking; learning how to earn
Back-to-basics curriculum	Essentialism	Three Rs; academic subjects	Specific knowledge and skills; drill; attainment of measurable ends or competencies
Higher standards curriculum	Perennialism, essentialism, reconstructionism	Academic subjects; computer literacy; academic excellence	Knowledge, concepts and principles; learning how to learn;

		and educational productivity	attainment of measurable ends or competencies
Students-Centered			
Child-centered curriculum	Progressivism	Student needs and interests; student experiences	Play oriented; creative expression; free learning environment
Activity-centered curriculum	Progressivism	Student needs and interests; student activities; school community activities	Active, experimental environment; project methods; effective living
Relevant curriculum	Progressivism, reconstructionism	Student experiences and activities; felt needs	Social and personal problems; reflective thinking
Hidden curriculum	progressivism, reconstructionism	Implicit processes; social norms	Hard to recognise, unaccounted for factors; cultural assimilation; conformity and control
Humanistic curriculum	Progressivism, reconstructionism	Introspection; choice	Individual and group learning; flexible, artistic, psychological methods; self-realisation
Values centered curriculum	Reconstructionism	Democratic values; crosscultural and universal values; choice and freedom	Feelings, attitudes, and emotions; existentialist thinking; decision making

CURRICULUM DEVELOPMENT

Curriculum at the National Level

Techniques for curriculum development include a wide range of activities, among them assessing the needs of learners, developing objectives, and selecting or creating instructional materials and activities. At the national level, curriculum-making is minimal and indirect. It is limited to federally financed curriculum projects at universities and a few educational regional laboratories, the curriculum influence of private foundations and nonprofit organisations, and the school materials and textbooks produced by publishing companies in cooperation with professional educators.

In this connection, specialised personnel—subject specialists or curriculum specialists, learning theorists, and editors—make most of the decisions on what should be taught and—to a lesser extent—on how. These specialists are influenced by professional opinion as well as by the popular media. They seek the advice of and listen to other professionals in the field of education, to textbook sales people, and to marketing surveys. In their attempt to plan and develop curriculum, they are particularly sensitive to the views of teachers, school administrators, and schoolboard members.

Curriculum at the State Level

Curriculum development at the state level is mainly limited to curriculum guides and booklets. These materials are prepared by a professional staff in state departments of education assisted by curriculum consultants and college professors. The purposes and goals set forth in these materials are usually formulated in committees composed of these professional educators and selected lay persons. State guides and booklets tend to focus on aims and objectives according to subjects and grade levels; they correspond with state laws and change when priorities and trends change. For example, today there is concern for developing curriculum in the area of multicultural education, sex education, international education, and handicapped education, and this is reflected in new state-produced curriculum materials.

Curriculum at the District Level

The most common arena for curriculum development is the local school district, although curriculum making at individual schools is increasing. School districts often employ personnel who specialise in curriculum development at the central office level; these specialists include among others subject-matter specialists, test consultants, representative teachers and administrators, and sometimes lay persons. They should and usually do consider local and regional history and culture in developing the curriculum, as well as current economic and social trends in focusing on goals, content, and instructional activities.

At the school level, the teacher or a group of teachers organised by subject or grade level often develop a curriculum that is appropriate for the students. In some cases, they may work with parents and administrators. At the high school level student representatives may be on the committee or team involved in curriculum development. Committee members are encouraged to keep in mind state and local district goals and laws pertaining to subject matter. Although many teachers at the classroom level rely on such outside sources as textbooks and courses of studies to determine the content and scope of the curriculum, they should modify it to satisfy the needs and interests of their students.

Textbook Adoption

Relying on Textbooks

Here it should be noted that textbook adoption has become an important issue confronting school districts and schools, and in a few cases (for example, Texas) it involves an entire state. To the extent that textbook publishers try to satisfy potential customers, it may be said that certain content and even pictures are omitted, added, or treated in a manner so as to attract the largest audiences. A sales adoption in Texas or in the Detroit school district has tremendous monetary implications, much more than an adoption in a school district enrolling only 1,000 students. To the extent that curriculum committees or teachers rely on textbooks as the major source of content in the classroom, curriculum-making decisions are made by those who write, publish, and select textbooks. In those cases, curriculum content is reflected by what is in the textbook. There is danger in this approach. When the textbook becomes the basis of curriculum making and curriculum content, revisions in curriculum (and instruction) usually occur only when the textbook is revised or when one textbook replaces another textbook.

INSTRUCTIONAL INNOVATIONS

High Hopes for Reform

Although many educators differ in their definition of curriculum, the majority recognise that curriculum and instruction are interrelated. To carry out the curriculum one must rely on instruction—programs, materials, and methods. The search for new programs and methods of instruction is continuous. The era of the 1950s and 1960s, in particular, saw a major effort to reform curriculum and instruction. It was regarded by many educators as an era that would transform the schools. As the New York State commissioner of education wrote in 1960:

> Never before have so many new approaches developed in such a relatively short period... we are learning that many of the old ways of operating our schools are not necessarily the best ways. New methods of organisation, the use of new technological devices and new concepts of the role of the teacher provide answers that numbers alone cannot provide.

The era of reform has carried over to the present. This

section describes a number of instructional practices or innovations that have been popular during the last twenty-five years.

TEAM TEACHING

The team teaching approach is rooted in the early organisational plans of the twentieth century, particularly the Gary Plan and the Batavia Plan. It was reintroduced and modernised in 1957 at the Franklin School in Lexington, Massachusetts, under the directorship of Robert Anderson with the assistance of the Harvard Graduate School of Education. From this experiment the team teaching approach became one of the most widely discussed and frequently adopted organisational programs.

Teachers Combine Their Abilities and Interests

Team teaching is an arrangement whereby two or more teachers combine their abilities and interests to complement each other and assume joint responsibility in teaching students. The original experiment by Robert Anderson involved both large teams, composed of five or six teachers, ans small teams, composed of three teachers. The titles *team leader* and *senior teacher* were used to designate teachers who had responsibility for leadership in the team. Each team was assigned a part-time clerical aide, and the two large teams also were assigned a quarter-time teaching-assistant.

As various schools across the country adopted the team concept, the team patterns varied. Most of the present plans provide for a learning situation where the master teacher or teacher with the most knowledge of the subject instructs a large group and where students have the opportunity to work in small groups with other teachers and to do individual work as well. An experienced or master teacher is usually teamed with less experienced teachers, student teachers, and a teacher aide.

Remuneration for Increased Responsibilities

Little Time for Planning

The teacher designated as a team leader is sometimes paid an additional remuneration for his or her increased responsibilities. This stipend is supposed to serve as a means of holding able teachers in the classroom, rather than losing them to administration. In most cases, however, the schools using the team approach do not distinguish either the role or salary of various team teaching members. Rarely does the team have an aide or clerical assistant. Cooperative planning of curriculum and instruction is essential; however, in some instances there is conflict over the inadequate performance of team members and there is little time for planning. Charles Silberman's description of team planning seems to be characteristic of most schools.

> An elementary school in one of the wealthiest suburbs in the United States claims to be using team teaching in its fifth grade. What this means is that some teachers are handling math and science, others English and social studies. It is called team teaching because the teachers allegedly "get together and discuss all the children." "Isn't that kind of conference difficult to fit into a full teaching schedule?" a visitor asks with feigned innocence. "Well, you know how it is," comes the reply, "We fit it in during lunch hour, or we stay around after three for a few minutes."

The team approach has been successfully adopted in some form by many school systems, but it seems to have failed to achieve its intended purpose in many other places. Educators are still in the process of learning how to make team teaching work effectively in the classroom.

TEACHER AIDES

Teachers aides, sometimes called paraprofessionals or auxiliary personnel, often are required to perform the tasks assigned to the educational assistant under differential staffing. However, the case for teacher aides can be considered independently of any particular model of faculty utilisation.

Teacher aides were originally used to offset the shortage of classroom teachers in the early 1950s. The idea of using teacher aides on a systemwide basis was first tried in the Bay City, Michigan, schools in 1953. From there it quickly spread across the country. In 1967 a nationwide NEA survey showed that almost one in five schoolteachers, or 19 percent, had assistants of some kind. About 14 percent shared the services of one or more aides with other teachers, and 5 percent had one or more aides of their own. Twice as many elementary school teachers as high school teachers reported having aides. The typical aide at that time earned about $2 per hour. Job qualifications varied among school systems. Most of them required at least a high school diploma.

Jobs for Minorities

Trend has now Diminished

A massive program to train several hundred thousand auxiliary personnel was funded by the federal government in the late 1960s. Impetus for the program stemmed from a desire to train minority teachers, to provide jobs in ghetto areas, and to fight the War on Poverty, coupled with the advent of Headstart and Follow-Through programs. Thus the ranks of teacher aides had swelled to 200,000 by 1970, and it was estimated that by 1975 the number was 400,000. This trend came to a halt, however, as federal spending decreased in the Nixon-Ford administration and as the demand for teachers waned in the 1970s.

Across the country, state departments of education have been slow to develop and apply certification requirements for teacher aides—partially because of the past oversupply of teachers and the extra costs involved for instruction. Many wealthy school districts have a healthy number of aides in relation to their student enrollments, especially at the elementary level, while many large school districts employ them sparingly.

At present New York City is one of the few school systems that is still committed to teacher aides, who are referred to as paraprofessionals. The school system employs twice as many paraprofessionals as any other school system—about 10,000. They have permanent status and are unionised with the teachers. They have full medical and hospital coverage, obtain free schooling at the colleges, and in 1984 generally earned between $6.00 and $8.65 per hour depending on their education and experience. Most important, a career ladder program has been developed for them; they may improve their education and job opportunities and move up the ladder to become regular teachers.

FLEXIBLE SCHEDULING

Although there are literally hundreds of different methods for grouping students and teachers, one of the most widely discussed proposals, which was introduced in the 1950s, is the concept of *modular scheduling*—a popular example of flexible scheduling. The idea, proposed by J. Lloyd Trump, is to organise the school around large-group instruction, small-group discussion, and independent study. About 15- to 20-minute units of time replace the regular bell schedule and permit greater flexibility and variations in scheduling.

Organising Large, Small, and Independent Groups

Large-group instruction includes activities carried out in groups of 100 or more students and occupies about 40 percent of the time, instruction is carried out by a particularly competent teacher, and he or she is provided with additional time for preparation. Small-group instruction consists of ten to fifteen students and occupies about 20 percent of the students' time. Most of this activity is related to the large-group instruction, with the teacher serving as a consultant or counselor.

Independent study consists of students in small groups of two or three, or as individuals, engaging in independent work on projects and research in laboratories, resource centers, libraries, and outside school. This occupies 40 percent of the students' time. Teachers and other personnel serve as consultants, and greater responsibility is afforded to the students.

Periodically the students are regrouped in order to cope with differences in student abilities and interests. Flexibility of grouping is a key concept. Students tend to enjoy the subject matter more, because of increased student interaction, independence in work and special projects, and flexibility in the delivery system. Teachers work ten to twenty hours and have more time for professional preparation and professional conferences. More time also is devoted to student conferences. The plan relies on a team teaching approach where high salaries are sometimes paid to team leaders and commensurately higher salaries to master teachers. A few schools have introduced some sort of flexible scheduling. Most schools, however, still maintain the older daily schedule.

Individualised Instruction

The 1950s and 1960s saw a renewed stress on individualised learning, with new content and materials designed for individual learning, new instructional activities to provide a one-to-one teacher-student relationship, new machines to aid in this process, and a new philosophy that students should proceed at their own rate of comprehension. Thus a supporter of the individualised approach noted: "For half a century we have been committed to individualised instruction.... Yet only now have (we) been able ... to act on our conviction with the prospect of success." With the advent of team teaching, teacher aides, flexible scheduling, and independent study, he concluded that education was ready to assume responsibility for preplanned individualised learning programs.

Principles of Programmed and Behavioral Instruction

One of the best known individualized programs of the late 1950s and early 1960s was the Project on Individually Prescribed Instruction (IPI), which was developed at the University of Pittsburgh and later became known as Adaptable Environments for Learning (AEL). IPI applied the principles of programmed instruction and behavioral instruction. The curriculum was stated in behavioral objectives with proficiency levels; each student was diagnosed, and an individual plan was developed for each subject; several materials were introduced to provide a variety of paths for mastery of any given objective; learning tasks were individualised for each student; and there was continuous evaluation.

Individualised Objectives and Rates of Learning

Other systems for delivering individualised instruction in elementary and secondary schools that appeared in the late 1960s are the University of Wisconsin's Individually Guided Education (IGE) and the Program for Learning in Accordance with Needs (PLAN). IGE is a total educational system for formulating and carrying out instructional programs for individual students in which planned variations are made in what each student learns, in how he or she goes about learning, and in how rapidly he or she learns. Instructional objectives are developed for each student; the student participates in a one-to-one relation with the teacher, teacher aide, or another student; and the program includes independent study, small-group instruction, large-group instruction, and various classroom activities. The actual mix of these activities for each student depends on the abilities of the student, the objectives to be attained, and the costs involved. IGE was developed as an alternative to age-graded education and to unstructured open education, but it can be implemented in either age-graded or ungraded schools and in either self-contained or departmentalised classrooms.

The five components of the PLAN system are as follows: (1) a set of educational objectives, (2) related teaching-learning units, (3) a set of tests, (4) guidance activities to enhance self-understanding, and (5) an evaluation system. Individualization is essentially accomplished by (a) ungraded materials appropriate to the student level of achievement, (b) alternative sets of materials for each unit of instruction, and (c) two-week modules, arranged according to each student's level of achievement.

Group Instruction Prevails

All three systems—IPI, IGE and PLAN—have been field tested and are used today to a limited extent. There have been various reports of success and significant gains in student achievement and comparative skills. The plans have not been implemented on a mass scale because of their cost and administrative obstacles. In many respects, these individualised approaches are the forerunner of today's diagnostic learning approaches, such as mastery learning, continuous progress, and direct instruction. Nevertheless, the majority of schools today are still geared to group instruction, group norms, and group expectations, rather than individual student differences.

INSTRUCTIONAL TELEVISION

In the late 1950s a great many educators saw the new medium as a panacea for many educational ills. Instructional television (ITV) was expected to solve the teacher shortage, enable master teachers to reach more students, and make it possible to substantially increase class size. In addition, television was expected to reduce some of the inequalities of educational resources, enable students in rural and small schools to receive high quality instruction, and make available instruction in specialised subjects. It also was supposed to provide a library of tapes and kinescopes that would be reused like library books.

Both the Ford Foundation and the federal government poured tens of millions of dollars into a variety of ITV experiments. In Hagerstown, Maryland more than one hundred live programs were transmitted each week from five studios to 37 elementary and secondary schools containing 90 percent of the 18,000 students of Washington County schools. In Southwest Indiana, lessons were transmitted to more than 23,000 students in 108 schools. These experiments served as models to guide other school systems in adopting educational television.

Criticisms of ITV

The experiments were initially perceived to be making a real contribution to education, and they became a vital part of many school systems; eventually, however, educational television was criticised for fragmenting learning, impersonalising it, and standardising it into mere information acquisition. Television failed to consider individual interests and learning rates; the costs were high; there were technical difficulties—and the effort was not considered worthwhile, since ITV mainly served as low-level occasional enrichment.

After a decade of intensive effort and expenditures, its most ardent advocates had to admit that ITV had not made a decisive impact on the schools. Recent reviews of the research on instructional television indicate that although children can learn from TV in the classroom, few people can agree on how to use it most effectively. The question that needs to be explored today, however, is why the medium proved so disappointing. Even "Sesame Street" and the "Electric Company," each of which reaches between 15 and 20 million children regularly and was originally intended to help disadvantaged children catch up with other students, had to be reassessed. "Sesame Street" and "The Electric Company" did improve the learning of disadvantaged children, but they helped more affluent youngsters at the same time and thus did little or nothing to close the gap between the two groups.

There is some indication that students react positively to the use of ITV in the elementary schools, but the history of ITV in high schools has been one of many unproductive experiments and unfulfilled promises.

Cable Television and Telecommunications

The most recent potential for instructional television involves cable television, telecommunication systems, and video disc players—hooked up to either home or school TV screens. Certainly school districts can telecast programs to various schools and classrooms for minimal or reasonable cost with their own district-wide system or via cable companies that must provide some educational programming for a nominal fee in most communities. It is possible, also, for students to share some instruction and to interact on the TV screen among themselves or with special tutors, teachers, or resource instructors, through special cable connections. At present, however, few school systems utilise these instructional methods.

PROGRAMMED INSTRUCTION

Although a number of auto-instructional devices were developed during the 1920s, their impact was inconsequential. Except for sporadic use mainly during World War II, such devices were virtually forgotten until B.F. Skinner stimulated a new surge of interest in 1954.

Stimulus-Response Reinforcement Cycle

The principles of programmed instruction were derived from Skinner's principles of operant conditioning, which were based on his laboratory work with animals. A relatively small unit of information called a frame is presented to the learner as a *stimulus*. The learner is required to make a *response* by completing the statement or answering a statement. By a feedback system, the learner is informed if the response is correct or wrong. If wrong, he or she is told why. If correct, the response is *reinforced*. The learner is then presented with another frame, and the stimulus-response-reinforcement cycle is repeated until a series of hundreds or thousands of frames is presented and the program is completed in a logical sequence of information. The instructional sequences are simplified to such a degree that if the percentage of errors of the average learner is more than 10 percent, the program usually is considered to be in need of revision.

Skinner called the device a "teaching machine." Since more attention was focused on the machine than on the instructional program, more machines than programs were produced during the first years of the movement, and many commercial companies produced them in ranges of $20 to $2,000. The concept caught on but as criticism of programmed instruction snowballed, the "boom" turned into a "bust." Even Sidney Pressey, the leading researcher who had worked with programmed instruction in the 1920s, attacked the procedures of the fifties as based on "a false premise that the important features of human learning are to be found in animals." He maintained that programmed learning procedures "fragmented learning,... [reinforced] rote learning" and dehumanised education.

Video Materials

Despite these criticisms, the principles of programmed instruction are in use today, at home, in school, and in various computer-assisted programs and video disc materials, which provide immediate feedback and instant access to information. In stark contrast to the old printed methods and workbook materials, programmed instruction can be individualised, so that students interact with new video materials on the TV screen. The instruction depends on the student's entry level and is designed to accommodate many styles and rates of learning. Writing the software is crucial. With computer systems, programs can be quite sophisticated and can provide individualised programmed materials and methods to suit almost any student.

COMPUTER-ASSISTED INSTRUCTION

Three Different Types of Instruction

The application of computer technology has increased steadily since the first commercial computer began operation in 1951. In education the computer is capable, first of all, of presenting individualised lesson material almost simultaneously with feedback and correction. The tutorial system offers a second approach, in which a computer takes over the responsibility for presenting inquiry learning. As soon as the student manifests a clear understanding of a concept or problem, he or she moves to the next exercise. The third and most sophisticated level of student-computer interaction is the dialogue system, which permits the student to conduct a genuine dialogue with and ask questions of the computer.

Criticisms of Computerised Instruction

There are several advantages to using the computer for instruction: the current emphasis on individualised instruction, the increasing amount of new knowledge to be learned, the growing need for periodic upgrading of one's education, and the unlimited diversity it presents for curriculum and teaching. Critics point out that the use of the computer limits human interaction in teaching and learning, that it leaves the role of the teacher unspecified, and that it provides little insight into student purposes, motives, or feelings. Most important, some educators believe that the values of individuality and human freedom are threatened by the widespread use of technology in education. Most of these same fears have been raised over the years with the introduction of other types of education machines—a perceived conflict between humanism and technology—but they remain important factors to consider.

Computers Enter the Classroom

Because of their lowered costs and their pervasiveness in the home, in the workplace, and in government, computers will be widely used in the classroom. Although computerised instruction did not have a widespread impact on education from the 1950s to 1970s, schools tend to mirror society. Computers are beginning to have a significant effect on the classroom of the 1980s. The trouble is, according to one observer, that no one really knows how to use computers well for educational purposes. Nevertheless, the potential is great and will occasion changes in the day-to-day operation of the classroom.

Computer Systems and Languages

Although microcomputers are easily adapted to school instructional settings, appropriate software is needed before the schools can expand their commitment to computer-assisted instruction. (Most present computer software was initially developed for nonschool use.) Other problems include the need to train teachers who will be versed in computer instructional design and programming. Concern also has been raised about the nature of computer systems and languages, that they are somewhat complex and turn off many students who become frustrated or lose patience. None of these problems are insoluble, but they are reasons for the slow school adoption of computers despite the widespread use of them in other sectors of society.

ADDITIONAL INNOVATIONS

More Innovations Between 1950s and 1980s

In addition to the aforementioned major innovations, many other innovations have been adopted only on a piecemeal basis. The following are representative innovations of the period between the 1950s and the 1980s:

1. *Resource center*. A specialised center with learning materials specially selected to meet the needs of the students and staffed with teachers, teacher aides, and other special personnel.

2. *School-within-a-school.* A large school organised into smaller units for administrative and/or instructional purposes.
3. *Open space facilities.* Classrooms and/or schools organised to permit students and teachers to move about and share space in various ways, ranging in size and purpose, but suggesting flexibility.
4. *Language laboratories.* Equipment used to present recorded voices as part of the audiolingual approach to learning a language.
5. *Telephone amplification.* Long-distance discussions held by students and/or the teacher with persons from outside the school, with amplification for the entire classroom to hear.
6. *Simulation or gaming.* An experience used to create a problematic situation, usually logical or reality-oriented, involving students in role playing and/or decision making.
7. *Pass-fail.* The option for students to take a specified number of courses, usually elective courses and no more than one course per term, on a pass-fail basis instead of for traditional grades.
8. *Nongraded programs.* A series of programs open to students without regard to grade level and/or sequence of courses. The students usually work at their own pace.
9. *Criterion-referenced tests.* Tests devised to measure specific learning changes, usually involving stated behavioral objectives and expected competencies.
10. *Independent study.* Work conducted by the student on a topic of interest, using school or nonschool resources with the teacher serving as a resource agent or guide.
11. *Community study.* Work done by students in the community, preferably with some health, social,

or business institution, in conjunction with their school program and under the supervision of a teacher and another person or group of people outside the school; the focus is practical, not academic.

12. *Instructional materials center.* A center that houses a variety of printed and audiovisual materials for student use.

The 1980s has witnessed renewed interest in developing new curriculum and instructional techniques to meet the current and future needs of our students and society. A genuine reassessment is underway that may lead to major changes in our schools. In the discussion that follows, we will look at some of the possible directions that curriculum and instruction may take in the future.

CURRICULUM TRENDS: AN AGENDA FOR THE FUTURE

Less Compartmentalised, More Integrated Curriculum

Opinions differ on the directions education will take, and library shelves are filled with volumes describing current and anticipated changes in society and education. Despite disagreements, however, considerable consensus exists on several broad trends that are likely to have a major impact on curriculum planning in the educational system. Some of the most important of these trends are listed below. The emerging curriculum responds to the urge to break away from traditional disciplines, to develop more interdisciplinary approaches. In the curriculum of the future, subject matter most likely will be less compartmentalised and more integrated and holistic. Although traditional subject boundaries will remain, there will be increased cross-subject material; knowledge will no longer be considered fragmented or linear, but multidisciplinary and multidimensional.

1. *Communication.* Technology will make it possible to

revolutionise the communication as information and understanding in the classroom. The technological revolution in communications has been proceeding for many years, but most observers agree that there is no real end in sight. Substantial improvements is communications capacity will continue at an accelerating rate for the next few decades. Predictable and envisioned improvements in technology less to such scenarios as the following.

Each student will have at his or her disposal a television receiver, either in his or her home or the publicly supported learning center. Closed circuit and cable telecourses will be commonplace, and video discs and video-taped "telelessons" will replace textbooks and written materials. Students will have available a dial-access facility that permits access, via laser or a telephone, to a central learning center equipped with high-speed computers that can communicate with computers in any learning resource center anywhere in the world.

Silicon Chips

2. *Computers.* We are in the midst of a technological and information revolution spawned by new networks and combinations of computer data bases—combined with telephones, satellite and cable transmission systems, and robots. Like the Industrial Revolution, this new revolution will ultimately affect how we work, where we live, and the quality of our lives. Terms such as *postindustrial society* and *third wave* connote the transformation that is now taking shape. Manufacturisation is certainly a key part of this revolution. Silicon chips the size of child's fingernail have been developed with enormous memory capacity and ability to calculate. Hence, some knowledge of computers is fast becoming essential; in the future, many high-paying jobs will require this knowledge. People without it may very well be relegated to lower-paying jobs or the themselves unable to move beyond a certain point in the workforce or management team.

The Fourth R

Computer literacy will stand beside the three Rs as a fundamental skill. Knowing how to retrieve information, as opposed to having access to information, will mark the difference between an educated person and a semieducated person. If we are to take advantage of the ever-increasing quantity of information, commonly referred to as the *knowledge-explosion,* we will have to rely on computer-based tools. We will need to distinguish between three levels of computer knowledge: (1) computer literacy, suggesting knowledge of how computers work and what they are used for; (2) computer competency, being able to use it as a tool in a particular field; and (3) computer expertise, suggesting the person whose profession is computing.

750,000 to 1,000,000 Computers in Schools

Teachers are waking up to the fact that computers are here to stay and can be effective tools of instruction. In 1980, some 50,000 microcomputers were used in the nation's schools; by 1990, the number should reach 750,000 to 1 million; in other words, there will be several computers to a school. It is also envisioned that most secondary schools will be offering students an average of 30 minutes per day at a computer terminal, not to mention that many elementary schools already have students learning on computers, and some 50,000 or more teachers will be teaching computers as their main subject.

What actually happens will depend to a large extent on the money available for the purchase of computers, the software available for student use, and the way computers are adopted into the curriculum.

What should be the objectives of using computers in schools?

Should they be restricted to students who have mathematical abilities? to certain grade levels? to particular subjects?

Should they be used to teach other subjects (that is, to provide drill or tutoring) or be used to teach about computing and programming?

Should students be charged user fees for using computers?

Training Teachers for Computer Use

Who will train teachers in computer use?

Do we reorganise the classroom and have computers at every desk, say, as in an office, or do we limit our expectations to a computer laboratory?

How we resolve these questions will determine to some extent the trends that take effect by 1990.

Second or Third Careers

3. *Lifelong learning*. The trend toward lifelong learning is occurring in all modern societies as a result of the knowledge explosion and rapid social, technological, and economic changes that persuade or force people to prepare for second or third careers and to keep themselves updated on new developments that affect their personal and social goals. Education will continue to become more of a "lifelong" enterprise and increasingly will take place outside the confines of the traditional school. Taking note of these trends, the Carnegie Commission has developed the concept of a "step-in, step-out" educational system for lifelong learning. This means that people could move in and out of educational programs throughout their lives.

Some observers believe that much of the learning that has been provided by elementary, secondary, and postsecondary schools may be provided by business and industry in the future. Still other scenarios envision educating adolescents and adults through a network of community resources and individually appropriate learning opportunities.

4. *International cooperation.* Although historically the United States has taken a relatively isolationist position, interdependence among nations no longer allows Americans to ignore what happens elsewhere or to remain ignorant of developments in far-distant countries. Educators will feel the need to place a greater emphasis on understanding other nations and cultures than they have in the past.

A Global Village

In an era of rapid change and ever-increasing global interdependence, we are forced to appraise the tendencies of the times and recognise that the oceans no longer protect us from the problems or realities of the rest of the world. For instance, more than 50 percent of our oil is imported from the Middle East, a most unstable part of the world where tribal and religious conflicts can and already have interrupted the flow of energy imports, with the potential of causing major disruptions in the United States. About 15 million Third World children died of hunger last year, and another 800 million or more (about 20 percent of humanity) go to bed hungry or malnourished. On a "small planet" like ours, other people's problems or strengths, sooner or later, affect us. We do indeed inhabit a global village; there is no escaping it.

Peace Education

Both the United States and Soviet Union possess enough nuclear war-heads to destroy the world. If a computer malfunctions or an unforeseen contingency develops, we are 30 minutes from nuclear destruction. Indeed, the effects of nuclear war have been vividly portrayed from the 1950s *(On the Beach* and *A Canticle for Leibowitz)* to the 1980s (*The Fate of the Earth* and *The Day After,* two television scenarios). The nuclear freeze and disarmament movements have swept across the United States, Western Europe, and Japan; they are filtering down into the schools and curriculum under the umbrella of peace education and the teaching of peacemaking strategies

Innovative learning in today's schools must be widely international if a country is to participate effectively in the world. Educators need to raise the right issues and ask the right questions. The schools must revive dying foreign language programs. They might expand travel exchange programs and perhaps make study in another culture a requirement for graduation. For the near future, schools and colleges may be restricted be budget problems, but the need will become more evident and money may loosen up in this area of curriculum.

5. *Environmental education.* Mounting concern over such problems as pollution, overpopulation, and depletion of food and natural resources has created demands for more knowledge and new programs in ecology and environmental education. Much of the relevant content has long been included in traditional earth sciences, biology, and geography courses and in conservation programs. The new demand calls for a more meaningful and better coordinated program that raises the theme of crisis. Many people—including educators—believe that the worldwide ecosystem is in jeopardy and can no longer support the growing world population.

The parade of grim environmental realities makes a long list, with extinction of large portions of vegetation, topsoil, natural resources, and animal life (*Homo sapiens* included) a real possibility sometime in the twenty-first century. If these threats are acknowledged as real, no educational system hoping to prepare students for the world tomorrow could fail to treat the environment as an important subject.

Rather than terrifying students about ecological disaster, the school system should help students understand that the environment is globally connected with humankind, which is a globally dominant species that has the potential wisdom to keep the environment safe from ruin. That is a more hopeful, less paralysing view of the world, and a challenge for curriculum specialists.

Spiraling Energy Costs

6. *Energy education.* Between 1973 and 1980, the total heating bill more than doubled for American consumers, despite reduced fuel consumption. The cost of heating is expected to double again by 1986, partially as a result of deregulation and partially as a result of increased foreign costs and profit-taking at home. Our entire society is faced with spiraling costs for all forms of fuel, electricity, and water. The need for an energy-wise policy, one that reduces consumption and waste and makes efficient and safe use of synthetic fuels, solar energy, waste products, and even coal is paramount if we are to maintain our economic health and standard of living.

We need to educate children for their roles as energy consumers and voters and as potential energy-related workers or technicians. Although there are many different opinions concerning the future direction of policies, consensus exists that it is essential to educate the public about energy; such an education starts at home and continues in the schools.

Cultural Richness and Diversity

7. *Ethnic education and cultural pluralism.* That a land growth of curriculum offerings in various ethnic studies followed on the feels of black studies is not surprising. The sense of neglect and the need for identity and recognition are by no means limited to blacks. There are several ways to look at the rise of ethnic consciousness. On the positive side is the hope that these programs will lead to greater understanding of various groups and will enhance the concepts of cultural richness and diversity and a ethnic self-esteem. On the negative side is the possible divisive effect of these programs on the body politic, loosening the ties that bind our society together.

The focus varies from state to state, ranging from little interest in ethnic studies to considerable legislation instituting various programs. In some cases, even though no laws or defined policy have been established on the state level, there is considerable local activity. Nearly forty states have published materials and media on the subject of ethnicity, nearly thirty states have formulated policy statements on ethnic studies, and nearly twenty states have mandated ethnic studies in school curriculum. This trend should spread, since immigration has recently increased as more Third World people are entering this country.

8. *Nonsexist curriculum.* Curriculum and instruction are also influenced by Title IX of the Education Amendments of 1972 and other laws and forces that aim to reduce sexism in education. Curriculum efforts in elementary, secondary, and postsecondary schools include a requirement that institutions develop programs to meet the athletic needs and interests of both sexes. There is recognition that women need to be trained placed, and advanced in leadership positions in schools and colleges as teachers, coaches, officials, directors, administrators, and members of governing boards.

Sex Bias in Textbooks

Educators are also working to reduce sexual stereotyping and other forms of sexism in textbooks and instructional materials. A comprehensive body of research indicates six forms of sex bias in textbooks invisibility, stereotyping, imbalance, unreality, fragmentation, and language which need to be corrected. Sex bias tends also to operate in teacher expectations, teacher interaction patterns, vocational counseling, career equation, and employment practices. Many people feel the need to bring sex equity from the periphery of conferences and meeting to the core and mainstream of school life, particularly as it relates to curriculum and instruction practices.

Proper Nutrition and Exercise

9. *Dieting and exercise.* With the exception of a few heart-conscious individuals, we have become a nation of junk eaters

and flabby people. Americans are literally addicted to a diet of excessive sugar, salt, fats, refined starches, and caffeine. The cumulative effect of American eating habits, coupled with lack of exercise, is directly related to a shortened life span. Schools ought to provide guidance about diet and exercise, eliminate junk food from lunches and vending machines, develop adult programs that encourage healthy growth and development, and encourage parents to supervise their children's food consumption and exercise program. Recent research linking good nutrition and exercise for children to good health, proper growth and development, positive social behavior, and healthier adult years should lead schools to incorporate increased nutrition and exercise into the curriculum.

10. *Sex education.* Despite objections from some community groups and sporadic controversy, sex education is filtering down to the elementary school curriculum. Because of mounting divorce rates illegitimacy, and venereal disease among our youth, many educators and citizen groups have deemed sex education essential. Traditional instruction units in hygiene, home economics, and family living have been supplemented with comprehensive explanations and prescriptions about dating, marriage, parenthood, and health problems.

Alternative Approaches to Sex Education

As sex education programs in school increase, controversy among home, church, and school will probably grow, as well. Course content, discussion, and pictures could be controversial issues in some communities, as could the schools' appropriate role and whether alternative modes of sex education are more appropriate. To be sure, sex education can be viewed as a health issue; a matter of moral values or religious beliefs; a family concern; a social, psychological or physical matter; or an educational issue. In our changing and pluralistic society, all of these views have merit. Curriculum specialists and teachers will have to wrestle with them.

The Conveyor Belt is moving for Us All

11. *Aging education.* Not only are we an aging society, but all of us are on the same conveyor belt—the only difference is that we got on at different times. Some people feel that the schools should teach students to understand the problems and prospects of aging—how to cope with it on an individual basis (even though it may seem distant when we are young) and how to help loved ones (parents and grandparents) deal successfully with this developmental stage of life. There is something to be learned from traditional societies that center around large kinship groups; postindustrial society should be educated about the worth of the aged—perhaps one of the greatest untapped resources.

Eventually, the curriculum should treat many of the problems of aging as a form of discrimination, as another "ism." This emphasis parallels changes in curriculum concerning racism, ethnicism, and sexism.

Reform of Vocational Education

12. *Career education.* There is a widespread reform of vocational education. The long-standing discontent with vocational education has finally led to the development of work motivation programs for *all* youth. Characteristic of these career programs is the extension of career guidance activities, the involvement of community groups and business groups, and the increased provision of career information and occupational training at the high school level.

Postindustrial and Information Society

We can expect to see greater emphasis on teaching job-related skills and on disciplining students according to the norms that guide the workplace. As the nation moves increasingly into a postindustrial and information society, the potential for job unemployment and underemployment is great. Increased use of computers and robots are expected to replace 15 to 25 million manufacturing jobs (and another 5 million service jobs) by 1990; the decline in American manufacturing jobs will roughly coincide in magnitude with the agricultural revolution and will represent about 5 to 10 percent of the workforce.

The workers who accept technology and are willing to retrain are far more likely to be employed than the workers who resist such innovation. Students who are counseled and educated properly will not emerge from school with obsolete knowledge and skills and will be better equipped for today's—and tomorrow's—job market. The situation in many of our educational (and employment) institutions is dismal now; we are unprepared to help American children and adults make the massive adjustments that lie ahead. There is no nationwide plan—educational, industrial, or governmental—that assesses the future occupational needs of society and focuses schooling and the nation's workforce on such needs; we are instead permitting the free market system and supply-and-demand swings of the workforce to dictate the future.

Viable and Obsolete Occupations

Society must prepare a future workforce, consisting of technicians, engineers, and managers, in the following areas: weapons and space; energy and nuclear systems; housing rehabilitation; hazardous pollution and industrial wastes; genetics; agricultural and processed food products; holographics and optics; tool and die, machine, and foundry systems; lasers and robots; allied health and geriatric services; and communication, mass media, computer, and information systems. In short, the schools must identify (in cooperation with industry and government, one would hope) obsolete occupations, assess the new technologies and services, and prepare students for viable careers.

What Kinds of People We Wish to Produce

13. *Values education.* The greatest danger in planning future curriculum is the subordination of human values to technological advances. Worthwhile human goals ought not

be replaced by computerized and mechanized techniques that may do more harm than good. For example, it may be undesirable to teach more facts about history if students are unable to use these facts to better understand the people they interact with and world in which they live. Similarly, drug education programs may only stimulate drug abuse unless students also understand how dangerous drugs are abused in everyday life. In short, when we plan curriculum, we need to be aware of the byproducts—both intended and unintended—and to weigh our immediate gains against their consequences. Apparent success could turn into disaster if the technological experts of tomorrow rush pell-mell into curriculum planning without knowing the effects of the new learning on the social and psychological development of the child, as well as on the attitudes and behaviors of teachers, parents, and community groups. The questions that we must always keep in mind as we move into the future are: "What kinds of people do we wish to produce?" and "What kinds of human behavior do we wish to encourage?"

Summing Up

1. Curriculum revision in the past was uniform and slow to change because the society was slow to change. Today the social changes are swift and curriculum modification must keep pace.
2. In organising the curriculum, most educators hold to the traditional concept of curriculum as the body of subjects, or subject matter. Nevertheless, a number of contemporary educators are more concerned with the experiences of the learner, and in this respect regard the student as the focus of the curriculum.
3. In developing the curriculum, educators engage in a process of planning and selecting the elements and procedures of curriculum. Curriculum development takes place at several levels; national, state, school district, and local school.

4. The 1950s and 1960s produced several instructional innovations. Many of these reforms are in use in today's classrooms and schools.
5. As we move into the mid-1980s, we must rely on new courses and new concepts to help us cope with change. Although many sensitive and frightening questions must be resolved in the future—the possibility of nuclear warfare, pollution of the atmosphere, fuel scarcity, racial polarisation, poverty—the basic curriculum questions remain the same. We ask ourselves: How can the schools meet the new challenges? How can schools best serve both the individual and society? What should be taught and how? And, is the curriculum relevant now and in the future?

Discussion Questions

1. Define curriculum and support your definition with at least three examples.
2. Describes a team-teaching program you would adopt for an elementary or secondary school. What problems might you encounter?
3. Summarise the rationale for flexible scheduling as it pertains to the learner and teacher.
4. How can the schools best adopt computers for instruction?
5. Discuss the problems and prospects of the curriculum trends discussed in the chapter. What other trends can you foresee?

Suggested Readings

Doll, Ronald C., *Curriculum Improvement: Decision Making and Process*, 4th ed. Boston: Allyn and Bacon, 1978.

An excellent overview on curriculum improvement, with emphasis on practical principles, problems, and solutions.

English, Fenwick W., ed. *Fundamental Curriculum Decisions.* 1983 ASCD Year-book. Alexandria. Va.: Association for Supervision and Curriculum Development, 1983.

Twelve chapters by authorities in the field, who examine various aspects of curriculum, emphasis is on contemporary issues.

Joyce, Bruce, Richard H. Hersh, and Michael McKibbin. *The Structure of School Improvement.* New York: Longman, 1983.

The authors discuss the pattern of relationships among individual components of school change and innovation, including teachers, administrators, curriculum specialists, and community members.

Tanner, Daniel, and Laurel N. Tanner, *Curriculum Development: Theory into Practice, 2nd ed.* New York: Macmillan, 1980.

A historical overview of curriculum coupled with a synthesis of research, theory, and practice.

Tyler, Ralph W., *Basic Principles of Curriculum and Instruction. Chicago: University of Chicago Press, 1950.*

A classic text on how to develop a curriculum.

5

Alternative Schooling

More important, we should have learned in the last decade that there is no magic in the single school system or in any set of curricular prescriptions, and that the most successful motivating device may simply be the sense that one has chosen what one wants to learn and under what conditions. In urban areas there is no reason why children in one neighborhood should be forced to attend one particular school for a specified period of time; why there should not be choice as to place, subject, style of teaching, and hours; why, for all children. French and history and algebra should have absolutely equal value: why, for some, art or dance or music should not be given more time than history; why reading a book is more of a humanistic activity than making a film or playing an instrument; why children should not be allowed to choose between permissive and highly structured situations (and many would choose the latter): why parents and children should not have the economic power to punish unsuccessful schools (by leaving them) and to reward effective ones; or why single, self-serving bureaucracies should continue to hold monopoly power in what is probably the most crucial, and certainly the most universal public enterprise in America. Wealthy children and middle-class parents have some options about schools; lower-class children have none.

Peter Schrag. *End of the Impossible Dream*

The 1960s was a time of optimism. The mood of the

nation was towards reform, and in education this mood was one of bold optimism. There was little question that reform could be achieved and schools implemented innumerable reform measures, including team teaching, flexible scheduling, programmed learning, multiple texts, nongraded schools, programs for the disadvantaged, computerised learning, and the "new" curricula. Educators were committed to the programs; change was just a matter of time. More dramatic, reform in education was seen as the keystone to curing many of the nation's social ailments.

The notion that reform of American public schools was necessary and imminent predates the sixties, beginning in the early fifties. First, there was the call for more intellectual rigor in the curriculum. Spokesmen such as Arthur Bestor and Hyman Rickover vigorously criticised the school system, arguing that students did not know enough history, physics and English; James Conant conducted an extensive study on the curriculum of the American high school, substantiating this view; Jerome Zacharias and other science educators, with the generous support of the federal government, rewrote the science curriculum. The return to "the fundamentals" and academic rigor did not subside in the 1960s, but it was flanked by another group of reformers Schrag refers to as democrats: those determined to integrate and humanize schools, while providing universal opportunity. The first group of reformers represented the aspirations of the enfranchised affluent, middle-class, who desired an Ivy League education for their kind. The second group demanded for the deprieved what they thought the privileged were getting. Now suddenly the optimism is gone. In retrospect, the sixties and seventies were decades of frustration and bafflement. The innovations, so highly regarded, did not foster basic change in our schools. Even if these reforms had lived up to expectations, people were no longer certain that the changes would have made any substantially improved economic opportunity of the disadvantaged, or the quality of life in the nation.

Meanwhile, the voices of reform shifted from those who are part of the institutionalised mainstream to those who were less sympathetic with the school system. These reformers disregarded any compensatory, innovative efforts in favor of overhauling the system; some, such as Ivan Illich, called for abandonment of the system. Nevertheless, the underlying theme of most critics—namely, greater respect for children and more diversity in approaches to learning—was hardly radical. But the words used by John Holt, James Herndon, Jonathan Kozol, Herbert Kohl, and others were imbued with outrage and indignation. Perhaps for this reason, more than any other, they failed to capture the public's support. Ironically, many of their ideas gradually become part of societal beliefs and school practices.

If there has been a "crisis in the classroom," for the past quarter of a century, the public has not responded with any sort of alarm or mandate for reform. When widespread change is desired, it is usually to retrench, as the renewed "back-to-basics" movement indicates. People by and large are content with the schools; the schools did well by them, so they reason, and the people assume that they probably can do even better by their children. Education is a process that we all endured, that most of us have assumed was beneficial, and that few of us clearly understood. The result is that, fundamentally, our public schools have changed surprisingly little since their conception over a century ago.

The most important effort at reform in the public schools in the early seventies was the "alternatives" movement. Despite good reasons for pessimism, alternatives offer some hope. Unlike nearly all the reforms of the fifties and sixties, alternative schools were offered as an option, not as a directive.

THE PROMISE OF ALTERNATIVE SCHOOLS

The alternatives movement has the potential for substantially different reform in the schools. Unlike earlier reforms, alternatives are not to be superimposed on reluctant and bewildered parents. With alternatives, the type of school a child attends is not presented as an edict but is left to the choice of parent and student. This is Schrag's message: "What I am arguing for, obviously, is a restoration of multiple options, and, as much as possible, multiple values." The alternatives movement is a promising step toward educational change because it offers students, parents and teachers a choice that takes into account a diversity of learning and reaching styles.

The meaning of "alternatives" needs to be clarified. The word "alternative" conjured various meanings to the public. The prevailing association is to the many radical schools often labelled "free" or "open." In this light, alternatives have been defined as schools or places that exist as an *alternative* to the traditional ("establishment") school. As Mario Fantini points out, when alternatives were first introduced to the mainstream, the bulk of the samples came from counterculture experiments, often in urban settings with minority children. This experience accounts for the "alternative to establishment" meaning cited above; it also helps explain the white middle class's skepticism of the term "alternatives." As a result, many establishment proponents of alternatives have substituted the terms "options" or "public options in education."

A more useful definition of "alternatives," in view of the direction the movement has taken in public education, is one offered by Fantini and the National Consortium on Options in Public Education. They think of alternatives as a *range of (school or classroom) options along a pedagogical contiuum.* Alternative schools that fit such a continuum can definitively be called free schools, open schools, traditional or standard schools, continuous progress or contemporary schools, and fundamental schools. There also exist less descriptive school types, such as multiculture schools, community schools, street academies, schools without walls, individualised learning schools, schools within schools, and so on. All these alternatives (options) can exist as a choice—not a fiat—for the community.

Alternatives also are designed to rely on evaluative feedback from parents and students; many include parents and students in policy-making. The continuum of types of schools and the policy-making involvement of parents and students are what many advocates of alternatives consider to be the seeds for truly fundamental changes in public education. These qualities, it is argued, are the essential strength of alternatives. Vernon Smith has immodestly described the movement as "The Quiet Revolution."

In this chapter, the meaning assigned to "alternatives" will be "a range of options along a pedagogical continuum." The last section in this chapter considers yet another way of looking at alternatives, as "alternative learning situations in a community that complement and supplement the schools."

A PERSPECTIVE ON THE ALTERNATIVE SCHOOL MOVEMENT

Early alternatives operated within the "alternative to" framework. By and large, the first alternatives were-called "free" or in some cases community schools. They were "free" in a sense that they attempted to create a free atmosphere of learning and development—the antithesis of the reality of most public schools. Typically, they were started by parents, teachers, and students, and privately financed, if only on a shoestring. Miriam Wasserman traces the contemporary roots of these schools to the freedom schools started for black youngsters in the South during the Civil Rights movement of the early sixties. The name became "free schools" when the schools were begun by people who believed that schools should concern themselves with the individual needs of youngsters and that the children should have some freedom to choose what and how they learn. Most of the schools are quite small, ranging from approximately ten to 250 students (the average size being about thirty-five). Although the schools are modestly financed, the staff-student ratio is a generous one to five. Allen Graubard, author of *Free the Children: Radical Reform and the Free School Movement*, reports that the number of free schools grew from twenty or so in 1967 to over 500 by 1972. It is not clear how the movement grew or declined since then, but it is clear that a "considerable number" of free schools close after one or two or three years. It appears that the movement leveled off, perhaps even declined in the late seventies.

People in the free school movement have been strongly critical of the public schools and the larger society that the public schools serve. They see the institution of school and the society as self-serving, self-supporting and reinforcing. In response, free schools themselves often are political and one must look as closely at their politics and ideology as their pedagogy and educational philosophy. As Graubard explains, it is necessary to distinguish between the apolitical and political free schools. Within the Summerhillian tradition, there is a distinct apolitical quality and the school looks, inward, sometimes consciously disengaging itself from the affairs of the larger community. (Summerhill is the famous British school started in 1921, and directed by A.S. Neill since its inception. Numerous Summerhill schools have been started on this continent by American advocates.)

In the more politically oriented middle-class schools, (typically located in suburban or rural settings), there exist strong elements of countercultural and counterinstitutional sentiment. The constituents of these free schools believe in permissive child-rearing, and they want their schools to foster creative, spontaneous, and relatively uninhibited and unrepressed individuals. To people coming from educationally and economically "enriched" homes, skill-learning in school is less vital, and anxiety over earning a living is reduced. It is this segment of the free-school movement, and their counterparts in the public schools, that were so critical of much of American society in the 1960s.

Jonathon Kozol carefully distinguishes another somewhat less political free school, this one typically found in the inner cities. In contrast to the counterculture, permissive free schools of the affluent, white middle-class, these schools are highly structured, with a premium on basic skill development. They are only political in the sense that they want the schools to liberate their children from the racism and indoctrination and do for them what schools apparently do for the dominant white (and middle-class) people. They do not want schools that promote a free, "do your own thing" learning environment. They want schools that will provide the literacy, skill, and professional training now provided white (and middle-class) students in the public schools. Kozol makes it quite clear that he believes the inner-city community school to be the true "free school."

Despite being outside the established educational system (or at best on the fringe, in the case of early streets academies), and despite being relatively small (by Graubard's estimate there are about 13,000 students or less than one half of 1 percent of all school-age children), the free-school movement has helped to spark reform in the system. The alternatives movement is indebted to the writers on radical reform; and to the work of early free-school parents and teachers.

In historical perspective, free schools appear to be direct descendants of the private experimentals early in the twentieth century; examples of these early schools include Caroline Pratt's Play School, Margaret Naumberg's Children's School, Marietta Johnson's Organic School and others. Figure 5.1 is a diagrammatic view of the relationship among these and other experimental school ventures, leading to the various alternatives that began to be institutionalised by the mid 1970s.

The Open Classroom

Another kind of experimental school concept that was a catalyst to the alternatives movement is the open classroom, modelled on the British Infant Schools. The term "open" is misused, used inconsistently, or used synonymously with free schools and open-space schools. Both resemble the open classroom only in minor ways, and many schools called "open" ought more accurately to be called free, open-space, or individualised-learning schools. In fact, the antecedent of American open schools; the English primary schools, have a variety of labels: somewhat unsatisfactory "informal education," the "free day," the "integrated day," the "integrated curriculum," and the "open school." The term "informal education," which the English tend to favor, is the most descriptive and least confusing.

Though not a majority of English primary schools, such schools do exist on wide scale in England. This approach to learning expanded rapidly after World War II. During the war, when it was necessary in Britain to keep children in schools for more hours during the day and days in the week, informal teaching became not just popular but essential. In 1967 the so-called Plowden Committee called attention to this approach and urged its adoption in the primary schools. As might be surmised from the labels "informal" and "open," the classroom atmosphere is casual; students are working simultaneously in small, groups or individually and on different material; students are integrated across grades; and different subjects are integrated.

Charles Silberman explains that informal education is less an approach or method than a set of shared attitudes and convictions about the nature of childhood, learning, and schooling. Teachers in informal schools begin with the notion of childhood as something to be cherished and are concerned with the quality of a child's school experience in its own right, not merely as preparation for later schooling or for later life. There is, in addition, the conviction that learning is likely to be more effective if it grows out of what interests the learner, rather than what interests the teacher. However, Silberman hastens to add that what chiefly distinguishes the

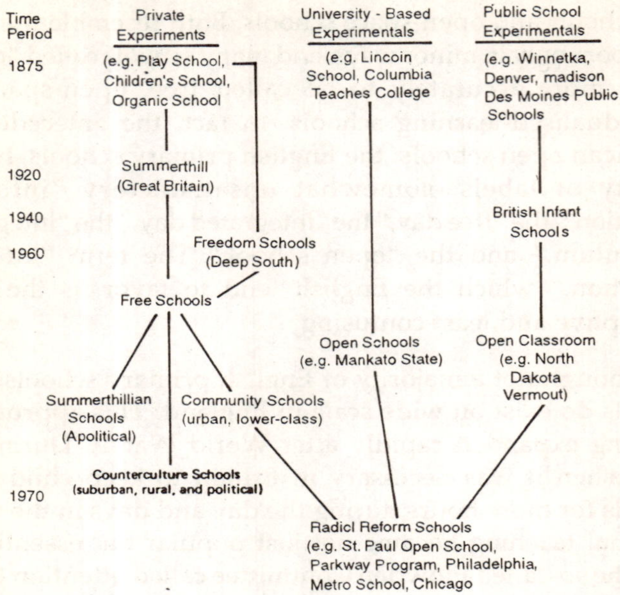

Figure 5.1. The Development of Experimental and Alternative Schools

contemporary English informal schools from the American child-centered progressive schools of the 1920s and 1930s, as well as the education advocated by romantic critics like John Holt, George Dennison, and Herbert Kohl, is the clear understanding of and insistence on the teacher's central role. Teachers are more than just sympathetic, intelligent, even creative adults in the classroom who permit children to discover what they may. As Silberman puts it, they are there to teach. The concept of British informal learning appears to have been introduced to Americans by Joseph Featherstone through a three-part series on the English schools in *The New Republic* in August and September, 1967. Since then Featherstone and a few other writers and educators such as David Hawkins, Vito Perrone, Roland Barth, Vincent Rogers, and Silberman have articulated the theory and practice of the informal classroom concept of Americans.

Although open or informal primary education developed in a very practical, intuitive manner in the classrooms of many teachers, the concept is supported by a substantial body of theory on the way children learn, the nature of knowledge, and the aims of education. The theoretical foundations for this concept can be found in the work of Jean. J. Rousseau, Friedrich Froebel, Maria Montessori, and Susan Isaacs, but most importantly in Jean Piaget's research on the mental development of children and John Dewey's philosophic treatment of instruction and learning. Both Piaget and Dewey hold that it is crucial for the child to act on his or her world. Actively manipulating, creating, and re-inventing, according to both Piaget and Dewey, are imperative to the child's understanding. It is not sufficient to tell developing children, nor even to demonstrate to them; genuine understanding occurs in the act of doing. According to Piaget, children proceed through stages of development in learning, with each stage reflecting a higher level of abstraction; but each child will develop in a particular learning area at the individual's own rate. In turn the child must work on a learning task at his or her own speed. Teachers must first decide what learning is important to the growth of a child, then arrange the classroom in such a way as to permit each child to learn at an individual's own pace and in his or her own way. Dewey's insight was that if intellectual growth is to take place, the teacher must take objects (and later ideas) from the material or external surroundings and bring them together with the experiences and interests of the child's (internal) world. Both Piaget and Dewey stressed that not only does that individual child act on material things, but each child does so with other children in a communicative or group fashion. This is important not only for social development, but also for intellectual development.

Although the idea of open classroom or school has been embraced largely by people from the liberal, in some cases radical progressive, tradition in education, the concept itself is essentially pedagogical and apolitical. As described, its practice is anchored in the substructure of educational psychology and philosophy. Unlike many free schools, political and ideological matters are at most tangential. Also, in contrast to the fashionable American open-space school, architecture is irrelevant. Open, informal classrooms have been created with equal effectiveness in new structures, ancient schools, church basements, and warehouses; in classrooms, auditoriums and corridors.

Many open-school spokesmen do argue from the stance of "alternatives to," or "replacements of" the traditional school, rather than "option along a pedagogical continuum" popular in the mid 1970s. Because it is rooted in sound teaching and learning theory, they ask, "why should informal education be merely one of many options?" The theoretical and empirical evidence supporting other kinds of schools, they argue, is far less substantive. However, there are political obstacles to wholesale implementation of major reform ideas. Permitting public choice among competing options is more acceptable, but not necessarily more responsible.

Figure 5.1 also illustrates a historical relationship among experimental or alternative schools and open, informal schools. The informal schools in this country are descendants of early public school experimentals, many of which emerged during the progressive era, roughly extending from the 1910s to the early 1940s. Notable examples of progressive public school systems include Quincy, Massachusetts, under Francis W. Parker in the 1870s, Winnetka, Illinois, schools under Carleton Washburne in the 1920s, Bronxville, New York, under Willard Beatty, and Shaker Heights, Ohio, under Arthur K. Loomis during the 1930s. A major catalyst to public school experimentals was the historic Eight-Year Study (1932-40), conducted by the Commission on the Relation of School and College of the Progressive Education Association (PEA). As a result of this experiment, progressive informal programs and classroom approaches were developed in Denver, Colorado,

Madison, Wisconsin. Des Moines, lowa, Grand Rapids, Michigan, and several other communities. With only slight differences, the aims, theory and practices of the earlier American Progressive experimentals and the informal schools in England (and America, notably in North Dakota and Vermont) are the same. The writing and work of John Dewey are the strongest links that bind the two forms. Although often misinterpreted and misconstrued, Dewey's teachings provided the basis for the early progressive schools.

After World War II, the mood of the nation was different. There was considerable disenchantment with progressive education (the PEA withered and died during the late forties), encouraged in no small part by the so-called Life Adjustment Movement, which in principal had little in common with progressivism. The public and many educators called for a return to the basics of learning and scholarship. While the dominant mood was a concern for "essentials," the progressive ideal merely lay as if it were dormant ready to surface at the proper time.

In some respects a reformulation and resuscitation of progressivism can be detected, paradoxically, in aspects of the essentialist reforms as early as the late 1950s. As manifested in the "new math," "new physics," "new social studies," and so on, the new curriculum movement, expecially as articulated by Jerome Bruner, has been labelled (often by its critics) as neoprogressivism. As Lawrence Cremin remarked, there are "patent continuities" between Dewey's *How We Think* (1910) and Bruner's *Process of Education* (1960). But there are important differences in the approach to instruction between these two groups—the early progressives and the more recent curricular reformers. One major difference stems from the false dichotomy (of which Dewey warned) of assuming either a child-centered or subject centered, school. While the progressive reformers erred in the one direction, the curriculum reforms of the 1950s and 60s opted for the other, subject-centered, side of the dichotomy. Whereas the early progressives needed much more to realise the delicate balance between subject matter and the child's needs, the reformers ignored the lessons to be learned from earlier attempts at curriculum reform.

By the late 1960s, progressive education—in the form of informal open classrooms—was reemerging. Not surprisingly, about a decade later, the pendulum had swung back to a preoccupation with the basic, essentialist curriculum. While the emphasis in education over time has shifted back and forth, the overall drift has been progressive. Even the traditional contemporary school has assumed a number of informal characteristics—small-group work, individual projects, activity periods, abundant materials, artifacts, animals, and other realia.

Today there are entire schools build on the informal concept of learning, as well as classrooms within schools. The approach has been more successful and extensive in elementary schools, but there also has been development at the secondary level. Other alternatives have sprung up, largely during the 1970s, some mainly elementary, some secondary, and a number across all grades. Alternatives such as the vocational-technical schools, are being revitalised, having existed for a better part of this century. Montessori schools, another alternative, have become increasingly popular after a long tradition of nearly a hundred years.

In one respect, a couple of alternatives—private "prep" schools and parochial (mostly Catholic) schools—have always been available to some families. More recent are street academies, dropout centers, and pregnancy-maternity centers, magnet schools, learning centers and educational parks, bilingual schools, and ethnic schools, in addition to free schools, open schools, community schools, and schools for individualised learning. Together these schools form a rather unsystematic panorama of alternative offering today.

A NEW CONCEPT OF ALTERNATIVE SCHOOLS EMERGES

Contrary to our traditional political and economic values, Americans have not been provided with diversity and choice in the selection of public schooling. In effect, the public has been offered one alternative, the standard traditional school. This school is bureaucratically organised, the classrooms are teacher dominated, and the curriculum emphasizes "essential" subject matter.

Several schemes for providing choice have been developed. All offer a range of alternatives with the intent of making schools more responsive and accountable to parents and students. Present channels for effecting change in public schools are very time-consuming and expensive. The political mechanism for making schools responsive operates through distant school boards and labyrinthian administrations. As such the process is cumbersome and largely ineffective. For those few people who have the time, energy, and know-how to battle organisations, some gains are made. A very few other bypass the obstacles by selecting private-school alternatives. The majority of families "pays their money and takes their chances" with the only school available. The alternative schemes are basically political, economic, and pedagogical in nature.

Diversity and Choice Through Decentralisation: A Political Proposal

Decentralisation of community control is most appropriate for urban settings, where turgid, monolithic bureaucracies operate the schools. This plan places control of neighborhood schools with the local citizens, who have the power to form their own school boards. Those neighborhood school boards in turn can effect important policies and decisions concerning school organisation, staff, and curriculum. While many cities have discussed plans for decentralisation and community control, New York City initiated several experimental local-control areas in 1968. The most publicised was the Ocean Hill-Brownsville community. Much controversy still surrounds the wisdom of community control within a large city, in part because of political struggles that have resulted.

With regard to alternatives, decentralisation is not intended to foster a range of alternative schools. Its purpose is to create a smaller, more responsive school system covering a relatively homogeneous population (for example, black, Mexican-American, Puerto Rican, lower-class white, middle-class white, or other ethnic groups) in a much larger heterogeneous city or school district. As in the present traditional system, children still attend their neighborhood school. But it is reasoned that this school is the proper "choice" for a child, because the children of the community share common educational and cultural needs, and the school is operated by adults in the community who are attuned to these needs.

The idea of vouchers for schooling dates at least to the economist Adam Smith's recommendation in the eighteenth century that public monies be given to private families to pay for educational needs. Smith, laissez-faire in economic matters, is often credited as being the father of capitalism. It is no surprise, then, that like Adam Smith many contemporary classical economists, notably Milton Friedman of the University of Chicago, enthusiastically support proposals to reduce, even eliminate government control in financial education. When it comes to support for educational vouchers, conservatives are joined by many liberal educators, including Christopher Jencks, James Coleman, and Theodore Sizer. Vouchers have a wide appeal in educational circles because they afford people the purchasing power (in the case of most liberal proposals, *equal* purchasing power) to select the school, and therefore the kind of education they desire. In addition, voucher plans allow schools to free themselves from the restrictions of their traditional monopolistic position; that is, a school is able to establish goals and programs of its choosing, within the framework of basic requirements applicable to all schools.

A voucher system operates in the following way: Educational vouchers worth the average per-pupil expenditure for the district are issued to all families with school-age children. The families, upon selecting a school for each child, give the voucher to the school. Schools then exchange the vouchers for money with which to operate their programs. This exchange is carried out by a designated *Educational Vouchers Agency* (EVA), which also regulates the plan. Conservative advocates of vouchers, such as Friedman, would have the EVA's impose few if any restriction on the participating schools and parents. Liberal supporters, including Jencks, carefully build in provisions to insure equality of purchasing power and to prevent discriminatory selection of students.

Several objections are raised to voucher plans. For one, opponents argue that the more affluent families would supplement the vouchers in acquiring a "better" education; on the contrary, a poor child, even with a voucher, still could not afford a suburban-type education. Second, opponents reason that ethnically, racially, religiously segregated schools would be encouraged. Third, they believed that private business persuasion and "hucksterism" would prevail, preying on parents and children who don't have an informative consumer's report on education. Finally, they argue that since vouchers are available to private schools, including those affiliated with churches, they would violate the First Amendment's prohibition against the "establishment of religion."

The Center for the Study of Public Policy at Harvard University, directed by Christopher Jencks, proposed an educational voucher system (for elementary education) designed to circumvent the above objections. The Center's plan calls for the establishment of an Educational Vouchers Agency (EVA) as described above. The EVA would issue vouchers to every family in a district with children of elementary school age. The vouchers issued families of "below-average" incomes would be compensatory, worth as much as twice the basic voucher. To become an "approved voucher school," a school would have to (1) accept each voucher as full payment for a child's education, charging no additional tuition, (2) accept any applicant so long as there was a vacant place, (3) in case of a surplus of applicants, fill at least half of its places randomly and the other half so as not to discriminate against minorities, (4) provide information on facilities and programs to the EVA and families, (5) maintain accounts of money received and disbursed, in a form intelligible to parents and the EVA, (6) meet existing state requirements for private schools regarding curriculum, staffing, and the like. Every spring each family would submit to the EVA the name of the school it wished to send each child to the following year. A child already enrolled in a voucher school would be guaranteed a place, as would any sibling of that student. So long as a voucher school had space, it would be required to accept any student who listed it as a first choice. Other regulations would prohibit any discrimination against racial minorities. Jencks and Judith Arien admit that the most worrisome objection to a voucher system is an EVA's willingness to vigorously regulate the marketplace so as to prevent any racial and economic discrimination. This objection, they add is one that holds equally for any reform including the existing system.

In 1972, the Office of Economic Opportunity (OEO) funded an experiment in vouchers with the Alum Rock School District in San Jose, California. The Office of Economic Opportunity wanted to study vouchers along the Jencks plan, but given its controversial elements, few schools were willing to participate. Alum Rock was the one exception, but it insisted on specific, less controversial modifications to the OEO proposal. Parents in this pilot project receive vouchers worth $680 for children in elementary school, and $970 for those in seventh and eighth grades. However, only one-third of the school district is involved, or just six schools and about 4,000 students; only public school programs participate; the Alum Rock Board of

Education retains control, although it is advised by an EVA committee (composed of parents); and the plan offers a choice of programs within a school, not among competing schools. In other respects the Alum Rock program retains features of the Jencks-OEO plan. Alum Rock officials have found that close to 40 percent of the parents are selecting non-traditional programs. Note that this means that 60 percent of the students are enrolled in the familiar standard program. The Alum Rock plan is something less than a 'real" voucher plan, but the results to date have been favorable. It is possible that this "consumerism" variant of alternative schools will grow in popularity.

Diversity and Choice Through Public Options: A Pedagogical Proposal

The third mechanism for choice in education today is through "providing for choice among a range of different schools along a pedagogical continuum. These schools take into account the apparent variety of teaching and learning styles. The major spokesman for this concept, Mario Fantini, remarks that one way to consider alternatives is to place them on a continuum according to the amount of freedom or independence afforded a student.

Fantini has designed what he calls an "overlapping continuum model" (illustrated in Table 5.1). At one end the learner decides what shall be learned, with whom, when, where, and how. This *free* school alternative enables each learner to select and use his or her own resources (of which the teacher is only one), whether these are inside or outside the schoolhouse. The free school alternative is most controversial and most difficult to legitimise in the framework of public schooling, an issue discussed earlier in this chapter. At the other end of the continuum, the student has little or no choice of teacher, content, methodology, time, and place. This is the familiar traditional school, or *standard* type, in which the learner is most dependent on the procedures and requirements of the educational institution.

Between these extremes there is a range of possibilities. As Fantini describes, the learners may be free to choose certain content areas (others, such as reading, writing, arithmetic, and physical education, are required of everyone; they may have some freedom in the approach to these areas (e.g., by reading, viewing video tapes, researching, discussing, listening to lectures); they may have some freedom to choose the time and place to learn, devoting extended periods, may be days, to one subject at a particular time; they may have access to resources in the community (including libraries, museums, artists, writers, and television and radio studios). Examples of the *open* categories include open classrooms (or American versions of British infant schools), Montessori schools, and possibly "schools without walls." Open-space schools featuring ungraded continuous progress, modular scheduling, and behavior modification are typical options in the *modified* category.

A number of large-city school districts have been experimenting with some form of alternatives plan at either the elementary level, secondary level, or both. Among these cities are Seattle, Washington, Quincy, Illinois, Rochester, New York, Grand Rapids, Michigan, Minneapolis, Minnesota, Berkeley, California, and Tacoma, Washington. Some were receiving support from the Office of Education while in the development stages. The Minneapolis Public Schools in 1972 initiated the Southeast Alternatives Program in the area around the University of Minnesota. Their plan uses the overlapping continuum as model. Elementary school students in the southeast area can attend any of four types of schools:

1. A *contemporary* school, Tuttle, which offers curriculum innovations but maintains a teacher-directed standard curriculum with a grade-level school organisation.

2. A *continuous progress* school, Pratt, in which each child advances at an individual pace without regard to grade level, and in which instruction is given by teams and based on a deliberately sequenced curriculum in basic skills.
3. An *open* school, Marcy, which offers an informally organised curriculum with children grouped across grade levels in the style of the British infant schools. This program combines the teachers' careful organisation of learning with emphasis on the children's pursuing their own interests.
4. A *free* school, Motley, which extends through the twelfth grade. Students, parents, faculty and volunteers develop courses; off-campus trips, work, and classes are an important part of the program.

A fifth school, Marshall Secondary School, completes the Southeast Alternatives plan. Marshall is a traditional school with an open school-within-a-school available to any of its students. The open program is both graded and ungraded at the junior high level, and graded only for senior high students.

As a result of the Southeast Program, other alternatives have developed in Minneapolis. These, as in other cities, include fundamental schools stressing basic skills and old-fashioned discipline.

The overlapping continuum scheme seems best suited for the elementary schools. Any community with a population as small as 6,000 could offer at least three different school options, and even community with just one elementary school could offer a variety of programs. Systematic development at the secondary level is less advanced but there is no reason why high schools or junior high schools in a city could not specialised in particular pedagogical positions, or why one larger high school could not offer several different learning options. School districts also may choose to develop alternatives with or without regard to grade level, such as the Berkeley plan. The Berkeley Unified School District generated some fourteen options that fall into four categories.

TABLE 5.1

Alternatives on a Freedom-to-Prescription Continuum

Free	*Open*	*Modified*	*Standard*
Learner directed and controlled. Learner has complete freedom to orchestrate his own education. Teacher is one resource.	Learner has considerable freedom to choose from a wide range of content areas considered relevant by teacher, parent, and student. Resource centers in major skill areas made available to learner.	Prescribed content is made more flexible through individualization of instruction; school is ungraded; students learn same thing but at different rates. Using team teaching, teachers plan a differentiated approach to the same content. Teacher and programmed course of study are the major sources of student learning.	Learner adheres to institution requirements uniformly prescribed; what is to be taught — how, when where, and with whom. Teacher is instructor-evaluator. Student passes or fails according to normative standards.
	Opening of school to the community and its resources.		
	Teacher is supportive guider.		
	Noncompetitive environment.		
			Competitive environment.
		Teacher-student planning.	
			School is the major instructional setting.
	No student failures. Curriculum is viewed as social system rather than as course of studies.		
Learner-centered	Teacher-centered	Subject-matter-centered.	Institution-centered.

1. *Multiculture* school, in which children are carefully selected on the basis of diversity of race, socio-economic status, age, and sex.

2. *Community* schools, in which much of the control, organisation, and teaching comes from outside the school (that is, from parents and other adults with useful knowledge and teaching skills), and where a significant portion of the curriculum is conducted in the community (for example in museums, theaters, courts, offices, and local businesses).

3. *Structured skill-training* schools which are primarily in the classroom, under the guidance of a single teacher (or a team) with emphasis on learning basic skills—reading, writing, and mathematics.

4. *Schools without walls,* in which students carry out many of their studies in the resources of the city, the school being just one resource. Professionals in many skill areas are used on the job and in the schoolhouses to teach (directly and indirectly), using their know-how and experiences. A principal goal of these schools is for students to grow in self-understanding and self-esteem while developing socially and intellectually.

There are many other examples of public school alternatives, in an increasing number of communities, that take the form of either classroom alternatives, schools-within-schools, or separate alternative schools.

Mario Fantini warns that the greatest danger facing alternatives is that they will become fads like many other reform ideas. If problems are to be minimised, Fantini recommends the following ground rules: do not superimpose, rather leave as a matter of choice for all participants, teachers included; do not publicise as a replacement to the existing schools; do not practice exclusivity, racial, economic or religious; do not make exaggerated claims of accomplishments that may be deceptive in the long run; aim at a broad set of common educational objectives, spanning cognitive and affective areas, including basic skills, talent development, and self-concept development; and do not ask for more than your share of the existing school funds. Some of the developed alternatives plans have enjoyed the support of the Office of Education, such as Minneapolis Public Schools, but it can be done without extra money—though free advice from the established programs is very helpful.

In the final analysis the case for alternatives reduces to the argument that schools can increase their capacity to individualise students' programs. A student's learning style and educational needs can be matched with the methods and goals of a particular school. In the process, parents and pupils, as well as teachers, are permitted to select the learning environment that they judge best suits them. Ultimately, the privilege and also the responsibility of selection rests with the client. Although schools and their personnel are on the hot seat to meet the client's needs or "go out of business," offering alternatives reduces institutional political conflict. If constituents don't like one option they can try another; the schools collectively adapt to the learner, not the reverse.

ALTERNATIVE SCHOOLING IN PERSPECTIVE

Assumptions and Critiques

The alternative schools idea appears to be grounded in a set of assumptions. One assumption of alternative proposals is that the singular, monolithic, traditional school has not served anywhere near all of the students effectively. This assessment is observed in the deteriorating dropout rate and average daily attendance as well as the achievement scores, particularly of low-income groups.

Still, as indicated in annual Gallup surveys, upwards of 60 percent of the American public are satisfied with the existing schools. If anything, the public today wants a more structured, basic school program. According to the polls, discipline remains the number-one problem in schools, and a growing number of people want to see basic skills reemphasised. Yet Fantini argues that this support still leaves unsatisfied a critical mass of up to 40 percent who apparently want and could effectively use alternative options to the traditional school.

A second assumption underlying alternative school proposals is that choice for students and parents is desirable. This usually is argued on the ground that choice of schooling is an individual right. Harry Broudy raises a serious question about this right in regard to education. He argues education is a *public* good and not merely a *private* one. The individual student and family are not the only benefactors of a sound education (or the victims of an inadequate education); society has a stake in the schooling of each youngster. Broudy adds that if the argument is not on the basis of individual right, then it is based on the assertion that the public good can be satisfied by whatever alternative parents choose. In other words, one forms of educational experience is potentially as good as another, or that nothing we do in education makes any difference. This claim, he states, overlooks historical evidence to the contrary.

A third assumption of alternatives is that they promote freedom for parents and children. Generally this freedom is in the form of freedom *from* the control of school authorities and *from* the constraints of the established school structure and curriculum. Broudy argues that some educational constraints cannot be avoided, and in fact are desirable. Contrary to the view that learning should be fun, joyous, and ecstatic, some things one must learn in school, Broudy explains, do not come naturally or easily—namely an understanding o the intellectual resources of a culture. In addition, our cultu imposes certain other demands on the individual as a conditi for coping with it: occupational, civic, and personal adequ The first is needed to earn a living, the second to plan o role in a social order, and the third to live as a fully develop authentic human individual. It is unrealistic and irresponsi

Broudy states, for any school to ignore these constraints. To be sure, some alternative schools do. Yet many advocates of alternatives, including Fantini, insist that all alternatives schools meet a common set of educational objectives, including career development, political socialization, and talent development, as well as basic skills.

A fourth, closely related assumption is that given a choice among competing alternatives, parents, and children can make intelligent selections. But intelligent choice presupposes that they can identify the best or most appropriate instruction. Because of lack of experience, the young student appeals largely to what feels right, which may be a useful guide but no guarantee of an intelligent decision. Many parents also lack the necessary knowledge, interest, and wisdom to make this choice. As a group, teachers and other educators should be more informed than parents with respect both to what is an appropriate education and to how to achieve it in the classroom. That there exist widely different viewpoints within the educational community tends to confuse the public.

When placed in the position of deciding what school to choose, parents often are at a loss and rely on the immediate and transitory interests of young students. Many appear to be asking for more than information about the alternatives; they want the experts to make the decisions.

Sound educative experiences, in John Dewey's terms, are not easily achieved. An educator who is a professional should be able to distinguish between "educative" and "miseducative" experiences. Interest and enjoyability are no guarantee that an experience will be educative. In assessing the potential of a learning experience, a teacher, unlike a parent, always considers (or ought to) whether or not a youngster is prepared to make the most of an experience, and where the experience is leading developmentally. The first consideration requires that educational resources be adapted to the needs and abilities of the learner, the second requires that no matter what stage of learning is involved, the teacher keep an eye on future stages as well as the present. These are simply what Dewey described as the principles of interaction and continuity.

Clarifying the Rationale

Alternative schooling is built on two major premises. The first is that students have different dispositions toward learning and different learning styles. Therefore, they require different learning environments and teaching methods. The second is that the list of competing objectives in education is endless, and really a matter of taste; therefore, options should be available. The first premise has considerable support, but still demands the continued attention of researchers and practitioners. The second is much more suspect. Philip Jackson and others take the position that educators who operate from this belief are retreating behind the relativist, and culturally sanctioned, democratic principle. In doing so they are abdicating their responsibility as educators. Jackson argues that professional educators, teachers, and administrators must keep at the forefront of their thinking the notions that education should be a "purposeful" activity, and should entail "life-enhancing experiences." Such queries take us back to the ideas of Dewey on the nature of educative experiences. Teachers can and must plan such learning into a child's experiences.

There are several central questions in considering the validity of educational alternatives:

Are all learning environments and teaching methods equally useful in providing educative experiences? In other words, if sound education in any school demands in some form, a command of basic reading, writing, and computing skills, as well as problem solving and inquiry skills, will an[y] of a number of different type schools function equally wel[l]

Are educators abandoning their responsibility [by] advocating alternatives?

Are parents and pupils good enough judges of the education that is best for them, or are they equally as good judges as the professionals?

Different types of alternative schools will surely have to compromise on their basic styles to accomplish these objectives. The free-school types probably will have to make special efforts toward skill-building, while the traditional and fundamental schools will have to make appropriate changes to develop problem-solving and inquiry abilities. But educators will not be irresponsible nor parents and students incapable if timely and competent guidance is provided.

ALTERNATIVES TO SCHOOLING: COMPLEMENTARY AND SUPPLEMENTARY INSTITUTIONS

Another concept of alternative education is to use the natural educative capacities of community organisations and institutions—museums, studios, parks, businesses, churches, professional and social organisations. This is the call for "configurations" or an "ecology of education." There is nothing new about this idea. These agencies in the past have played an important part in "informal" education. School until the twentieth century was considered only one environment where learning took place, and a minor one for most youngsters. As the enrollment and time spent in formal education increased, learning became associated with the activities of schools. What took place informally, outside schools, was falsely considered to be quite different, namely work, play, hobbies, amusements.

During the early history of this country, informal or incidental learning was the dominant form of education. For both children and adults, the influence of the informal agencies declined as industrialisation, urbanisation, and automation inexorably replaced the shopkeeper, craftsman, and rural, small town way of life. With the urbanisation and more recently the suburbanization of life, the natural surroundings of the young have become less utilitarian and educative. In an earlier era, adults during their daily living and working were naturally teachers; valuable learning experiences were to be found everywhere, on farms, in homes, in shops, and on the streets of every community. The call to include organisations, professionals, and other working people in the education network is recognition that these agencies potentially play a critical role in education, and that children gradually have been cut off from the natural, incidental learning of life and society around them.

Over time, schools have been asked to assume greater and greater responsibility. Schools have done this with considerable success, considering the difficulty, perhaps impossibility of the total task. Schools may be providing services and educational experiences that never existed in the past, but there exist important experiences that schools cannot provide, or only provide artificially. The schoolhouse is but one of numerous educational agencies in a community.

The new direction in the alternatives movement is a systematic attempt to return some of education to a variety of informal agents, both organisations and people. In this context, Richard Saxe defines alternatives as planned experiences designed as activities to accomplish one or another objective of the curriculum and which do not take place within the regular classroom. Investigating the functions of a local bank, writing a paper at a nearby newspaper office or publishing house, examining chemical processes at a paper mill, brewery, or other factory, surveying community problems, and studying the history of a city through the architecture of its buildings and homes are all alternaitves to the routine classroom lectures, discussions, and homework. The strength of these activities is that they bring learning into a natural and perhaps more efficient setting. In effect, subject matter is related to practical affairs; that is, theory and practice are merged, and within and specific subject matter various areas of study (such as economics, politics, and architecture) are integrated. Subjects are not a secondary matter, rather, the notion is to start with reality and view it through the spectacles of disciplined study.

When possible, Saxe comments, the best agent should be employed for an educational experience. Still, according to this point of view, alternative educational agencies are a supplement and a complement to the schools, not a replacement. "Schools without walls," such as Philadelphia's Parkway Program and Chicago's Metro School, as well as many community schools, are examples of alternative schools operating in this framework. Education in the community with workers as teachers, and with organisations as schools, is a growing dimension of the alternative movement. In another sense, we need to design into our educational systems the facilities that Ivan Illich and Everett Reimer call learning networks. These are homes, meeting places, workshops, clubs, and so on, where people of all ages can systematically gather to learn how to build houses or repair automobiles or discuss literary works or make philosophic inquiries.

Alternative programs are not confined to urban areas and other communities. The wilderness programs, conducted by enterprises such as Outward Bound, are a growing complement to community alternatives. Outward Bound programs exist in many regions, some associated with public or private schools and some with independent agencies. The programs associated with school systems include summer sessions, semester seminars, minicourses, or just weekend outings. The wilderness settings in turn include mountains, rivers, lakes, woods and forest areas, and even oceans, where a variety of skills, including mountaineering, hiking, rafting, and camping are learned. Outward Bound, however, does not exist as merely a diversion from in-school activities; it has specific cognitive, affective, and psychomotor aims. For biology, botany, geology, ecology, sociology, and many other subjects, much potential academic study is available, and in an integrated, interrelated fashion. Time spent intensively living and working together provides a forum for interpersonal growth. Finally, the athletic and other physical skills of existing in a wilderness setting are legion. The threads that connect mental, emotional, and physical learning and that interrelate academic areas (seemingly disparate dimensions of life and study in a school-oriented society) are the valuable lessons to be gained from the outdoors.

CASE STUDY: ALTERNATIVE SCHOOLS

The school administrators for the community in which you teach submitted a plan for the development of several alternative schools. The board of education recently approved the plan which will go into effect this coming year. The plan calls for several different elementary schools, including two traditional schools, two continuous progress schools (open space), an open school, a Montessori school, and a free school. The free school will be K-12; all others will be K-6. The school district is small enough to allow parents and students anywhere in the district to choose any one of the schools. Transportation will be provided students who live farther than one mile from the school they wish to attend.

The parents and students of the community also will be offered a choice of three junior high schools: a standard school with traditional course offerings; an open-space school based in large part on student contracts and programmed learning; an open/informal school with combined teacher-student decision-making in the curriculum. Junior high and senior high students wanting a free school environment can attend the K-12 free school in the district.

The single high school in the community has four wings, which now in effect will become four-schools-in-one-school with a different curriculum for each wing. Students may select any one of these four curricula. One wing or school will be the traditional comprehensive school emphasizing basic skills in both academic and vocational studies; a second will be traditional, but with a heavy academic or college prep orientation; a third will be largely vocational, with the minimum required general education courses and a heavy emphasis on work study courses; the last school within-the-school with be an informal program made of an array of academic courses (e.g., history, literature), special interest courses (pottery, black studies, wilderness ecology), and vocational courses (welding, typing, mechanics), in the form of either regular semester or mini-courses.

The school administration is offering the teachers of the community a choice as to which school they prefer. A major effort will be made to insure a proper mix of teacher with school; it is guaranteed that no teacher in the system will be placed in a school that is incompatible with his or her teaching philosophy and methods. Considering the school level at which you teach, elementary, junior or senior high, which would you choose? Why would this be the best setting for you? Why do you consider this school a desirable option of the district's alternative plan? What problems might occur in implementing the overall plan? How would you and other faculty members handle the problems with respect to your school?

THOUGHT QUESTIONS

1. Peter Schrag, in the opening quote of the chapter, remarks that, "Wealthy children and middle-class parents have some options about schools, but lower-class children have none." What options exist for the middle-class youngster? Should we concentrate on providing more options for lower-class students, or on developing programs for all youngsters?

2. Fantini describes four options along the freedom-to-prescription continuum. Which describes the classroom in which you are working? Which type of classroom do you hope to conduct, and why?

3. A number of advocates of the "open classroom" argue that this concept has the most solid empirical learning base,

and should be the learning environment of most, if not all, students. What support is there for this position and what objections?

4. Considering that the free school is a politically oriented, counterculture concept, does it have a legitimate position among public school options? Consider carefully arguments on all sides on this question and support a decision?

5. Assessments of the experiments on educational vouchers are just now becoming available. What does the evidence to date suggests about the success, the strengths, and the weaknesses of the idea? Should the voucher plans be modified to more closely fit the liberal proposals of Christopher Jencks and others or the conservative proposals of Milton Friedman, or should the idea be scuttled?

6. Are parents and pupils the best judges of an appropriate education? Are educators abdicating their professional responsibility if they leave the decision of what school students should attend to the family?

7. Harry Broudy questions whether or not alternatives really promote-freedom for the public. What is the distinction between "freedom from" controls or constraints, and "freedom to" behave in an intelligent fashion? Of the legitimate constraints demanded as a condition of living in a society, are there any that all schools must be held accountable for? Would you add to or subtract from Broudy's list?

8. Given the increased concern for basic skills education, can this objective be achieved in all types of alternatives? Explain. Are the other educational objectives Mario Fantini outlines (career development, political socialization, talent development, and critical thinking) being met in schools today? Are they as important as basic skills?

9. Discuss the strong points of a community-based education program. Should the school remain as the primary

place of learning in such a program, or should it merely be one of many relatively equal learning centers in the community?

10. How are outdoor, wilderness experiences justified as an integral part of a public education program? How can they augment the academic education of a student, the total education of a student?

PRACTICAL ACTIVITIES

1. Visit an alternative school (a) free, community or open school). Write a description of the physical structure curriculum, and administrative organisation, as well as treatment of students; teacher roles, and teaching methods. Comment on how the school compares with the one you are working in, or with those with which you are familiar.

2. Visit an open-space school in your area. Discuss the physical structure, curriculum, administrative organisation, treatment of students, teacher roles, and teaching methods. If possible, do so by comparing and contrasting this school with a traditional school and other alternative schools.

3. Assume you are teaching in a high schools. Set up a plan for a school-within-a-school in your building. Consider the number of students and teachers, faculty teaching fields, faculty organisation, courses offered, space needed, and grading system.

4. Design a comprehensive alternative schools plan for the district in which you will be teaching. Use either the elementary, middle, junior high, or senior high school level to illustrate. What types of schools would you include? Describe them briefly. How would student and teachers be selected for the different schools? Which school would you want to teach in? Why?

5. Design an educational system for your community in which the school is but one center of learning. What businesses

clubs, organisations, and public facilities could be tapped? How would these agencies fit in? What businessmen, enterpreneurs, craftsmen, and other professionals would you enlist as teachers?

6. Take the subject you will be teaching (if you are an elementary teacher, select one subject area) and outline a curriculum, learning resources, and room arrangement for "opening" or informalising your classroom. Explain your rationale for this arrangement. (For example, how does it help students to learn and you to teach?)

7. Participate in an outdoor or wilderness program offered at your college, or in the community. Of what value was the program to you? What place should such experiences have in the public schools?

8. Design a wilderness program for your school. What would the setting for the experience be? How long would the program be and how many students would participate? Write five on six major objectives (knowledge, attitude, and skill) for the program.

6

School Reform

Focusing Questions

What are the characteristics of effective schools?

What does research say about the school improvement and reform process?

What types of instructional approaches can improve achievement?

What proposals are being made to reform high schools?

How can schools cooperate with other institutions?

What is the role of magnet and alternative schools?

Are nonpublic schools more effective than public schools?

How can rural schools be made more effective?

Should the United States emulate Japan?

There has always been considerable variation in instructional patterns and effectiveness among the many thousands of elementary and secondary schools in the United States. Research in the 1970s and 1980s has now enabled educators to identify unusually effective schools and to describe some of the characteristics associated with their success. In addition, many potential reforms and improvements are currently being proposed to increase the effectiveness of U.S. schools. The purpose of this chapter is to summarise some of the major developments and issues involving the improvement of instruction in elementary and secondary schools. We will examine findings about the nature of effective schools, the school reform process, promising approaches for improving instruction, and a number of other important themes frequently discussed under the heading of school effectiveness.

CHARACTERISTICS OF EFFECTIVE SCHOOLS

The push for greater school effectiveness has become a national growth industry in the 1980s, generating hundreds of research studies as well as thousands of discussion papers and school- and district-level improvement plans. This section describes some of the most important findings from this vast flood of materials.

EFFECTIVE TEACHING

One conclusion supported by recent research on effective schools is that teachers in these schools made use of effective instructional practices. Studies that focus on this idea are referred to as *effective teaching* or *effective instruction* research. This section summarises what this research has to say about classroom management, effective instruction, and grouping of students.

Classroom Management. Research on classroom management indicates that effective teachers utilise a variety of techniques to develop productive discipline and to motivate students. Effective teachers do the following:

Successful Classroom Management Techniques

1. They make sure that students know what the teacher will not tolerate.
2. They make certain that students know what to do if they need help or if they complete assignments early.
3. They follow through with reminders and rewards to enforce the rules.

4. They provide a smooth transition between activities.
5. They give students assignments of sufficient variety to maintain interest.
6. The monitor the class for signs of confusion or inattention.
7. They use variations in eye contact, voice, movement, and academic activities to focus attention during lessons.
8. They do not respond to discipline problems emotionally.
9. They arrange the physical environment to complement their instructional objectives and methods.

Effective classroom management relies on a systematic strategy that starts with advanced preparation and planning before the school term and is reinforced throughout the year.

Delivery of Instruction

Effective Instruction. During the past decade, research has identified what appear to be the most important considerations in delivering instruction effectively in elementary and secondary schools, particularly with reference to improvement of students' comprehension skills. Some of the considerations emphasised in recent research are as follows:

1. Effective teachers provide an overview of what is to be learned.
2. Readiness activities emphasise the linking of new information to prior knowledge and the preteaching of difficult vocabulary.
3. Emphasis is placed on examples and applications of concepts, principles, and vocabulary terms.
4. Explanations are provided of examples utilised in instruction.
5. Teachers monitor students' comprehension.

6. Learning cues, including cautions concerning probable errors, are provided.
7. Strategies for vocabulary learning and/or metacognitive learning (understanding and monitoring one's own learning) are taught.
8. Students engage first in guided practice and then in independent practice.
9. Stress is placed on continuous feedback to correct learning errors and provide positive reinforcement.

Homogeneous vs. Heterogeneous Grouping

Grouping of Students. Research on grouping of students for effective instruction is complex and controversial. As we noted in Chapter 11. Research indicates that homogeneous grouping by ability—a common strategy in the past—has failed to improve the performance of low achievers. On the other hand, heterogeneous grouping generally has not been successful unless it has utilised effective individualized and small-group methods that allow students to proceed at their own pace (continuous-progress instruction). Unfortunately, individualized, continuous-progress instruction has seldom succeeded, because it requires an enormous amount of planning, effort, and instructional resources to be effective. When teachers have neither adequate assistance nor resources for providing students with continuous individual guidance, students tend to spend a good deal of time in unproductive seatwork.

A comprehensive discussion of the problems involved in grouping students for more effective instruction is beyond the scope of this text. However, the most important considerations can be summarised as follows:

Key Considerations

1. Homogeneous grouping of low achievers can be successful if adequate steps are taken to eliminate low expectations, stigmatisation (students' feelings

that they can't learn because they are in a "dummy" class), and related problems.

2. The number of low-achieving students must be kept small enough for the teacher to instruct them effectively.
3. Either homogeneous or heterogeneous grouping can be effective, provided there are appropriate arrangements for scheduling of students, preparation of teachers, provision of supplies, and related matters.

ELEMENTARY EDUCATION

Most of the recent research on effective schools has focused on elementary education. Authors of various studies generally have identified specific characteristics of effective elementary schools and have usually defined effectiveness at least partly in terms of outstanding student achievement.

Edmonds's Research

Studies of School Effectiveness. One of the best-known studies is that of Ronald Edmonds and his colleagues, who define an effective school as one in which workings-class students score as high as middle-class students on basic skills tests. Based on analysis of such schools, Edmonds identified an effective school as one in which there is (1) strong leadership, (2) an orderly, humane climate, (3) frequent monitoring of student progress, (4) high expectations and requirements for all students, and (5) focus on teaching important skills to all students.

Other observers and groups frequently extend this type of list to include one or more additional characteristics. A good example is the analysis utilised by the Connecticut School Effectiveness Project, which describes an effective school as having the following characteristics:

Characteristics of Effective Elementary Schools

1. A *safe* and *orderly environment* that is not oppressive and is conducive to teaching and learning.
2. A *clear school mission* through which the staff shares a commitment to instructional goals, priorities, assessment procedures, and accountability
3. *Instructional leadership* by a principal who understands and applies the characteristics of instructional effectiveness
4. A climate of *high expectations* in which the staff demonstrates that all students can attain mastery of basic skills.
5. High *time on task* brought about when a high percentage of students' time is spent "engaged" in planned activities to master basic skills.
6. Frequent *monitoring of student progress* using the results to improve individual performance and also improve the instructional program.
7. Positive *home-school relations* in which parents support the school's basic mission and play an important part in helping to achieve it.

Instructional and Organisational Arrangements

Additional insight has been provided by a 1982 report by Levine and Stark on instructional and organisational arrangements at high-achieving inner-city schools in Chicago, Los Angeles, and New York. Community District 19 schools, in Brooklyn, New York, introduced a comprehensive reading approach that emphasised the Chicago Mastery Learning Reading Program (CMLRP), which is specifically designed to teach higher-order comprehension skills. After implementing the new reading program, the percentage of students in grade 2-8 reading more than a year below grade level fell from 45 percent in 1979 to 26 percent in 1983. The Los Angeles schools in the study had participated in the Curriculum Alignment

Project, in which the staff attended workshops that helped them coordinate instructional methods and materials with tests on specific skills emphasized in each grade and classroom. When such training is successful, teachers are less likely to rely solely on textbooks regardless of whether they are too simple or too advanced for students; instead, they are more likely to select from texts and other available materials or create new materials that are most appropriate for teaching a specific skill to a particular group of students. Drawing on the CMLRP, Curriculum Alignment training, and similar approaches, the unusually effective schools in this study exemplified the following characteristics:

Alignment of Objectives, Materials and Testing

1. Teaching objectives, materials, and testing were painstakingly aligned with each other. Teachers were selecting and emphasising the most important learning objectives, looking for the best instructional materials to teach them, reducing duplication in instruction across grades, and moving away from page-by-page teaching of the textbook. Thus they were overcoming some of the instructional problems.
2. Substitutes for the "pullout" approach had been introduced to provide compensatory education for low-achieving students. Rather than pulling students out of class for additional instruction that was not coordinated with the regular classroom, arrangements were made to fully coordinate compensatory and regular instruction.
3. Relatively great emphasis was placed on teaching higher-order cognitive skills.
4. Steps had been taken to ensure that appropriate instructional materials were easily and immediately available to teachers.

Minimised Record Keeping

5. Systematic efforts had been made to minimise teachers' record-keeping work.
6. Emphasis was placed on improving the quality of students' homework and on increasing parent involvement in student learning.

Many Additional Characteristics

Several individuals and agencies have gone further in "mining" the research to identify characteristics thought to be present at unusually effective schools. A good example of a thoughtful document of this type is the list of effective practices prepared for the Alaska Effective Schooling Program in cooperation with the Northwest Regional Educational Laboratory. After defining *practices* as "procedures, approaches, and attitudes" that focus the entire school on helping children learn, the authors described 129 specific practices under 33 headings.

Definitions Differ

Evaluation of Effective Schools Research. A number of points should be kept in mind. First, one should recognise that there is widespread confusion concerning the definition of an effective school. Reports and plans are being discussed all over the United States, but there are nearly as many definitions of effective schools as there are people discussing them. Some people have in mind a school with unusually high academic achievement (taking account of social class), but others are thinking about a "self-renewing" school that can identify and solve internal problems, a school that promotes students' personal growth, a school that has shown improvement in academic achievement, or a school that concentrates on developing independent study skills and love for learning. And some people apparently have in mind no specific definition at all when they write or talk about making schools more effective.

Research Emphasises Inner-city Schools

Second, most of the more rigorous studies have been concerned entirely or largely with inner-city schools. Those schools identified as unusually effective in such studies generally have been poverty schools in which academic achievement is higher than that at most other schools with similarly disadvantaged students. It is more difficult to identify unusually effective schools outside the inner city, where high achievement is more common. In addition, the key components of effectiveness outside the inner city may differ somewhat from those at poverty schools.

Little Experimental Research

Third, nearly all the research on effective schools is correlational. That is, researchers have identified characteristics (correlates) of unusually effective schools, but few studies have manipulated a particular variable, such as leadership qualities of the principal or expectations for students, to determine the effect on achievement gains. This failure makes it difficult to be sure that work to improve a given characteristic will make any real difference.

Methodological Problems

Fourth, other methodological problems have left much of the research vulnerable to criticism. For example, schools identified as effective in a given subject (say, reading) during a given year may not be effective on other measures or the next year. In addition, controls for students' social class and family environment frequently are not adequate to attribute high achievement to school characteristics. This can happen, for example, when magnet schools enrolling inner-city students are judged as unusually effective, but further research would show that their students came from highly motivated poverty families dissatisfied with their neighborhood schools.

More Specificity Needed

Fifth, the general level of most characteristics cited in the literature is such that they tend to "beg the question" of what teachers and principals should do in the schools. For example, saying that a school requires good leadership and a productive climate does not provide much direct guidance on how to accomplish these objectives. It is probably necessary to state may characteristics at a general level because more specific recommendations would not fit all schools. Nevertheless, many educators believe that much of the school effectiveness literature is still too vague to offer real assistance in the schools. (On the other hand, it should be recognised that some of the effective school characteristics, such as Levine and Stark's findings on the negative effects of "pullout," have relatively specific, practical implications based on considerable support from research.)

Importance of School-level Emphasis

Consistency throughout the school

Sixth, the emphasis in effective schools research clearly is on school-level or schoolwide practice, rather than on teaching individual classrooms. The research says that teachers in effective schools use effective instructional practices (as described above), but it is the school-level emphasis that makes the movement potentially potent in overcoming the obstacles to improvement (that is, the "regularities" of traditional schooling) described in Chapter 10. The effective schools movement views the school as an institution in which consistent and coordinated change can yield large gains in student performance. For example, one of the frequent problems in schools is that many students—particularly low achievers—are reluctant to engage in difficult learning tasks oriented toward higher-order skills, and many teachers accommodate them by emphasising rote learning, which at least contributes to an orderly environment. This type of situation is unlikely to change significantly unless all or most of the teachers in a school work together to raise expectations and requirements for better performance on meaningful learning dimensions.

SECONDARY EDUCATION

Little Research Available

Few studies have focused on identifying the characteristics of effective secondary schools. One reason for the shortage of research is the small number of inner-city secondary schools that stand out as having high achievement. Hard as it has been to find unusually successful inner-city elementary schools (in terms of academic achievement), finding successful secondary schools has been almost impossible.

Intermediate Schools. In the past few years, a few inner-city secondary schools have demonstrated that their students' achievement can be raised to relatively high levels. After searching to find high-achieving inner-city *intermediate schools* (defined as junior high schools including grades 7, 8 and 9 or middle schools including grades 7 and 8), Levine and his colleagues identified five such schools in four big cities. In addition to finding that these schools had the same general characteristics that researchers had identified for effective elementary schools, the investigators concluded that effective inner-city intermediate schools in their sample strongly emphasised the following commonalities:

Characteristics of Effective Intermediate Schools

1. Organisational arrangements facilitated improved reading performance among low-achieving students.
2. Teachers emphasised achievement of higher-order cognitive skills.
3. Guidance and personal development of students were emphasised.
4. Expectations and requirements for student performance were high throughout the school.

One interesting and important fact about the successful intermediate schools was that each had somewhat different approaches and mixtures of approaches for attaining the goals implicit in the four characteristics described above. Some of the approaches used by these schools included the following:

Arrangements for Low Achievers

1. Effective arrangements for low achievers
   a. Small classes of low achievers taught by highly skilled teachers
   b. More time devoted to reading, language, and math
   c. Individual and small group tutoring
   d. School-within-a-school units for low achievers.

2. Emphasis on higher-order skills
   a. Availability of elective courses emphasising these skills
   b. Instructional materials designed to teach higher-order skills
   c. Improved coordination between electives and regular courses
   d. Instructional strategies designed to develop thinking and comprehension skills.

3. Emphasis on guidance and personal development
   a. Large numbers of counselors and guidance personnel
   b. Elective courses emphasising personal development
   c. Utilisation of community agencies
   d. Group counseling

Institutional Expectations

4. High institutional expectations
   a. Contracts with students and parents
   b. Required summer school for failure in any subject

c. Schoolwide point systems for students
d. Weekly or biweekly report cards

Structural Changes

All five schools made *structural* changes to improve the performance of their students, particularly their low achievers. By *structural change,* we mean major modifications in the school schedule as well as in the way students and teachers are assigned to classes. For example, one of the schools had changed the typical pattern so that classes of low achievers were much smaller than average classes; another had assigned seventh and eighth graders to only two teachers each for English, social studies, science, and math; and several had reduced the time devoted to science and social studies in order to increase the allocation for reading and math. Such changes appear to be prerequisite to school effectiveness at the secondary level.

Conforms with Middle School Philosophy

Most characteristics of effective inner-city intermediate schools probably are important in effective nonurban schools, although the importance of a given characteristic may vary somewhat from one type of school to another. The emphasis on students' higher-order thinking skills and personal development is a standard component of middle school philosophy; from this point of view the successful inner-city schools identified by Levine and his colleagues had not done much more than make major structural changes needed to implement goals frequently recommended by experts on the education of adolescents.

Senior Highs are Complex
Existing Literature is Questionable

Senior High Schools. Unusually effective senior high schools have been even harder to identify than effective intermediate schools. Because the goals and programs of most senior high schools are so diverse and complex, it is difficult to conclude that one school is generally more effective than another, even when the social class of the student body is taken into account. In addition, hardly any senior high schools serving a representative poverty population stand out as being relatively high in achievement. Thus the most frequent definition of effectiveness at the elementary and intermediate levels is not applicable. Several authors have attempted to draw conclusions from descriptions of inner-city senior high schools that they identified as unusually successful. Close examination of their writings, however, generally indicates that these schools either constituted high-dropout environments where only a relatively small and selective group of students advanced beyond the ninth grade or they utilised extremely rigorous discipline policies that led many students to transfer (or drop out) and thus provide a better learning environment for those who remained. The latter strategy may be defensible on several grounds, particularly if a school district establishes small alternative schools for students eliminated from regular high schools. However, schools employing this strategy offer little guidance for identifying the characteristic of senior high schools that successfully serve a comprehensive population with a high proportion of alienated or low-achieving students.

Developments at South Boston High School

One of the few senior high schools for which concrete data indicate unusual effectiveness is South Boston High School. Reform of South Boston occurred over several years during a time of continuing turmoil in the Boston school system, but by 1980 impressive data were available on improvement in the performance of students.

Between 1979 and 1980, for example, average reading scores went from the 16th percentile to the 40th percentile in the ninth grade and from the 18th to the 32nd percentile in the tenth grade. In addition, the percentage of graduates attending postsecondary education institutions increased from less than 8 percent in 1976 to 40 percent in 1980. Changes that appear to have been most important in accounting for these and other improvements at South Boston included the following:

Changes at South Boston

1. A new principal and administrative team made major changes in traditional organisational patterns and insisted that staff re-examine their instructional methods.
2. More than two-thirds of the faculty were replaced by teachers willing to discard ineffective traditional methods.
3. Nearly all ninth and tenth graders were placed in reading and writing courses rather than in traditional English classes.
4. Students were placed in mathematics courses rather than in "business mathematics," which for the most part repeated beginning arithmetic.
5. A number of in-school and out-of-school alternatives were established. These alternatives include a self-contained school-within-a-school that emphasized academic learning and a mini-school that emphasized experiential learning and individualized instruction.
6. Work-study programs based on learning opportunities in the community were made available to many students after the ninth grade.
7. Discipline, including strict attendance and tardiness policies, was very firm but also fair.
8. An effective in-school suspension program was introduced. This approach differs from many in that participating students are fully isolated from the remainder of the school during their period of suspension.
9. Guidance in personal development was emphasised for students in the ninth and tenth grades.
10. School pride and spirit were systematically emphasized.

General Characteristics Supported in Previous Research

Since no two schools share exactly the same problems and possibilities, one cannot say that a successful senior high school should implement the identical changes as were introduced at South Boston. However, some of the South Boston characteristics, such as systematic emphasis on school spirit, firm but fair discipline, and emphasis on development of reading and math skills, have received considerable support in research on effective high school approaches for improving student performance, particularly among low achievers. In addition, South Boston illustrates the importance of structural change.

Examples of Structural Changes

After studying the literature on high schools (both junior and senior) that are trying to improve the performance of low achievers in reading and other subjects, Levine and Sherk identified some of the most viable and promising structural changes.

School-within-a-school

1. *School-within-a-school for low achievers.* Students who can read but are more than two or three years below grade level are assigned to a school-within-school serving 80-120 students and staffed by four or five teachers (English, reading, math, science, and social studies) and a coordinator. If teachers in this type of program are specially selected for their ability and willingness to work with low achievers, participating students can make very large gains in reading and other basic skills. This approach is illustrated in a 1983 booklet by Wehlage.

Grouping by Previous Reading Achievement

2. *Intragrade grouping by previous achievement.* An alternate approach to providing effective reading instruction for low achievers is to group across grade levels for English. Grouping should not involve a large number of levels, in order to avoid potential disadvantages of homogeneous grouping. High

schools in Detroit, Kansas City, and elsewhere are developing promising approaches, which generally involve three levels: (1) nonreaders; (2) poor readers—often the majority of students in the inner city; and (3) students at or above grade level. Nonreaders are taught in very small groups, and a major effort is made to provide appropriate instruction for poor readers.

Dewey High School

3. *A longer and different school day.* Possibilities for changing the school day to facilitate student achievement in various subjects are exemplified by the John Dewey High School in Brooklyn, New York. Dewey appears to have successfully provided effective educational opportunities for its diverse student body through such interrelated changes as a lengthened school day, establishment of independent learning centers in every major subject, and provision of smaller classes and extra assistance for low-achieving students.

Cleveland Heights High School

4. *Achievement centers.* The achievement center is a promising approach under development at Cleveland Heights (Ohio) High School. After specific learning objectives are identified for a given grade and subject area (for example, tenth-grade English), an achievement center is established for both remedial and developmental purposes. A student who does not have skills prerequisite for a particular unit or who needs special assistance in developing his or her full potential will attend the achievement center instead of or in addition to the regular class. Achievement center placement generally replaces the regular class for about two weeks, and close coordination is maintained between achievement center staff and the regular teacher.

Five-school Project

5. *Instructional teams.* The potential value of instructional teams as a basis for secondary school organisation is suggested

in a recent study of five diverse schools. The study attempted to identify and assess approaches for implementing flexible instructional programming, individual goal setting for students, multiple learning options, and other arrangements designed to ensure productive learning. Organisational arrangements included the establishment of instructional and advisory units consisting of four academic teachers and about 120 students.

SOME CONCLUSION ABOUT PROJECTS TO IMPROVE SCHOOL EFFECTIVENESS

Effective Schools Projects are Widespread

Improvement at Milwaukee Elementary Schools

Attempts to improve instruction in elementary and secondary schools, both in the inner city and elsewhere, are being based on effective schools research. For example, educators in Chicago, Detroit, Milwaukee, Memphis, New York, and St. Louis are trying to create successful inner-city schools by introducing the practices identified in previous research. Departments of education in California, Connecticut, Florida, New Jersey, Ohio, and other states are providing services to help low-performing schools become more effective. Among eighteen Milwaukee elementary schools that have been participating in a project to raise achievement in the inner city, the percentage of fifth-grade students reading in the lowest performance category decreased from 55 percent in 1979 to 37 per cent in 1983, and the comparable decline in math was from 42 percent to 21 percent. In the past, successful inner-city elementary schools were "mavericks," whose success was attributed mainly to the efforts of an atypical principal. It now appears to be possible to create such schools through careful planning and implementation of improved arrangements for curriculum and instruction. Further information on the Milwaukee project has been provided by Maureen Larkin, who has analysed differences between the schools that improved a great deal and those that improved least. She described the following characteristics and practices of the high-improvement group.

Articulation of Objectives and Standards

> *The more effective schools had clearly articulated their grade level objectives and minimum standards in each subject area.*
>
> The staff...participated in the development of the grade level objectives and standards and communicated to students and parents that mastery of these objectives was prerequisite for success at the next grade level.

Emphasis on Homework

> *The more effective schools developed a schoolwide homework policy that expected all students to complete daily homework assignments.*
>
> ....The principals and teachers enforced the policy by monitoring the doors at dismissal and sending empty handed students back to their rooms.
>
> *Teachers in these schools planned to teach the entire grade level curriculum content to all of the students.*
>
> Teachers used content coverage schedules to plan on a yearly, weekly, and daily basis.

Other Encouraging Reports

Although hundreds of projects designed to make public schools more effective are underway in the United States, very few have collected the long-term data on student performance needed to determine whether most are likely to be ultimately successful. On the other hand, encouraging preliminary reports are coming in from a number of locations. Initial assessment of the Maryland School Improvement Through Instructional Process Program indicates that two-thirds of the teachers participating in the active teaching component (which incorporates principles of effective teaching) or the mastery learning component believe that the project has improved their performance. Provided that effective schools projects make good utilisation of what is known about the school improvement process, they may well lead to widespread gains in student performance.

THE SCHOOL IMPROVEMENT AND REFORM PROCESS

Promulgating, legislating, and even packaging change is not the same as actually changing. Analysis of past efforts to improve schools has resulted in a much better understanding of the steps that must be taken to ensure that reform efforts have a significant and lasting impact. Among the lessons that can be deduced from past innovative efforts are the following:

Failure to Implement

Improper Implementation

1. *Adaptive problem solving.* Implementation of an innovation frequently either is not carried out successfully (that is, the innovation is never truly implemented) or has little or no effect on students because a host of problems arise to stifle practical application. For example, experts may devise a wonderful new science curriculum for fourth graders and school districts may purchase large quantities of the new curriculum materials, but teachers may choose not to use the materials, may use them improperly because they do not fit the existing curriculum or schedule, or may not know how to use them. Innovations are not likely to be implemented successfully unless the organisation introducing them is *adaptive* in the sense that it can identify and solve day-to-day implementation problems.

2. *School-level Focus.* because the innovating organisation must identify and solve day-to-day problems, the focus in bringing about change must be at the level of the individual school building where many of the problems occur.

Shared Vision

3. *Leadership and shared agreements.* Implementation of a significant innovation requires change in many institutional arrangements, including scheduling of staff and student time, selection and utilisation of instructional methods and materials, development of new behaviors and attitudes on the part of teachers and students, and mechanism for making decisions. The building principal, who is responsible for arrangements throughout the institution, usually is the key person in successfully implementing change. In addition, the faculty must have a "shared culture," or shared vision of the kinds of changes that are possible and necessary to improve their instructional program; otherwise, the staff is unlikely to seriously consider proposals that require significant change in existing behaviors and arrangements.

Some Schools Need Organisational Development

Some sites require much more time and effort to develop shared agreements than do others. At some schools there is considerable agreement that achievement must be improved and that this requires change in many current arrangements; here the problems of change management are largely technical. At other schools, lip-service given to the need for improvement does not denote any real willingness to change existing practices. If this is the case, the first emphasis must be on organisational development designed to help faculty better evaluate what they are doing and make informed decisions on how to improve their program.

4. *Teacher involvement.* Because people who are expected to alter their working patterns will not cooperate fully unless they have a voice in designing and implementing change, teachers who are to use innovative methods and materials in the classroom must have an opportunity to help select and evaluate them.

Tendency toward Equilibrium

5. *Multiple obstacles.* Major changes require not only good deal of time and many resources but also a systematic examination of all their implications and a plan for overcoming the many obstacles that will arise; otherwise they will be swallowed up by forces that tend to maintain stability. As one observer has noted, "Organisations legitimately seek a state of equilibrium in order to sustain themselves.... Schools can tolerate only so much change and still attend to the business of `keeping school,' and planned change programs should be sensitive to that need."

Ownership Important

Insistence on Change

6. *Combination top-down and bottom-up approach.* Because years of research underlined the importance of teacher participation in decisions, researchers in the 1960s and 1970s tended to emphasize a "bottomup" approach in the change process in order to encourage a sense of "ownership" among teachers asked to devot much time and energy to implementing improvements in curriculum and instruction. However, research in the 1980s has tended to underline the importance of "top-down" components in initiating change successfully. Insistence on and support for change by administrators, school board members, and others at the school, district and state levels frequently are required to initiate meaningful action at the classroom level. Two major, independent studies of innovation efforts have concluded that top-down initiation and support of the change process frequently is required to institutionalise long-term improvements. Organisational development specialist Matthew Miles has delineated the stance of top-level administrators who communicate to principals and teachers an understanding that "we are going to try a new approach, you are going to implement it, and we are going to help you." Miles believes that administrative *pressure* and *support* frequently lead teachers to develop *mastery*

of an innovation. Mastery helps develop the *commitment* to implement the change effectively.

Top-down and Bottom-up Mixtures

Of course, the support provided to improve instruction at the school level must be extensive and well-planned, with considerable emphasis on local adaptation and decision making. From this point of view, successful change seems to require a mixture of top-down initiation and bottom-up decision making. This mixture will vary with the situation in particular schools and districts, the nature and stage of the change, and other considerations. For example, large urban districts typically function in a relatively turbulent and difficult environment that requires relatively more initial top-down initiative; implementing a change—such as individualised instruction—that involves fundamental reform of all arrangements throughout a school requires relatively more emphasis on bottom-up adaptation.

Projects Depend on Problem Identification

7. *Data collection.* One particulary important component in carrying out the change process is the collection of data identifying possible deficiencies in a school's arrangements and outputs. Other things being equal, faculty will be more likely to change their behavior and arrangements if data clearly indicate a need for such change. For this reason, leading efforts at organisational improvement generally have emphasised the collection of appropriate data to identify needs and directions for institutional improvement. Many effective school projects utilise questionnaires, interviews, and document analysis to prepare comprehensive school profiles, which attempt to pinpoint problems in a school and specify the issues that need to be addressed in designing change.

Collegial Staff Development

8. *Training of Staff.* Staff development (formerly called in-service education) is a core activity in the school improvement

process. Staff development to support improvement should be centered on the school as the basic unit, *not* on the individual teacher. In the case of an elementary school, the entire staff should participate; in secondary schools, departments may be the appropriate unit for some activities. Staff development should be an interactive process in which teachers and administrators work together at every stage. Collaborative planning develops collegial responsibility for improvement. Staff development generally is most successful when it takes place during the regular school day.

PROMISING INSTRUCTIONAL APPROACHES

Many New Approaches

Many instructional approaches developed during the past decade show great promise for improving the quality of education in elementary and secondary schools. We already have mentioned several such approaches, including bicognitive instruction and the Kamehameha Early Education Program described in Chaper 12. We do not have space to describe or even list all of the instructional approaches that educators are now developing and implementing in elementary and secondary classrooms. Instead, we will illustrate some of these exciting possibilities by describing three evolving instructional approaches that appear to be successful when they are implemented effectively.

STUDENT TEAM LEARNING

Learning Teams

Student Team Learning (STL), along with other forms of cooperative student learning, constitutes one of the most powerful instructional approaches developed in recent years. The STL approach incorporates a set of techniques in which students work in four- to five-member learning teams receive recognition based on the degree to which all team and members have individually mastered a common body of information or skills. The class follows a regular sequence of activities: a period of lecture-discussion; another period of team study, in which team members use worksheets to practice the materials and to assess one another; and a third period in which students are either individually quizzed or compete against members of other teams in an academic game.

Student scores are based on improvement over their own past performance or on their game scores in competition with equals; both of these systems make it possible for all students to do well if they work hard. Team scores are the average of members' individual scores, and the most successful teams are recognised in class newsletters or on bulletin boards. Student Team Learning methods thus constitute a relatively comprehensive program, based on psychological theories of group performance and group rewards, but also containing many separable elements, such as rewards for improvement, a regular schedule of teaching-study-quiz, and public recognition for successful performance.

Positive Research Results

Research on Student Team Learning has shown positive results over a range of student outcomes in such areas as reading, math, science, and social studies. Properly implemented, STL results in significant gains in academic achievement as well as improvement in attitudes toward school, self-concept, and other noncognitive objectives of cooperative learning. Research indicates that low achievers can benefit academically from team learning and that cooperation in the classroom may "fit" the learning style of many minority students. In addition, team learning can contribute to positive interracial attitudes while avoiding the disadvantages of homogeneous grouping.

Team Assisted Individualisation

Robert Slavin and other developers of STL have been preparing and testing a modified version called Team Assisted

Individualisation (TAI), which combines the advantages of team learning, mastery learning (described on next page), and individualised instruction. Early research on TAI in teaching mathematics in grades three through six indicates that it can bring about large gains in student achievement and student attitudes.

TEACHER EXPECTATIONS AND STUDENT ACHIEVEMENT

Another promising and increasingly popular approach for improving teaching and learning, particulary among low-achieving students, is Teacher Expectations and Student Achievement (TESA) training, which was developed under the auspices of the Los Angeles Country Superintendent of Schools.

Improved Interaction Needed

Extensive research has shown that teacher interaction with students perceived as low achievers is less motivating and less supportive than interaction with students perceived as high achievers. In addition, high achievers get more opportunities—and more time—to respond to questions. When high achievers do have difficulty, teachers tend to give clues or rephrase the question more frequently than they do for low achievers. Training in TESA is designed to help teachers overcome this type of classroom pattern. It consists initially of five workshops scheduled about one month apart, emphasizing fifteen important teaching skills, such as equitable distribution of instructional time, individual help for students, higher-order questioning, and acceptance of appropriate student responses.

Teachers Help Each Other

Following each workshop, participants observe each other four times. While being observed, teachers consciously attempt to practice the interactions addressed in the workshop with all students. The observation data are provided to the teacher, who can utilise them to re-examine his or her teaching practices. TESA thus reflects research indicating that staff development is most effective when it allows teachers to observe and assist one another in real classroom settings. Workshops in the TESA approach are offered regularly as part of school improvement projects in many school districts.

MASTERY LEARNING

Steps in Mastery Learning

The major steps of the instructional sequence used in mastery learning are (1) to *define* a specific objective, (2) to *teach* the skill or understanding in the objective, (3) to administer a criterion-referenced *test* to assess mastery of the objective, (4) to *provide corrective instruction* for students who have not mastered the objective and enrichment, acceleration, or other alternatives for those who demonstrated mastery, and (5) to *re-test* the group that needed additional work. Benjamin Bloom and his colleagues have emphasised whole-group instruction during the first teaching component. Some other advocates and developers have emphasised small group and individualised teaching.

Mastery-type Learning

Many approaches other than mastery learning (as defined above) emphasize mastery teaching and testing of specific learning objectives. Such approaches, which are almost synonymous with curriculum alignment (coordinating objectives, methods, materials, and testing) can be viewed as mastery-type learning. They are often referred to as outcomes-based education. As described earlier in this chapter, curriculum alignment, and outcomes-based emphasis, and mastery learning are characterisitc of effective schools.

Very Large Achievement Gains

Research on mastery learning (as defined by Bloom)

indicates that it can be a very powerful force in improving student achievement, particularly among low achievers. Mastery learning can bring about achievement gains, in many subjects and at many grade levels, comparable to the 2 standard deviation gains attainable through tutoring students as individuals or in very small groups. This means that mastery learning can raise the student now at the 50th percentile to the 90th percentile or above, and the low achiever now at the 10th or 15th percentile can improve to the 50th percentile or above. Mastery learning itself can give gains of 1 standard deviation. Gains of 2 standard deviations are possible when mastery learning is combined with enhancement of students' entry skills on concepts prerequisite to the instruction, emphasis on appropriate cues and feedback-reinforcement and on students' active participation, and/or work with parents to improve the home learning environment. Bloom concludes, moreover, that these gains can be attained for higher mental-process skills, not just low-level mechanical learning.

School and District Gains

Bloom's research has been conducted mostly with individual classes using teacher-made tests, but recent research indicates that comparable results can be attained using standardised tests in entire schools and school districts. Jones and Spady have exmined mastery learning in Johnson City, New York; Red Bank, New Jersey; and several other school districts. According to their findings, enormous gains in academic achievement are being registered when mastery learning is implemented effectively. Jones and Spady agree with Bloom's conclusion that effective implementation depends on paying adequate attention to students' entry skills (in other words, it is imperative to teach prerequisite skills if necessary), careful scope and sequencing of objectives and instruction, and utilisation of some of the principles of effective instruction (for example, clarifying major goals, reinforcing correct responses, encouraging student participation). Mastery learning implemented on a shcoolwide or districtwide basis, they further conclude, yields gains when combined with emphasis on quality of instruction that approach the 2 standard deviation level obtainable from tutoring.

Pitfalls in Mastery Learning

Like direct instruction, however, mastery learning seems to be particularly susceptible to ineffective implementation caused by overemphasis on narrow, low-order skills that are relatively easy to teach and test. Teachers implementing mastery learning frequently bog down in keeping records of student performance on a multitude of separate skills. Perhaps because mastery learning is so susceptible to these and other pitfalls, it sometimes fails to bring about substantial gains in student achievement. Like any other instructional approach, it will not be successful if it ignores findings on the school improvement process discussed elsewhere in this chapter.

Combined Approaches

It is important to emphasise that the instructional approaches described above are not mutually exclusive. They all tend to draw on a larger knowledge base that delineates characteristics of effective instruction, and they generally can be combined with each other or with related approaches to constitute a larger program of instructional improvement. Thus for example, STL can be incorporated as a learning approach in mastery learning, and the teacher-student interactions emphasised in TESA can inform the implementation of mastery learning or STL Indeed, many schools are emphazing several approaches in their school effectiveness improvement projects.

Visions of Future Achievement Gains

Given the very large gains in student achievement, particularly among low achievers, that have been registered in some schools implementing recently developed instructional approaches, it now is possible to conceive of a national pattern in which nearly all students are high achievers. Most students.

can achieve at a level currently attained by only the top 15 or 20 percent. Of course, being able to conceive of such a pattern does not mean it is going to happen, and most observers would say that such a prediction is unrealistic. To a significant extent, substantial improvment in our schools will depend on the degree to which change efforts reflect what is known about the school improvement process.

HIGH SCHOOL REFORM PROPOSALS

In addition to the proposals for high school improvement in the national reports discussed in previous chapters, proposals for comprehensive reform of high schools have been offered by several prominent educators. Two of the most highly publicised proposals for reform of this kind have been offered by Ernest Boyer and by Theodore Sizer.

BOYER'S HIGH SCHOOL

High School, written by Ernest Boyer, is a report prepared for the Carnegie Foundation for the Advancement of Teaching. Published in 1983, *High School* is based in part on a three-year study in which twenty-five educators collected data at fifteen diverse senior high schools. Eighteen pages of proposals for improvement and reform are offered with reference to twelve major themes:

Twelve Themes Emphasized

1. Goals must be stated more clearly, focusing on mastery of language, a core of common learning preparation for work and further education, and community service.
2. Emphasis on language development should stress writing, speaking and listening.
3. The core curriculum should expand from about half the units required for graduation (as at present) to about two-thirds.

4. More should be done to help students make the transition to work and further education.
5. Students should participate and learn in the community.
6. Working conditions of teachers must be improved.
7. Improvements must be made in teaching methods and materials.
8. Technology should be used to enrich curriculum.
9. More flexibility is needed in school size, the use of time, and other organisational arrangements.
10. Principals should have a greater leadership role that includes selecting and rewarding teachers.
11. More "connections" are needed with other institutions.
12. There must be a public commitment to excellence.

Smaller Load for Teachers

Among Boyer's most important recommendations were those dealing with teachers' working conditions. These recommendations included proposals that high school teachers should have a daily load of only four regular classes and one small seminar, should have an hour a day for class preparation, and should be exempt from monitoring halls, lunchrooms, and recreation areas.

SIZER'S HORACE'S COMPROMISE

Horace's Compromise. The Dilemma of the American High School, based partly on Theodore Sizer's visits to eighty high schools, is the first of three reports in a study sponsored by the National Association of secondary school Principals and the National Association of Independent Schools. In this book, a teacher named Horace must choose between "covering" the prescribed curriculum and in-depth teaching of important concepts and understandings.

Similarity to Adler's Paideia Proposals

Unproductive Tacit Understanding

Somewhat similar to Mortimer Adler's Paideia proposal discussed in Chapter 6, Sizer's book recommends that high schools concentrate on using didactic instruction, coaching, and Socratic instruction to devleop knowledge, skills and understandings, respectively. The curriculum should be divided into four major areas: inquiry and expression; mathematics and science; literature and the arts; and philosophy and history. Sizer advocates a system of mastery learning in all subjects. He also emphasized more active learning, and reduced emphasis on "coverage" and on what he views as mindless approaches to minimal competency testing. He particulary wants to eliminate the tacit understanding between students who say "I will be orderly ... if you don't push me very hard" and teachers who respond "You play along with my minimal requirements and I will keep them minimal."

Teams of Teachers and Students

Perhaps the greatest virtue of Sizer's proposals is that they explicitly recognise the difficulties of high school teaching. He states flatly that special arrangements such as a school-within-a-school should be provided for high school students who cannot read, write, or do math, and he also emphasizes structural changes that will be needed to improve students' higher-order cognitive skills. Regarding the latter objective, he has pointed out that teachers cannot provide appropriate coaching in skill development for 150 to 180 students a day; accordingly, he advocates that teams of seven or eight teachers should work with groups of about 100 students in teaching the four curriculum areas specified above. At a minimum, he says, high school teachers should have no more than 80 students a day. Sizer would make these teacher-pupil ratios possible by eliminating the separate functions of teachers now assigned to counseling, the arts, physical education, and other specialised areas. Regarding the change process, he implicitly criticises many of the 1983 national reports.

Contrast with National Reports

The proposals by Boyer and Sizer pay much more attention to the realities of schooling and research on the school change process than do the national reports cited in Chaper 13. Focusing change effort on the building level is one of their central themes, as is the difficulty of improving education when teachers are overburdened with too many students. Thus these proposals are, from some points of view, much more "radical" than those of the national reports. As one might hve expected, the bulk of reform activity taking place nationally seems to center on relativley "easy" changes involving such national report recommendations as increasing graduation requirements and modifying teacher certification regulations. It will be interesting to see whether future reform efforts proposals for fundamental change such as those offered by Boyer and Sizer.

OTHER THEMES INVOLVING SCHOOL EFFECTIVENESS

Practically everyone who wants to change education says that the reason is to make schools more "effective." We do not have space (or the inclination) to describe all the themes that are under discussion nationally as art of the effort to improve the effectiveness of the schools. The most important such themes that have not been adequately described elsewhere in this book will be discussed briefly in the following pages.

COOPERATION WITH OTHER INSTITUTIONS

Many schools and school districts are attempting to improve the quality of education in elementary and secondary schools by cooperating with other institutions, particularly business and industry. Some of the most promising efforts along these lines include the following:

Adopt-a-school Programs

"Partnership" or "adopt-a-school" programs in which

a business, a church, a university, or some other community institution works closely with an individual school in providing assistance such as tutors or lecturers, funds or equipment for vocational studies, computer education, or other subjects, help in curriculum development, and provision of community learning opportunities.

Boston Compact

Cooperation in preparing young people for productive lives in a modern society. One of the best current examples is in Boston, where a "compact" has been made through which the schools are trying to improve basic skills and attendance of secondary students, and business are providing part-time jobs for students and full-time employment opportunities after graduation.

Joint conduct of activities such as health education, drug education, and counseling of high school students.

Joint conduct of school improvement projects in which the emphasis is on helping faculty utilise research to improve curriculum and instruction.

Coordination with Community Institutions

In addition to providing specific assistance to the schools, community institutions in many locations are coordinating their efforts with the schools so as to improve the delivery of educational services and reduce duplication and waste in expenditure of government money. Mario Fantini has argued forcefully that the schools may have taken on so many responsibilities (such as development of athletes, vaccination of children, and driver education) that their attempts to improve academic achievement are frequently diffuse and half-hearted. Fantini concluded that much progress in instruction might be made by reassigning nonacademic responsibilities to other agencies. For example, education in the use of modern technology might best be provided by conducting classes at leading businesses, and driver education might be shifted to insurance companies.

Not Many Large Pay-offs Yet

Teachers College Dean Michael Timpane has reviewed recent increases in support of and cooperation with the schools. He has called it a "rediscovery" of the public schools by business. One 1983-84 survey of public school-private sector interaction in twenty-two big cities identified many examples of productive cooperation, including cases where businesses had helped obtain millions of dollars of additional funding for education. The author tentatively concluded, however, that large "pay-offs" are "much rarer than the mythology that sustains prospectors." More needs to be done to coordinate school efforts with those of other institutions.

MAGNET AND ALTERNATIVE SCHOOLS

Growth of Magnet Schools

Another major effort to improve and reform the public schools has involved the establishment of magnet and alternative schools. *Magnet schools* attract enrollment on a voluntary basis by offering special instructional programs or curricula designed to appeal to students in more than one neighborhood attendance area. Most magnet schools attract students by providing either a special field of study (for example foreign languages, preparation in a career field such as health care) or a distinctive approach to instruction (for example, either "open" education or "traditional" education). Some magnet schools, such as the Bronx High School of Science of New York City, have existed for many years. Such schools usually were not referred to as magnets until the 1970s, when many big-city districts established magnet schools to increase voluntary desegregation. Rather than serving only an academic elite, magnet schools today generally are designed to provide students of all ability levels with an opportunity to participate in a specialised or alternative instructional program not available in their local schools. This approach has been a major thrust of activity in many cities. For example, since 1977 Milwaukee has established magnet schools in visual and performing arts applied technology; marketing and business; college preparation; finance and commerce; communications and media; health sciences; and other areas.

Recent Decline in Funding

Growth of magnet schools was greatly accelerated by passge of the 1976 amendment to the Emergency School Aid Act (ESAA) providing for the funding of desegregated magnet schools. By 1980, hundreds of school districts had established one or more magnet schools. However, support for establishment of magnet schools declined considerably in the 1980s when the amount of federal money targeted for voluntary desegregation was drastically reduced.

Many Types of Alternative Schools

Alternative schools provide alternatives to learning opportunities available in the average public school. From this point of view magnet schools are a type of alternative school. So, too, are many parochial and other nonpublic schools; schools for special-needs students, such as the physically handicapped or the emotionally disturbed; institutions such as street academies, storefront schools, high school "outposts" designed to make education more relevant for inner-city students; and schools without walls, which draw heavilty on community resources for learning.

Characteristics of Alternative Schools

A national survey of alternative schools has indicated that, compared with more traditional schools, they tend to have the following characteristics: enrollment of students who have not succeeded in traditional schools or want a different kind of education, greater individualisation, more independent study, more openness to the outside community, small size, high staff morale, high attendance, satisfied students, freedom from external control, and high concern for noncognitive goals of education.

Alternative Schools Provide Choice

Advocates of the alternative school movement point out that generally only one model of education is available to parents in any given public school neighborhood. Some advocates argue for creating alternative schools within the system; others argue for greater alternatives outside the system, contending that the only true alternatives *are* outside the system. Inside *or* outside the existing establishment, alternatives would permit parents and students to choose the school that best suits them.

Criticism of Alternative Schools

Arguments against altarnative center on the fact that there is little empirical evidence that alternative schools make a difference in achievement and other goals. Moreover, many of these alternative schools have the reputation of de-emphasising cognitive skills while focusing mainly on affective education. Critics also worry that the proliferation of alternatives outside the sytem may increase divisiveness and polarization, including the encouragement of privte all-white or all-black schools. Proliferation of alternatives within the public system, on the other hand, may "drain off" the most motivated students from "regular" schools and divert attention of parents and educators from the task of improving the system as a whole.

EFFECTIVENESS OF NONPUBLIC SCHOOLS

The question of whether nonpublic schools are more effective than public schools in bringing about high academic achievement and accomplishing other goals has emerged as an important issue in education. As we mentioned in Chapter

8, proposals have been made to provide families with vouchers and tax credits to support attendance at nonpublic schools, and some movement is occurring in these directions. To some extent, the desirability of such proposals as public policy hinges on the argument that nonpublic schools tend to be more effective than public schools.

Study by Coleman

Coleman Study Conclusions

Debate regarding the effetiveness of nonpublic schools has been spurred by publication of an important study by James Coleman and his colleagues comparing nonpublic and public schools. Among the major conclusions of this study were the following: (1) when family background factors are taken account of, students in nonpublic schools have higher achievement than students in public schools; (2) nonpublic schools provide a safer and more orderly environment; (3) except for Catholic schools, nonpublic schools are smaller, have smaller class size, and encourage more student participation that do public schools; (4) nonpublic schools require more homework and have better attendance; and (5) superiority in school climate and discipline (for example homework, attendance) account for the higher achievement of nonpublic students.

Criticism of Coleman Conclusions

Most of the subsequent analysis and scrutiny of this study's conclusions have been critical of the authors' major findings. Other researchers have concluded that taking better account of family background variables eliminates the achievement superiority of nonpublic students, that taking account of achievement level upon entry to high school also eliminates the achievement difference between public and nonpublic students, and that higher scores of students in nonpublic schools are associated primarily with relatively high proportions of enrollment in college-track programs.

Coleman Defense

Coleman and his colleagues have defended the study's methods and conclusions. In particular, they have argued that nonpublic schools enhance achievement by placing a relatively high percentage of students in college-bound programs. Since public and nonpublic schools differ greatly on this factor, and since it is difficult to isolate student motivation differences even after one has taken account of family background and social class, researchers will probably continue to argue over the relative effectiveness of public and nonpublic schools.

Meanwhile, several researchers have published other studies concluding that nonpublic schools are superior in effectiveness. For example, Andrew Greeley analysed data on Catholic schools and reached essentially the same conclusions as did Coleman, moreover, a recent in-depth study of Catholic schools concluded that their rigorous academic core curriculum has been beneficial to their students, regardless of background. Issues involving the effectiveness of nonpublic versus public schools, and policy implications drawn from research on these issues, are likely to remain important.

RURAL EDUCATION

Little Research and Attention

The particular problems of rural schools have received little attention during the past fifty years. This neglect has recently been rectified to some extent by a small group of scholars who have been trying to determine what should be done to provide high quality education in a rural setting.

Thoughtful analysis in thirteen rural communities has helped clarify the characteristics and problems of rural schools as well as innovations that might make rural schools more effective. Paul Nachtigal and his colleagues who carried out the study reached a number of conclusions.

1. Typical rural schools are closely linked and interdependent with their communities.
2. The critical elements for rural school improvement are very much community dependent in terms of both what is done and how it is carried out. For this reason, staff development arrangements that are effective in urban areas tend not to work well in rural areas.

Rural Schools Diverse

3. Because there is tremendous diversity in rural America, school improvement efforts also should be diverse.
4. Improvement efforts in rural areas should emphasise helping local school and community persons define and redefine their particular problems.

Advantages of Smallness

5. The small scale of rural schools offers potential advantages. Teachers can know students personally and individualise instruction, teachers and principals can work closely with community groups, and schools can draw on community resources to improve learning.
6. Technology such as television and microcomputers can improve instruction in rural schools.

Reassessing Benefits of Consolidation

Other authors have also attempted to determine how to make rural schools more effective. One analysis of appropriate training for persons who hope to teach in rural areas indicated that such training should prepare teachers in a larger number of content areas for a broader age range of students than to conventional programs. Other eductors have analysed ways in which rural schools can assist in community development or redevelopment. In general educators are carefully reassessing the desirability of consolidating schools to gain efficiency versus the advantages that can be present for teachers and students in very small schools.

SHOULD THE UNITED STATES EMULATE JAPAN?

As Japan's economy has challenged the United States in both international and domestic markets, eductors as well as lay leaders have begun to assess the role of Japanese education in that nation's economic gains. They wonder whether the United States should emulate some aspects of the Japanese educational system

Japanese Students High in Achievement

That the Japanese system has many admirable outcomes is supported by several sources of data. The International Studies of Educational Achievement mentioned that Japanese students score consistently high across subject areas, particularly science and math. One study of mathematics achievement concluded that U.S. students fall further behind the Japanese for every year in school; by fifth grade, the lowest Japanese classes score higher than the highest U.S. classes. Preliminary analysis of international data has also indicated that Japanese students have half as many absences for reasons other than illness as U.S. students and that the typical Japanese student spends much more time on homework than the typical American student. Only about 1 percent of the Japanese population is functionally illiterate, even though Japanese is much harder to read and write than English.

Problems in Japanese Education

On the other hand, Japanese students feel less control over their future, are less likely to feel they are worthy persons, and are less likely to plan for and enroll in college than are U.S. students. In addition, violence and suicide have become serious problems among Japanese adolescents who are unable to meet high standards in the classroom. Many Japanese educators believe that their system overemphasizes rote learning and multiple-choice examinations to such an extent that it stifles creativity and higher-order learning.

Drawing on the work of several scholars, John Cogan has identified the following major features of the Japanese system of education:

Characteristics of Japanese Education

1. Public interest in and support for education are high.
2. Schools have demanding requirements and standards, but they also emphasise art, music, and physical education to develop the "whole person."
3. Students spend about 240 days per year in school, as compared to 180 days in the United States.
4. Teachers have public respect and professional security.
5. Children are taught to be responsible for their schools and for one another.
6. Schools have orderly climates.
7. Parents and teachers emphasise the importance of education for long range success.

Hard to Transplant

Cogan thus points out that the Japanese educational system has many strengths, but he also concludes that rigid emphasis on national examinations distorts the curriculum toward low-order skills, generates violence and widespread alienation among adolescents, and fundamentally constitutes an enormous selection-and-sorting process that disenfranchises a high percentage of children and youth. Some educators and lay leaders in the United States have singled out Japan's longer school year, rigorous examination standards, and high level of classroom discipline. They have argued for similar goals in U.S. schools. Cogan agrees that we may be able to adopt some of these policies, but he points out that it is dangerous to take practices that are thought to work in one culture and transplant them to another. He concludes that "Americans would be wise to fully investigate the nature of education in Japan before jumping on a 'let's go Japanese' band wagon."

Improvement Efforts Elsewhere

It should be noted that some other industrial countries also seem to be making great strides in some aspects of elementary and secondary education. For example, Germany has long had outstanding arrangements for vocational education through a school-business apprenticeship system, France and Venezuela are initiating national efforts to encourage the intellectual development of preschool children, and England is attempting to modify its national examination system to stimulate mastery learning in the schools. It is important that U.S. educators learn more about such efforts and adopt those international practices that can improve our own system of education.

Summing Up

1. Research indicates that schools that are unusually effective in improving student achievement have initiated effective instructional practices. They exemplify other characteristics on a schoolwide basis—among them outstanding leadership, high expectations for students, focus on important learning skills, and an orderly, humane climate. Research also has identified somewhat more specific characteristics such as alignment between teaching and testing, emphasis on higher-order skills, and high time on task.
2. Effective secondary schools possess the characteristics identified as being important in research on elementary schools, but they also have

introduced fundamental structural changes, particularly as regards more successful delivery of instruction for low-achieving students.

3. It now seems possible to create effective schools, provided one recognises and utilises what has been learned about the school improvement and reform process.
4. Student Team Learning (STL), Teacher Expectations and Student Achievement (TESA) training, mastery learning, and other recently developed approaches for improving instruction, when successfully impemented, can bring about very large gains in student achievement.
5. Greater cooperation with other institutions and establishment of magnet and other altenative schools may help to improve the éffectiveness of our educational system.
6. Some recent research indicates that nonpublic schools are more effective than public schools, but many researchers question the validity of this conclusion.
7. The United States can learn much from educational developments in Japan and other nations, but caution should be exercised in borrowing from other societies.

Discussion Questions

1. How can schools and school districts become more effective than they are now? What kinds of resources are needed to make this possble?
2. How do instructional innovations such as mastery learning, TESA, and STL address problems of school effectiveness? Which effective school characteristics do they focus on?
3. What does the research say about the relative effectiveness of public and nonpublic schools?

4. Why should educators be somewhat cautious in reading and interpreting the effective schools research? What mistakes are most likely to be made in interpreting this research?
5. What might be done to raise the average student to the 90th percentile or above in academic achievement? Do you think this is likely to happen at many schools? Why or why not?

Suggested Readings

Brookover, Wilbur, et al. *Creating Effective Schools.* Holmes Beach, Fla.: Learning Publications, 1982.

Chapters are devoted to improvement of school climate, high expectations for learning, and other aspects of effective schools.

Dianda, Marcella R. *The Superintendents' Can-Do Guide to School Improvement.* Washington, D.C.: Council for Educational Development and Research, 1984.

Step-by-step analysis and description of what can be done to make schools more effective.

Fullan, Michael. *The Meaning of Educational Change.* New York: Teachers College Press, Columbia University, 1982.

Combines excellent analysis of both the theoretical basis and the practical implications of research on the school change process.

Goodlad, John I. *A Place Called School.* New York: McGraw-Hill, 1984.

A thoughtful analysis of the problems and possibilities for reform in elementary and secondary schools, beginning with a chapter entitled "Can We Have Effective Schools?" and concluding with two excellent chapters, "Improving the Schools We Have" and "Beyond the Schools We Have."

Joyce, Bruce R., Richard H. Hersh, and Michael McKibbin. *The Structure of School Improvement.* New York: Longman, 1983.

Detailed analysis and recommendations regarding possibilities for improving education in accordance with recent research on effective schools and the school improvement process.

Nachtigal, Paul M. *Rural Education*. Boulder, Colo.: Westview, 1982.

Thoughtful analysis of the special problems of rural education and promising avenues for possible improvement.

7

Futures

> Society will be transformed from the "primary" or agricultural level to the "secondary" or industrial level to the "tertiary" level—that of a "learning society."

As a species, humankind is unique in several respects, one of which is the ability to transport itself mentally from present to past to future. To understand fully oneself and one's world, requires that perspectives from the past and future both converge on the present. Conjectures of the future are partly factual and partly imaginative, a combination of extrapolation and intuition.

Education also is influenced by concepts of time—as in the use of instructional and learning objectives, the administrative emphasis on planning and policy studies, the tradition of relying on "olders" to be the teachers of "youngers," and the custom of grouping students by age for instruction. Most of all, education is cumulative and antientropic; it is cumulative both in the residue retained by the individual and in the collective value to society of diversely educated individuals; it is antientropic in that the knowledge created in the process is an energy source (actual and metaphorical) equal to if not greater than the energy expended to create it.

Knowledge seekers are time travelers, in the sense that learning is a process, a "continuous reconstruction of experience," to use John Dewey's phrase. Learning is an integration of past experience with one's present condition, together with the potential for future applications. For the teachers of children and adolescents, the future is the broad realm in which their clients will spend 80 or 90 percent of their lives. The students of the young teacher in the late 1970s will probably experience more than half of the twenty-first century.

The twenty-first century will require a crucial attitude for the survivors aboard Earth: to view the human condition from a global perspective. More and more, one's immediate, local needs and concerns are inextricably entwined with those of other human beings in any other places on the planet. The energy crisis can be viewed as a practice round for other immanent cases of global confrontation, all signaling the advent of the era of global interdependence.

A Framework of the Future

If we wish to enter the twenty-first century in advance of its arrival, we not only need to acquire a global orientation, but we need a framework and some tools for probing the future. Further, since our special interest is the future of education, and since education is but one societal institution, we need to look to both national and global futures for clues about education's future. Finally, because biological and technological inventions and discoveries tend to affect all social institutions, we need to see what effects and applications these have in education.

As a framework for approaching the future, we use as a model a three-sided pyramid or tetrahedron (Figure 7.1). The base of the pyramid represents the infrastructure of the future—current and emerging values and attitudes that form the consciousness base for the present and the future. The visible side on the left represents current and emerging state of knowledge, including technology. The visible side on the right represents current and projected problems, crises, and those fears which tend to incapacitate or immobilize. Then there is the invisible side of the pyramid, hidden by the exigencies of the present and the placid appeal of a once-secure past. This unseen side is the future, partly known and determined by emergent aspects of the base and two visible sides, and partly at the mercy of our intuition and caprice, but still amenable to human intervention, to plans, and to self-fulfilling and self-defeating prophecies.

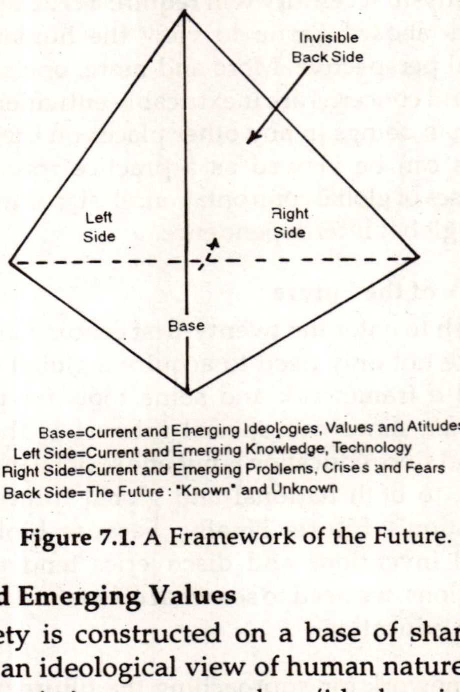

Figure 7.1. A Framework of the Future.

Current and Emerging Values

A society is constructed on a base of shared common values and an ideological view of human nature and human society. All societies possess a values/ideology infrastructure, which is in a state of relative stability and flux. By this is meant that a society's values/ideology base is constantly evolving, the pace varying from nearly stable to revolutionary change. When the pace is rapid, one observes (1) a set of dominant values on which the present society is based, and (2) a different set of emergent values among which are those values upon which the future society will be built. Thus, in the United States today, there are present a set of traditional, dominant values *and* a set of emergent, future values. Of course, any society of the future—national or global in nature—will reflect a synthesis of both traditional and emergent values, and not a total substitution of emergent values for traditional ones. Even cataclysmic social upheavals, such as those which occurred in Russia (1917) and China (1949), do not eliminate completely the values that prevailed prior to the revolutions. The general principle is that since values are broad cultural-meaning patterns, they are relatively stable. Even at the threshold of the 1980s, in the United States and in Western nations in general, even in the midst of rapid technological change and knowledge growth, the values/ideology base of a culture, a society, a nation remains relatively stable.

"The unity of a culture consists in the fact that all valuations are mutually shared in some degree." In the United States today, in the face of new, emerging values, and despite the rhetoric of "cultural pluralism," a cement of shared values binds individuals and groups to the common-wealth, to the national society.

In his classic study, *An American Dilemma,* Gunnar Myrdal called this body of mutually shared values an "American Creed." What this creed is comprised of, however, is difficult to determine. Myrdal only alludes to the tenets of the "creed," without ever attempting a formal analysis. For him, the "creed" embodies a group of ideals: "the essential dignity of the individual human being.... the fundamental equality of all men,.... certain inalienable rights to freedom, justice, and a fair opportunity"; a concept of democracy elucidated in the Declaration of Independence, the Preamble of the Constitution, the Constitution, and the Bill of Rights; Woodrow Wilson's fourteen points and Franklin Roosevelt's four freedoms; "a humanistic liberalism developing out of the epoch of Enlightenment"; the perfectibility of man, reliance on the will of the majority, the use of several processes by which the consent of the governed is obtained. All of these rested upon the foundations of rationality, science as method, and democracy—the American trinity. Myrdal asserted that "the main norms of the American Creed as usually pronounced are centered in the belief in equality and in the rights to liberty."

American society derived the "creed," in Myrdal's judgment, from at least three sources: (1) the eighteenth-century philosophy of the Enlightenment, (2) the Judeo-Christian tradition and moral code, and (3) the principles embedded in English law. The Enlightenment provided the concepts of perfectibility, rationality, science as method, and democratic nationalism. From the Judeo-Christian tradition, especially from European Protestantism, came the ideas of individualism, bourgeois capitalism, and freedom or free will. Finally, English law yielded political democracy, the "principles of justice, equity, and equality before the law," and the "concept of a government 'of laws and not of men.'"

We have generated our own list of traditional value orientations which seem to us to undergird American society:

1. Values of the Puritan/Protestant Ethic
   a. Self-denial and endurance of distress
   b. deferred gratification
   c. sex taboos or sexual constraints
   d. thrift
   e. striving to achieve/hard work yields success
   f. punctuality
   g. self-control
   h. "survival of the fittest" (the elect of God)
   i. volunteerism and charity

2. Values of Capitalism
   a. unlimited demands (wants) with limited supply leads to scarcity
   b. competitiveness
   c. profit motive

d. contrive demand or "invention is the mother of necessity"
e. social class distinctions based primarily on wealth
f. materialism, acquisitiveness, and conspicuous consumption
g. meritocratic hiring and promotion
h. desire for upward socio-economic mobility and fear of downward mobility
i. protection of private property ownership rights

3. Values of Democracy
   a. enhancement of human dignity
   b. rational consent of the governed
   c. majority rule
   d. constitutional guarantees of individual and minority rights and of "due process"
   e. freedom or liberty or independence
   f. equality and equity
   g. conjoint living

4. Values of American Nationalism
   a. patriotic loyalty
   b. parochialism and exlusionary attitudes
   c. territoriality and desire for hegemony
   d. preference for monolingualism (English)
   e. friendship, paternalism, arrogance, or animosity toward other nations.

5. Values of Western Philosophy
   a. rationalism
   b. empiricism
   c. scientism
   d. dualistic analysis
   e. humanism
   f. reductionism and quantification

Since the 1960s, many observers of American society have noticed value shifts occurring among adolescents and young adults. Such shifts may presage a new, emerging value base for the total society. One could view these challenges and alternatives to traditional values as the first, tentative, experimental manifestations of an emergent ethic. This gradual movement from traditional to emergent values seems to have the following general directional flows:

From	*To*
self-denial, endurance of distress, and deferred gratification sexual taboos and constraints	pursuit of immediate pleasures or hedonism sexual permissiveness and openness
self-control; striving to achieve, or hard work yields success	self-actualization and self-expressiveness; acceptance and expression of feelings; self-realization
"survival of the fittest"	"survival of the wisest"; the individual's survival is entwined with species, global survival
progress equated with growth; promotion of increased consumption and number of consumers	limits to growth; search for ecological balances; stress on qualitative, rather than quantitative aspects of progress
competitiveness; a win-lose, either-or attitude materialism, acquisitiveness, and conspicuous consumption	cooperation; conflict resolution and reduction; win-win attitude focus on essentials; greater desire for quality and durability of goods
social class distinctions based primarily on wealth	greater concern for equality and equity; class distinctions based on multiple criteria (de-emphasis on accumulated wealth) which will tend to blur class lines
preoccupation with private property ownership rights	increasing pressures to insure basic human rights—nationally and globally; greater concern for

	"the commons' which are shared collectively (e.g., water, parks, air, neighborhoods)
government by isolated elected officials in state and national capitals	government by association, involvement, and participation of the entire citizenry; increased interest-groups pressures
nationalism; exclusive national sovereignties as loci of loyalties; independence of nation-states	world order models; transnational economic groupings as bases for regional political groupings (e.g., European Common Market); regional and world federalisms; interdependence of nations
freedom or liberty or independence: individualism	mutuality of concern: cooperative processes; greater attention to interpersonal relations and quality of conjoint living
rationalism, empiricism, scientism, dualistic analysis, reductionism, and quantification	renewed reliance on faith and feeling; practice of meditative modes; global humanism; blending of Taoist and Buddhist world views with those of Judeo-Christian tradition: abandoning the search for value-free knowledge; greater trust in all human ways of knowing

Pointing to three obsolescent premises upon which the industrial-state era is based (as contrasted with pre- and postindustrial eras), O.W. Markley suggests that the coming post-industrial society era will require a new "image of mankind." The outworn premises are (1) "that human progress is synonymous with economic growth and increasing consumption," (2) "that mankind is separate from nature, and that it is the human destiny to conquer nature," and (3) "that economic efficiency and scientific reductionism are the most trustworthy approaches to fulfillment of the goals of humanity."

For Markley, "an adequate image of mankind for the postindustrial future" would possess six conditions:

> (1) an *ecological ethic,* emphasising the total community of life-in-nature and the oneness of the human race, (2) a *self-realization ethic....* (3) be *multi-leveled, multi-faceted,* and *integrative,* suiting various culture and personality types, (4) [provide for the] *balancing and coordination of satisfactions* along many dimensions rather than.... along one narrowly defined dimension such as the economic, (5) convey a *holistic* sense of perspective...., [and] (6) be *experimental, open-minded,* and *evolutionary.*

Lester Brown believes that "the sixties witnessed a quickening of the social conscience of people" over such issues as war (particularly Vietnam), racism, sexism, overpopulation, poverty, and hunger—issues calling for empathy and political action. This social concern led to the formation of new values, especially among the young of all nations, and as a result "a new ethic may be emerging."

For Brown, this "new ethic encompasses a new naturalism [emphasizing] harmony with nature....," a recognition of "the finiteness of our biosphere...., a new childbearing ethic" in response to threats to our "very life-support systems...., [and] one designed to eventually stabilize population..., a much greater emphasis on distribution and sharing" of the world's material wealth and technology, the attitude that "I am my brother's keeper" in order "to eliminate territorial discrimination" as well as "religious, racial, and sexual discriminations...., [a broadening of] the social scope of decision making.... [by being] much more cooperative, acting in terms consistent with the collective welfare....," and the expansion of loyalties "to include all mankind."

Dorothy Skeel's study "How Do Children Rank Their Values?" revealed that "sixth grade children in varying geographic areas and sub-cultural groups across the United States do not have difficulty in deciding what values are most important to them. Nor do they show any apparent misunderstanding in the meanings of those values." The composite rankings for all subjects in the study appear in Table 7.1. "Terminal" values and "instrumental" values were defined in this study as: *terminal*— 'preferred end states of existence that people strive for"; *instrumental*—"preferred modes of behavior."

What was also significant in the Skeel study "is the low correlation between what teachers value and what children in all geographic areas and subcultural groups value. Is this low correlation a result of the age difference, the fact that the adults have thought through their values or had them challenged, or are values changing?"

Current and Emerging Knowledge

For over two million years our human ancestors have been learning, and, more significantly, accumulating knowledge for the use of each successive generation. Moreover, *Homo sapiens* has employed an ever-widening range of ways of knowing, of methods of creating relatively reliable knowledge. In our search for knowledge, we stand on the shoulders of those who have preceded us. And this will also be true for those who succeed us.

This is not to say that all paradigms and models of knowledge and all ways of knowing are already known. Knowledge growth occurs *both* by evolutionary development and by revolutionary "leaps," "shifts," discoveries, or inventions.

What we as a species know at any point in time cannot be known or comprehended by any one human being or computer. Our collective knowledge is stored in a variety of respositories: books and other visual media, libraries, cultural technologies (e.g., a factory or a corporation), specialists in academic

TABLE 7.1

Rankings of Terminal and Instrumental Values for All Children's Groups (N=312)

Rank	*Terminal Values*	*Rank*	*Instrumental Values*
8	a comfortable life (a prosperous life)	8	ambitious (hard working, aspiring)
6	an exciting life (a stimulating, active life)	14	broadminded (open minded)
16	a sense of accomplishments (lasting contribution).	15	capable (competent, effective)
1	a world of peace (free of war and conflict)	5	cheerful (light-hearted, joyful)
7	a world of beauty (beauty of nature and the arts)	3	clean (neat, tidy)
11	equality (brotherhood, equal opportunity for all)	11	courageous (standing up for your beliefs)
2	family security (taking care of loved ones)	7	forgiving (willing to pardon others)
3	freedom (independence, free choice)	4	helpful (working for the welfare of others)
5	happiness (contentedness)	1	honest (sincere, truthful)
17	inner harmony (freedom from inner conflict)	17	imaginative (daring)
12	mature love (sexual and spiritual intimacy)	13	independent (self-reliant, self-sufficient)
15	national security (protection from attack)	16	intellectual (intelligent, reflective)
9	pleasure (an enjoyable, leisurely life)	18	logical (consistent, rational)
10	salvation (saved, eternal life)	2	loving (affectionate, tender)
13	self-respect (self-esteem)	12	obedient (dutiful, respectful)
18	social recognition (respect, admiration)	6	polite (courteous, well-mannered)
4	true friendship (close companionship)	10	responsible (dependable, reliable)
14	wisdom (a mature understanding of life)	0	self-controlled (restrained, self-disciplined)

disciplines (e.g., physicists or linguists), and an individual's genes, mind, unconscious, and feelings. Our contributions to and uses of species knowledge must always be specific, partial, and selective, even though we may seek more simplified, generalized, and comprehensive understanding. Furthermore, each human society in each of its historical areas "chooses" a focus for its efforts in producing and using knowledge. It selects certain arenas for investigation and prefers certain modes of inquiry, procedures, techniques, or methodologies. This selectivity derives primarily from the economic, political, and other needs of a society in a particular stage of development. Thus, in a preindustrial society such as ancient Egypt, the primary arenas for the creation of new knowledge were in agriculture, religion, religion-related architecture, and military science, and the chief creators of knowledge were the clergy and the governmental aristocracy. Or, in the case of a Western industrial society such as the United States in the nineteenth century, the knowledge created from both basic and applied research was mainly in fields related to industrialisation and corporate capitalism, such as physics, chemistry, metallurgy, mechanical engineering, medical science and technology, and especially that peculiarly American province of physical/mechanical inventions by tinkerer-inventors.

In general, we can conclude that knowledge is appropriate and sufficient to a particular time and place, to the survival of a people; and yet its nature is to continually be incomplete, to always challenge human beings to extend its alterable frontiers, to steer its growth and flow in those directions most useful to a society's images of the future.

In industrialised, technologized societies like the United States, the premises underlying the creation of knowledge are probably either almost obsolete or inappropriate for postindustrial societies. Drawing on the work of James Conant, Markley lists these "outdated" axioms:

> Reason is the supreme tool of man.

Knowledge, acquired through the use of reason, will free mankind from ignorance and will lead to a better future.

The universe is inherently orderly and physical.

This order can be discovered by science and objectively expressed.

Only science deals in empirically verifiable truth.

Observation and experimentation are the only valid means of discovering scientific truth, which is always independent of the observer.

In the 1960s and 1970s, one or more of these premises has been called into question by several philosophers and social scientists. Herbert Marcuse insisted that sole reliance on the rational-scientific mode led to "one-dimensional" beings, while Theodore Roszak described the "wasteland" created by dependence on scientific and technological world views, and applauded the movement toward a counter-culture which could lead to a new, balanced, holistic conceptions of knowing and knowledge.

Questions have been raised about the claims to knowledge of such "mystical" methods and conceptualizations as meditation, Gestalt psychologies, extrasensory perception, Zen and Yoga techniques, intuition, and feelings-as-truth. Criticisms abound on the proliferation of specialized disciplines, the creation of discipline-specific technical terms, and the reductionist tendency to fragment wholes by analysis. Also, "recent developments on numerous fronts [have challenged] the idea that the objective world explored by the various scientific probes is essentially separate from and independent of the subjective experience of the investigator."

Factors affecting knowing and the known in the future will probably include (1) the creation of new knowledge based on current assumptions are paradigms, (2) the emergence of new paradigms and models which incorporate subjective experience, values, and other elusive dimensions, (3) the development of new procedures for "discovering" knowledge, among which are policy research and forecasting skills, and (4) new technological inventions, some mere amplifications of present systems, and probably a few startlingly new ones.

The Frontiers of Knowledge

When physicists learned during the first two decades of the twentieth century that light took the forms of particle and wave, they then knew that paradox and uncertainty had reemerged as ingredients of their science. In a sense, electrons were found to be both there and not there, to be both trace and geometric pattern. The universe began to become more mind than material, more idea than matter, more dynamic than static, until

> now we know that we are part of an immense galaxy [the Milky Way] of about 100,000 million stars, arranged in a disc-shaped spiral 100,000 light years in diameter, about three-fifths of the way out from the center of the disc, and moving further out at a mere 35 kilometers per second, [toward] the "edge" of the universe.... now billions of light years away and full of strange wonders: quasars, pulsars, and black holes; and even stranger, though logical, postulates of antimatter, time flowing backwards, negative mass, and particles travelling faster than the speed of light.... Modern physics and cosmology have placed the human in a universe inestimably more rich and extraordinary than the mechanical vision ever prepared him for....; the cosmic man of modern physics bears strong resemblance to the image of man-in-universe of Eastern philosophies.

In the biological sciences, the more promising search has to do with population, ecosystems, cellular, molecular and atomic levels of analysis, developmental-evolutionary factors and patterns, and extraterrestrial organisms. Or consider the implications of cryogenics (ultra low temperature effects), of recombining the structures of DNA molecules to modify the nature of existing organisms or species or to create new organisms, and of cloning or the capacity to replicate organisms.

Then there is brain research. In regard to the effects of biochemical substances on the mind, Kenneth Clark suggests:

> We might be on the threshold of that type of scientific, biochemical intervention which could stabilize and make dominant the moral and ethical propensities of man and subordinate, if not eliminate, his negative and primitive tendencies.

Also in this category is split-brain research, which focuses on the differing functions of the left and right hemispheres of the brain. Tentative conclusions point to the left side of the brain as being "analytic and reductionist," while the right side is "more holistic and integrative."

Another area of increased scientific interest is "in the ways altered states of awareness can affect perception, thinking, feelings, and behavior." This research probes consciousness "indirectly" through the use of such indicators as hypnosis, biofeedback training, dreams and dreaming meditation or relaxation training, psychedelic drugs, and subliminal stimulation.

New Paradigms or Models of Knowledge

Willis Harman forecasts that by 1994 we will have a new knowledge model or pattern.

> The new knowledge paradigm will be hospitable to some sort of systematization of subjective experience, the domain which has heretofore largely been left to non-science—the humanities and religion. Science will include the study of those experiences from which we derive our basic value commitments.... Thus the paradigm will allow a much more unified view of

> human experiences now categorized under such diverse headings as "creativity," "intuition," "mysticism," "psychic phenomena," "religious experience."—The new paradigm will also permit a more unified view of the processes of personal change and development which take place within the contexts of psychotherapy, education, "growth centers," religion, and crisis confrontation.

Difficult as it is for students and scholars to accept, it seems an inescapable conclusion that the current modes of organizing knowledge by separate, specialized academic disciplines will not be appropriate for the future. If the construct "quality of life" is the focus for investigation, it is clear that no single academic specialty is sufficient to comprehend and inquire into such an all-encompassing concept. What is called for is a multi- or interdisciplinary approach, or the creation of one or more new, comprehensive, integrating fields of study.

Only dim clues exist to point our way toward holistic approaches. Some potentially rewarding directions are general systems theory and the principles of cybernetics; general semantics and the search for a metalanguage; zetetics or the study of the ways human beings create knowledge, their modes of inquiry; the advancement of policy studies and research, or the process of individual, group, and mass problem-solving and decision-making; the relationships among high-level concepts such as growth, number, time, form, space, entropy, love, beauty, and goodness; and the study of "limiting" principles such as uncertainty, coincidence, paradox, and unpredictability (or synergy.)

The Frontiers of Technology

The technological base of a culture comprises the tools and techniques used to carry out the functions of the culture's social institutions. These social institutions are the family, the educational system, the economy, the political system, the health and welfare system, and the religious or moral system.

By defining a culture's technology as a collection of tools and techniques, we emphasize that technology embodies both physical, material objects (a set of tools) *and* processes, procedures, and organizational structures (a set of techniques). Such a definition suggests that an automobile, a factory, and a corporation are all technological inventions, as are solid state circuitry, Congress, voting and elections, jet airplanes and space satellites, computers and computer programs, schools, school district bureaucracies, and school curricula. Technology includes "hardware" and "software," that is, machines and processes, e.g., a teaching machine and the substantive lessons programmed into it.

That the existing state of technological development in industrialised nations causes ambivalence among both leaders and citizens is an indication that technological advance is a mixed blessing. We enjoy the convenience provided by cars and jet planes, but not the pollution and energy drain associated with their use. We admire the precision and efficiency of automated tasks, but not the resultant worker alienation, job insecurity, and increased unemployment. We applaud the discovery of miracle drugs and the procedures and inventions that make organ transplants possible, but then shrink from the concomitant problems of an aging population. We are coming to suspect that further technological development may threaten our quality of life, may cancel many of our material and physical comforts, and may even jeopardize our individual and collective mental health.

Often our naive faith in the gadget, the machine leads us to expect miraculous discoveries and inventions to appear in timely fashion and save us from the brink of disaster. Or conversely, we may become so jaded with the trends in technology that our cynicism blinds us to possible shifts toward a more benign and humane technology. Neither of these outlooks is particularly helpful for coping with either the development or control of technology, now or in the future. Perhaps a more useful attitude toward future technological developments should combine hope and cautiousness, with a questioning hesitation that asks, What will the discovery or invention mean for a definition of being human, what impact will it have on global interdependence and quality of life, what will it mean for human relations at all levels from the interpersonal to the intersocietal, and what will it mean for the long-term survival of the species?

By the twenty-first century, we can expect a new, vast array of technological products and processes. Some will be expected and some unexpected; some will be hardware and some software; and most significantly, some will have limited, inconsequential effects on human conditions of living, but some will have profound implications for the quality of life on earth. Following are *some* of the technologies that today's forecasters envision:

1. There will be improvements in the type and use of contraceptives for fertility control. Oral and male contraceptives will be perfected. National and international fertility control programs will be implemented.
2. Continuing progress in medical science (e.g., prosthetic devices, surgical procedures, vaccines), will allow U.S. citizens to expect an average 100-year life span. Improvements in cryogenics could make possible longer, interrupted life spans.
3. Pharmacology will develop a number of nonnarcotic and nonaddictive personality modification and control drugs. Also, there will be drugs to enhance intelligence and learning.
4. Weapons research will grow apace with the more benign technologies, producing *both* lethal and incapacitating biochemical weapons. (A weapon on the drawing board even in the late 1970s is the neutron bomb, which kills human beings but doesn't destroy buildings.)

5. New generations of computers and new computer applications will be developed, including home computer terminals and new versions of computer-assisted instruction.
6. Artificial forms of life will be created as outcomes of research on self-replicating molecules, recombinant DNA, and procedures for cloning.
7. Genetic control products and procedures will be developed that will eliminate many hereditary defects and allow for "choices" by prospective parents of a range of hereditary human characteristics for their planned offspring. also, ova/sperm banks will be established.
8. Household robots will be created, first to do just a few simple tasks, and then many complex chores.
9. Space exploration of our galaxy and solar system will continue, with a manned landing on Mars and a space colony established equidistant from Earth and its moon to collect solar energy and transmit it to Earth.
10. There will be improvements in and increased use of nuclear energy—both fission and fusion reactors. Other energy sources will be investigated for availability and economic feasibility: sources such as geothermal and solar energy, wind, and evaporation.

Current and Emerging Problems, Crises and Fears

The second visible side of the "framework of the future" pyramid comprises the problems, crises, and fears now being faced by humankind; and also the barely visible emergent issues which will likely impinge on us in the near future. Both current and emerging social problems grow out of the imbalances and excesses of the industrial era in human socio-politico-economic development, and also out of the dislocations and uncertainties of the transition to a postindustrial society.

At present, the most industrially and technological developed (some would say "overdeveloped") nations, the United States, Soviet Union, Japan, and almost all nations of Western Europe, are in various stages of transition from an *industrial* to a *postindustrial* society. These nations have already evolved through their preindustrial eras and nearly through their industrial eras, and have begun to encounter the problems of advanced industrialization and the first symptoms of postindustrial development. Basically, a preindustrial society is one that relies on agriculture and manual labor for its survival; an industrial society combines manufacturing with farming, but both rely heavily on technology and industrial organization and process; and a postindustrial society is one where farming and manufacturing are largely technologically automated, and where human occupations have changed from goods-producing types to service-providing and knowledge-producing types.

In essence, the transition from industrial to postindustrial society is a change from maximizing growth and quantitative factors to optimizing growth (which may mean stability or even some decreases) and emphasizing qualitative factors. Industrial nations have become expert at "doing," which has led to excesses. The new society will require expertise in "undoing" and in "doing well."

In this period of transition for Western nations, the developing or less developed nations will be affected mainly by the problems of attempting to accelerate industrialization (with limited capital and resources, and often in the face of overpopulation) and by the effects on their population of comparisons between the quality of life in their nations and that in the most developed nations. Such comparisons, of course, may yield envy and demands for redistribution of wealth and resources, but also they may lead to the wisdom to avoid many of the problems of the more "advanced" societies. Few nations, however, will avoid the traumas of transition which in the late twentieth century plague those nations moving toward a postindustrial era.

In addition to the overall movement of developing nations toward industrial development and of developed nations toward postindustrial society, a number of other conditions contribute to late twentieth-century crises, problems, and fears. Worldwide urbanization brings overcrowding, unemployment, and disillusionment. The modern nation-state, in order to deal with intranational and international interdependence, complexity, and conflict, tends toward the centralization of authority and decision-making, in turn alienating citizens from their government making them feel less and less able to influence public decisions. Social problems become more and more complex, involving dozens and even hundreds of related factors, and calling for considerable expertise to arrive at feasible, desirable solutions. And each problem is never totally solved, but leads to a new problem, setting in motion a problem-solution-new problem sequence that seems to go on forever. These conditions tend almost to overwhelm many citizens and even some leaders, too often stimulating feelings of hopelessness and helplessness.

The increasing pace of change characteristics of this century, especially the rapid accumulation of scientific and technological knowledge, creates the twin plagues of human obsolescense and fear of the future. These diseases are further complicated by the intrinsically dangerous nature of many new technologies: the overkill potential of nuclear weapons, the potential thermal and radiation effects of fission and fusion nuclear reactors, the potentially destructive effects of many biological and chemical products, and the threats to human values of techniques of "mind control" genetic engineering, and imposition of order.

Historical accident, timely inventions, and exploitation of readily available, inexpensive natural resources (including human labor) have enabled some nations to develop economically, technologically, and industrially more than other nations. These uneven growth patterns have also been affected by such factors as how much devastation a nation experienced in war, and how it was hindered or enhanced by its status as a colony or as an imperial power. Clearly, twentieth-century colonialism and imperialism are more economic than political or military. All these historical and contemporary forces have led to unequal distribution of wealth (both within and among nations); unequal access to education, medical care, natural resources, leisure, and food; and differential distribution of over-population (within as well as among nations).

World citizens will undoubtedly continue to face a myriad of socio-politico-economic problems, virtually all solvable only partially or by spawning new problems. Among problems likely to persist past the end of the twentieth century on a worldwide scale, in the developed or developing nations are:

1. starvation, hunger and inadequate nutrition.
2. depletion of natural resources, such as arable land, water, air, and fossil fuels,
3. inequality of material wealth and natural resources within and among nations,
4. national, regional and local overpopulation,
5. threats of nuclear war, threats of wars of "acquisition" (by the rich nations for natural resources or markets for goods), and wars of "redistribution" (by the poor nations to obtain wealth, natural resources, or food),
6. death due to plagues, other diseases, and inadequate medical care,
7. crime and other violations of property and human rights,
8. shortages of many kinds, including energy, medicines, fertilizers, and an array of "necessary" and "unnecessary" products and services,

9. credibility gaps: between political leaders and scientific experts on the one hand and the citizenry on the other,
10. illiteracy and its opposites—overeducation and overspecialisation,
11. an increase in specific psychoses and neuroses, including fear of the future, insecurity, and hopelessness.

There are other problems, however, which differ in kind from those in above list. These we call "consciousness problems" such as:

1. lack of a comparable substitute vision for waning Western secularism, Judaism, Christianity, Marxism, humanism, and primitivism,
2. racism, sexism, elitism, ethnocentrism, nationalism, chauvisnism, and paternalism,
3. lack of global and future orientations or predispositions,
4. overemphasis on competitiveness, unbridled individualism, and hedonistic presentism,
5. lack of replacements for the presently prevailing concepts of "ascending progress," "self-evident superiority," and "unlimited growth,"
6. need to harmonize the dualisms of intellect v. feeling, analysis *v.* commitment, nature *v.* nurture, victory/mastery *v.* harmony/acceptance, values *v.* science/rationality,
7. lack of epics and myths of universal, global, species-wide appeal,
8. lack of positive images and symbols of collective, communal living,
9. tendency for individuals to immobilise themselves: "I'm unable to cope!"

To return for a moment to the futures pyramid in Figure 7.1, interactions will occur along all its edges. The nature of the future is determined by these interactions: among the values/ideology base, the knowledge/technology plane, and the problems/crises side. As future trends appear in barely visible outlines, these also interact with all the other planes—chiefly by self-fulfilling and self-defeating "pushes."

Educational Futures

Thus far, almost no mention has been made of education and schooling in the future. As a social institution, education primarily reflects and conserves the values, norms, and practices of a particular society; only secondarily, and then rarely, does it initiate change and innovation on its own. Thus, educational futures are drawn mainly, and by implication, from societal futures, on all levels from family, through state and nation, to planet. For example, Harry Broudy has suggested that the major future demand *by* U.S. society *on* schooling will be for vocational competence, civic competence, and humanness (i.e., individuality, personhood, and freedom). Dwight Allen concluded that "to get past [rigid prerequisites and lockstep credentialing]...., we need to implement nonlinearity, simultaneity, and random access to education...., by allowing students to learn what they want, when they want it,.... to make education self-directed, continuing, and enjoyable."

A growing number of educators have become interested in the study of educational futures, or as it is sometimes referred to, educational policy studies or policies research. Their forecasts vary, both in terms of the educational topics they choose to study and in terms of their actual projections. Among the topics education futurists have selected for study and research are curriculum content (i.e., knowledge, skills, values, and attitudes), materials and methods; school and curriculum organization patterns; preservice and in-service education of teachers; schemes for financing public, private, and parochial schools; teachers' organizations or unions, and salaries and benefits; student demographic characteristics; educational media and technology; politics and control of education; global, international education; functions of nonschool educative agents, such as publishers, commercial television, families, and community agencies; and school buildings and other learning environments.

What follows are some of the educational futures envisioned by a sampling of late twentieth-century futurists:

Theodore W. Hipple. This prognosticator sees these changes in schools and schooling in the "distant and not-so-distant future":

> An enlarged and broadened base for financing public education will evolve.
>
> Teachers' salaries will continue to increase, though the percent raises will be barely ahead of inflation.
>
> Alternative schools (both the "fundamental" and the "open" varieties), schools-within-a-school, and schools-without-walls will flourish, especially beyond the elementary school level.
>
> A school will become a community center, as well as a user of community facilities and human resources.
>
> The time students spend in schools and classrooms will be shortened, while student time in out-of-school, community agencies and programs will increase.
>
> Older students will teach younger students, under adult supervision and for pay or for credit as volunteers.
>
> Curricula will incorporate computers and data retrieval systems, and will emphasize such learning "economies" as concept learning and basic communication and problem-solving skills.
>
> Teaching methods will change to accommodate more small-group and independent-study modes.

David J. Irvine. According to this educational futurist, an educational system of the future should be able to:

deal with large numbers of students,

accommodate to new and different population patterns (e.g., metropolitan government or abolition of state boundaries),

capitalize on the many "non-school educational forces which exist in society e.g., marketplace, corporations, museums, colleges, libraries, clubs, and commercial television stations),

accommodate to changes in natural resources available, such as air, water and fuel,

provide learning-to-learn and other survival skills,

allow greater learner autonomy in deciding educational needs and programs,

teach a variety of human relations skills: intrapersonal, interpersonal, and multicultural,

provide means for individual determine overriding purposes in their lives, and

move students away from the dichotomy between work and play.

Wilbur J. Cohen. This dean of the school of education at the University of Michigan and former Secretary of Health, Education, and Welfare suggests that educational futures will occur mainly in "ten areas of change";

formulas and bases of financing school expenditures,

emphasis on early childhood education,

continued desegregation, busing, and concern for quality in urban education, expanded collective bargaining,

substitutions (e.g., equivalency tests and competencies checks) for teacher certification, continued innovation and experimentation (e.g., voucher plans and challenges to compulsory attendance laws),

continued teacher surplus, but with shortages in selected areas (e.g., special education),

greater parent involvement and student participation in decision-making,

dissatisfaction with and greater expectation from public education.

changing community institution—family, government, and economy.

Harold E. Mitzel. "I predict that the impending instruction revolution will shortly bypass the simple idea of individualising instruction and move ahead to the more sophisticated notion of providing *adaptive education* for school and college learners. By adaptive education we mean the tailoring of subject matter presentations to fit the special requirements and capabilities of each learner."

Margaret Mead. In her volume *Culture and Commitment* this noted anthropologist claims that people learn from each other in three age-related modes, but that one of these modes has been dominant in most past cultures. The three modes are prefigurative learning—the old learn from the young; configurative learning—children, adolescents, and adults learn from their peers; and postfigurative learning, historically the typical mode—the young learn from the old. Mead suggests that today in industrial, technological societies like the United States, postfigurative learning is the norm of formal schooling, but that in other contexts (e.g., the adolescent subculture) cofigurate learning (peer learning) is the rule, and this is a crucial determinant of the phenomenon of the generation gap. In the future. Mead observes, there will be a need for all three modes of learning to occur in a culture.

Taking a broad perspective on education in the future,

two general, long-term trends seem to pervade public education in every nation. These are (1) the tendency of systems of schooling to first maximize the number of persons served by the system, and then to maximize the quality of service to special client groups and to individual clients, and (2) the tendency of curricular and decision-making orientations to shift from local, to national, to worldwide concerns and arenas.

Using the United States as an example, the historical pattern has been for each level of public education—elementary, secondary, and higher—to grow toward serving a maximum number of potential clients or students. This has been a progression "upward," of saturating each level in turn. By 1900, well over 50 percent of the elementary school age population was in elementary school (public, private, or parochial), and about 10 percent of the high school age youth were in secondary schools. By 1970, over 95 percent of the potential elementary school clientele were in school, while over 90 percent of the corresponding youth group were in secondary schools. Today in the United States, the elementary and secondary schools have virtually reached their quantitative limits, except in their adult education programs, where they compete with higher education for new clients.

From at least the 1950s and more so in the 1960s and 1970s, elementary and secondary education focused more and more on qualitative factors. This is especially so far federal legislation and funding during the sixties and seventies. For example, the Elementary and Secondary Education Act of 1965 supplied funds to state and local education agencies to improve the quality of education in several ways: to improve instruction and support services in schools with a high percentage of poverty-level students, to improve the holdings of school libraries, to improve state department of education services to local schools, and to foster exemplary, innovative instructional curricular practices. Other federal categorical-aid acts (as distinguished from general-aid acts) have provided funds for assisting local school districts with desegregation problems, for bilingual education, and for the education of the handicapped. Undoubtedly the future will see greater support at all levels for special-client groups and for the development of individualised approaches to education.

Two other broad tendencies of educational systems are toward the centralization of authority and power at "higher" levels—from local school districts to state departments of education to federal or national government; and the broadening orientation of curriculum from local to national to global. For example, the U.S. Congress in the late seventies was pressured by many groups, such as private and parochial school educators and big-city superintendents and school boards, to enact legislation to provide general financial aid to all forms of elementary and secondary education in the nation. At the same time, school curricula more and more reflected national concerns (e.g., the push to get back to fundamental skills) and the necessity for global citizenship (which was highlighted by the energy crisis, but which grows out of the recognition of interdependence in multiple worldwide contexts).

Case Study: A Problem in Space Travel

Imagine that you are a first-class passenger on a huge spaceship travelling through space at the speed of 66,000 mph. You discover that the craft's environmental system is faulty. Passengers in some sections are actually dying due to the discharge of poisonous gases into their oxygen supply. Furthermore, you learn that food supplies are rapidly diminishing and that the water supply, previously thought to be more than adequate, is rapidly becoming polluted because of fouling from breakdowns in the craft's waste and propulsion systems.

To complicate matters, in the economy sections, where passengers are crowded together under the most difficult of situations, many are seriously ill. The ship's medical officers are able to help only a fraction of the sick, and medicines are in short supply.

Mutinies have been reported, and although some of the crew and passengers are engaged in serious conflict in one of the compartments, it is hoped that this conflict is being contained successfully. However, there is widespread fear as to what may happen if it cannot be contained or resolved within that compartment.

The spacecraft has been designed with an overall destruct system, the controls of which have been carefully guarded. Unfortunately the number of technologists who have gained access to the destruct system has increased, and all of the crew and passengers have become uneasy at the evidence of instability in some of those gaining this access.

What can or should be done to save the spaceship and its inhabitants?

Thought Questions

1. For each of the following potential developments, decide if you think it "will occur" or "won't occur" by the year 2020. Also, regardless of whether you think it will or won't occur, decide if you think the development would be "desirable" or "undesirable."

Potential Development	will Occur	Won't Occur	Desirable	Undesirable
A cure for cancer				
Extensive use of home computers				
Existence of space colonies as satellites of moon and/or earth				
World government or world federation				
A life expectancy in U.S. of over 100 years				
Production of test-tube babies				

Nuclear war

The three-day work week in United States

Elimination of use of individually owned and operated automobiles in U.S.

Almost total reliance on nuclear and solar energy

Zero population growth in U.S.

The death of capitalism

Continued urban growth

Farming and Mining of the seas

Genetic manipulation and control of DNA (e.g., cloning, elimination of birth defects)

2. Which one of the following four metaphors comes closest to your conception of the future? If none seems appropriate, create one of your own. Explain!

1. The future is a great *roller coaster* on a moonless night. It exists, twisting ahead of us in the dark, although we can only see each part as we come to it....
2. The future is a *mighty river*. The great force of history flows inexorably along, carrying us with it. Most of our attempts to change its course are mere pebbles thrown into the river: they cause a momentary splash and a few ripples, but they make no difference. The river's course *can* be changed, but only by natural disasters like earthquakes or landslides, or by massive, concerted human efforts on a similar scale. On the other hand, we are free as individuals to adapt to the course of history either well or poorly....
3. The future is a *great ocean*. There are many possible destinations, and many different paths to each destination. A good navigator takes advantage of

the main currents of change, adapts his course to the capricious winds of chance, keeps a sharp lookout posted, and moves carefully in fog or uncharted waters....

4. The future is entirely random, a *colossal dice game.* Every second, millions of things happen which could have happened another way and produced a different future... Since everything is chance, all we can do is play the game, pray to the gods of fortune, and enjoy what good luck comes our way.

3. Supply evidence to support or refute each of the following hypotheses:

> The value base of American society has remined rather stable and constant for the past 200 years, and will likely remain so far at least another 200 years
>
> American values have evolved over hundreds of years, but are today being challenged and will probably change considerably between now and the year 2000.

4. On the blank lines, indicate whether each of the following potential educational developments in the United States will occur "by 1984", "by 1994," "by 2020," "by 2050," or "never."

1. a complete environmental-education curriculum, kindergarten through grade twelve
2. year-round school, broken up by holidays every quarter-year
3. abolition of compulsory attendance laws in most states
4. abolition of public schools
5. emphasis on global/futures education
6. gradual decrease in public school enrollments
7. elimination of the local property-tax base for funding public schools; all funds derive from state and federal governments

8. the option to "test out" of high school in all states
9. few, if any, significant changes in public education
10. use of computers to replace some teachers for almost half the school day
11. extensive use of drugs to enhance student learning and to increase students' abilities to learn
12. special schools and programs for the elderly
13. greater uses of educational TV and computer-assisted instruction in homes
14. free child-care and prekindergarten education
15. abolition of teacher tenure

Practical Activities

1. With respect to the following future possibilities, ask a number of children or adolescents in what ways their lives would be affected if each possibility were to occur:

you could travel to other planets as you now can visit other cities or countries

you were only allowed to work for a pay a maximum of twenty hours per week

You were required to retire from paid employment at age forty-five

you were expected to live to age 150

you could communicate with others by the use of extra-sensory perception (ESP)

twenty babies the exact genetic duplicate of you were artificially produced

automobiles were only available for rent or lease

gasoline for cars was priced at $4.00 per gallon

your occupation became obsolete every ten to fifteen years

You and your family could only dispose of one small garbage can full of garbage each month

you lived in a city under the ocean

you could only obtain food in capsule form

you were only allowed to raise artificially produced "sons" and "daughters":

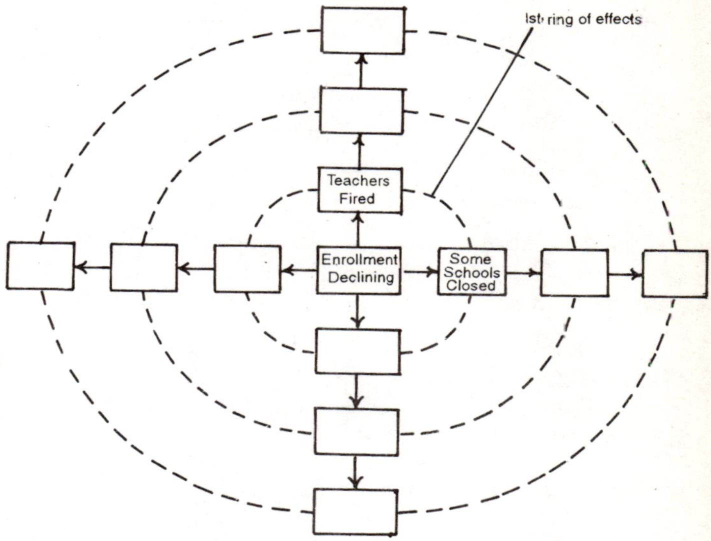

Figure 7.2. A Future Wheel

Write up a summary of your findings

2. Build a futures wheel! using Figure 7.2 as a starting point, complete the first, second, and third rings. In your projections, assume that a suburban school district is losing its student population at the rate of 2 percent per year. In 1976, there were 120,000 students in this district, and by 1979 this number had decreased to 113,000.

3. Write a science fiction short story, drama, or scenario that describes the lives of children and adolescents in their homes and schools in the year 2000.

4. Write a unit or lesson plan on "Alternative future" to teach in a class.

5. Become an active member of some organization which you feel is dealing with a crucial issue involved with future world survival (e.g., peace coalitions, Planned Parenthood, ecology groups, energy groups, etc.). Describe the organization, its importance, and your involvement.